Frederic Courtland Penfield

Present-Day Egypt

Frederic Courtland Penfield

Present-Day Egypt

ISBN/EAN: 9783337324407

Printed in Europe, USA, Canada, Australia, Japan

Cover: Foto ©ninafisch / pixelio.de

More available books at **www.hansebooks.com**

PRESENT-DAY EGYPT

By
Frederic Courtland Penfield
United States Diplomatic Agent and Consul-General
to Egypt, 1893-97

Illustrated by
PAUL PHILIPPOTEAUX AND R. TALBOT KELLY
And from Photographs

"I shall now speak at greater length of Egypt, as it contains more wonders than any other land, and is preëminent above all the countries in the world for works that one can hardly describe." *Herodotus*

NEW YORK
THE CENTURY CO.
1899

Copyright, 1899
By The Century Co.

TO KATHARINE:
WIFE, COMRADE, AND CRITIC

Preface

I STOOD once before a window in Venice wherein an artisan was at work. Arranged before him were smalts and innumerable bits of glass of every hue, some brilliant, many dull, and none suggestive of value or purpose. Apparently following no definite design, the workman seemed to draw mechanically upon the materials at his command, choosing alike from the dull and bright pieces, until it could be seen that the object on which he had been employed, now completed, was a mosaic of attractive pattern — not a masterpiece in any sense, but perfect enough to find a purchaser from among the group of onlookers.

In fashioning this mosaic volume of information concerning the reawakened Nile country, I may have drawn too generously upon the supply of lusterless material, and dulled naturally brilliant atoms by misplacing them in the pattern. The finished article, I am conscious, is far from a masterpiece, and is journalistic rather than literary; but it may still be attractive enough to satisfy the inquiring reader interested to learn about the atoms making up the Egypt of to-day.

"Present-Day Egypt" is prepared neither for

Preface

the Egyptologist, antiquarian, nor historian: these are favored already with a bibliography straining the shelves of every library. Aiming at being a discursive budget of information and comment,—social, political, economic, and administrative,—the volume presents a series of faithful pictures of the Egypt that is interesting to the winter visitor, health-seeker, and general reader, desirous of learning something, and not too much, of contemporary conditions in the oldest country in the world. "Present-Day Egypt" is written in no partial or partizan spirit, and advances no theory of the purpose of the Pyramids, nor attempts to explain the riddle of the Sphinx.

FREDERIC C. PENFIELD.

NEW YORK CITY, September 18, 1899.

AUTHOR'S NOTE.—The poem, "The Rose of Fayum," on pp. 348 and 349, is incorporated in this volume through the courtesy of Professor Clinton Scollard, and of Messrs. Copeland & Day, publishers, Boston.

Contents

CHAPTER		PAGE
I	IN FASCINATING CAIRO	1
II	IN FASCINATING CAIRO (*Continued*)	40
III	ALEXANDRIA, SEAT OF EGYPTIAN COMMERCE	78
IV	PARADOXICAL BUT EFFECTIVE ADMINISTRATION	104
V	THE EXPANSION OF PRODUCTIVE EGYPT BY IRRIGATION	145
VI	THE STORY OF THE SUEZ CANAL	184
VII	ISMAIL PASHA AS KHEDIVE AND EXILE	218
VIII	TEWFIK PASHA AND THE ARABI REBELLION	245
IX	THE PRESENT KHEDIVE AND KHEDIVAL FAMILY	272
X	GREAT BRITAIN'S POSITION IN EGYPT	298
XI	WINTERING IN EGYPT FOR HEALTH'S SAKE	336
INDEX		369

List of Illustrations

	PAGE
PROCESSION OF THE SACRED CARPET, CAIRO . *Frontispiece*	
From drawing by Paul Philippoteaux.	
GENERAL VIEW OF CAIRO	3
From drawing by Paul Philippoteaux.	
PUBLIC LETTER-WRITER (LETTER FROM BIANCA TO GIOVANNI)	9
From drawing by Paul Philippoteaux.	
MARRIAGE PROCESSION AND SABER DANCE, CAIRO	17
From drawing by Paul Philippoteaux.	
A BURIAL, CAIRO	25
From drawing by Paul Philippoteaux.	
A HOWLING DERVISH	31
From drawing by Paul Philippoteaux.	
TYPES OF MALE AND FEMALE BEDOUINS . .	37
From drawing by Paul Philippoteaux.	
BRASS-WORKERS AT THE SOUTH GATE OF THE KHAN HALIL, CAIRO	43
From drawing by Paul Philippoteaux.	
WOOD-WORKERS	49
From photograph by Zangaki.	
WOMEN OF THE NILE	57
From drawing by Paul Philippoteaux.	
THE ROSETTA STONE	67
COURT OF EL-AZHAR, CAIRO . . .	73
From photograph by Bonfils.	
WATER ENTRANCE OF RAS-EL-TEEN PALACE, ALEXANDRIA	81
From photograph by Zangaki.	
PLACE MEHEMET ALI, ALEXANDRIA .	87
From photograph by Zangaki.	

List of Illustrations

	PAGE
NATIVE WOMAN AND CHILD	93

From photograph by G. Lekegian & Co.

CLEOPATRA (FROM THE TEMPLE OF DENDERAH) . 99
THE SPHINX 107
   From photograph by Zangaki.
AFTER PASSING DRAWBRIDGE, CAIRO . 113
   From photograph by Zangaki.
MAP OF THE NILE AND NORTHEASTERN AFRICA . 121
   From drawing by F. E. Pierce.
THE PYRAMIDS, SEEN FROM NATIVE VILLAGE . 129
   From photograph by Zangaki.
AN OFFICIAL GROUP IN GROUNDS OF THE UNITED STATES DIPLOMATIC AGENCY AND CONSULATE-GENERAL, CAIRO 135
VISCOUNT CROMER, BRITISH DIPLOMATIC AGENT AND CONSUL-GENERAL 141
   From photograph by J. Heyman & Co.
GENERAL VIEW OF THE FIRST CATARACT, LOOKING SOUTH FROM ASSUAN 149
   From drawing by R. Talbot Kelly.
LOG-SWIMMING DOWN THE ASSUAN CATARACT. . . 155
   From drawing by R. Talbot Kelly.
PHILÆ AS IT IS 161
   From drawing by R. Talbot Kelly.
PROBABLE APPEARANCE OF THE CATARACT ON THE COMPLETION OF THE DAM 167
   From drawing by R. Talbot Kelly.
TOURIST-BOAT LEAVING SHELAL FOR THE CATARACT . 173
   From drawing by R. Talbot Kelly.
NATIVES HAULING A BOAT UP THE "GREAT GATE" . 179
   From drawing by R. Talbot Kelly.
BRITISH TROOP-SHIP PASSING THROUGH SUEZ CANAL . 189
   From photograph by Zangaki.
A DAHABIYEH ON THE NILE . 197
   From photograph by G. Lekegian & Co.
EGYPTIAN PROTOTYPE OF FERRIS WHEEL. HUNDREDS OF YEARS OLD 205
   From photograph by Zangaki.
A SIMPLE FORM OF IRRIGATION 213
   From photograph by Zangaki.
OBELISK AT HELIOPOLIS . . 221
   From photograph by Zangaki.
KOM-OMBOS (RECENTLY EXCAVATED) 227

List of Illustrations

	PAGE
EXTERIOR OF TEMPLE AT DENDERAH	233
From photograph by G. Lekegian & Co.	
THE FUNERAL CORTÈGE OF EX-KHEDIVE ISMAIL, IN CAIRO	239
From photograph by V. Giuntini, Cairo.	
PREDECESSORS OF KHEDIVE ABBAS II	249
From photograph by G. Lekegian & Co.	
TULIP COLUMNS AT KARNAK	255
From photograph by G. Lekegian & Co.	
AVENUE OF SPHINXES AND PYLON, KARNAK	261
From photograph by G. Lekegian & Co.	
EGYPTIAN BRIDE GOING IN STATE TO NEW HOME	267
From photograph by Zangaki.	
HIS HIGHNESS ABBAS HILMI PASHA II, KHEDIVE OF EGYPT	275
From photograph by J. Heymau & Co.	
ABDIN PALACE, CAIRO. CITADEL IN DISTANCE	281
From photograph by Zangaki.	
THE SULTAN'S HIGH COMMISSIONER IN EGYPT, GHAZI MOUKHTAR PASHA	287
From photograph by Abdullah Bros.	
BISCHARINS IN UPPER EGYPT	293
From photograph by G. Lekegian & Co.	
LORD KITCHENER, SIRDAR OF THE EGYPTIAN ARMY AND GOVERNOR-GENERAL OF THE SUDAN	301
A NILE FARM	309
From photograph by Edward L. Wilson.	
THE NILE BARRAGE, NEAR CAIRO	317
AT THE BASE OF CHEOPS	323
GHIZEREH BANK OF THE NILE, CAIRO	331
From photograph by Zangaki.	
TEMPLE OF ABU-SIMBEL, NUBIA	339
From photograph by A. Beato.	
SCENE IN THE FAYUM	345
From photograph by G. Lekegian & Co.	
LUXOR	353
ASSUAN	361
From photograph by G. Lekegian & Co.	
MAP OF EGYPT AND THE SUDAN	367

Present-Day Egypt

Present-Day Egypt

CHAPTER I

IN FASCINATING CAIRO

FROM its founding in 969 by the Fatimite califs, as an offshoot of the tented settlement of Fostat, to the present rule of Abbas Pasha, seventh khedive, or viceroy, of the dynasty of Mehemet Ali, Cairo—capital of Egypt, metropolis of the African continent, and chief seat of Mohammedan teaching—has a romantic history. Scene of famous exploits of great personages, from Saladin to Napoleon, of sanguinary conflicts between Christianity and Islamism, and the memorable massacre of the Mamelukes; cradle of religions and cults; home of the "Arabian Nights" tales; the place where lasting principles of philosophy and science were conceived, and where Bible scenes were laid, Cairo has become the meeting-ground of winter idlers from every clime.

The visit to Egypt has become almost as essential to Americans—and fully half of the eight thousand winter visitors are from the United States—

Present-Day Egypt

as the pilgrimage of good Mohammedans to Mecca. The Mohammedans' religion takes them but once to the sacred city of the prophet, but pleasure draws those favored by fortune to the Nile capital time after time. Cairo is more than interesting: it is fascinating. The antiquarian, the student, and the savant have always been at home there; and the invalid—real or imaginary—seeking a climate, finds in and about the khedival city the superlative of air and temperature.

Artists never weary of reproducing Cairo's picturesque scenes and vivid colorings. The ether of the skies, the splendor of the setting sun, the Turneresque afterglow, and the delicate browns of the desert, can be best suggested in water-colors, for, like Venice, Egypt demands a master hand in oils.

The traveler of impressionable nature yields to the fascination of Cairo's quaint Eastern life, as perfect as if met far beyond the Orient's threshold, and doubly satisfying, because found within a half-hour of the creature comforts of hotels conspicuously modern. To walk the streets of an Oriental capital wherein history has been made, between meals, as it were, and delve by day in museums and mosques perpetuating a mysterious past, and dine *de rigueur* in the evening, with the best music of Europe at hand, explains a charm that Cairo has for mortals liking to witness Eastern life provided they are not compelled to become a part of it. If Egypt disappoints, the indecisive idler can in four or five days be back in Paris or on the Riviera.

GENERAL VIEW OF CAIRO.

In Fascinating Cairo

Every turning in the old quarters of the Mohammedan city has its story. The remnant of a fortified gateway, a dilapidated mosque, a Cufic text, each has its history, perhaps carrying one back to the days when Saladin went forth from El-Kahira to meet Richard and his crusaders on the plain of Acre; or the mind's eye sees the good Harun-al-Rashid, freshly arrived from Bagdad, stealthily pursuing his midnight rambles. A hundred associations such as these are wrapped about the crumbling ruins of medieval Cairo, to this day rich with exquisite achievements of Saracenic art. Huge monuments of the earliest history of the world fringe the horizon as one looks from the ramparts of the citadel, teaching us how the years of Cairo are but as days in the sight of the Sphinx and the Pyramids. To the left is desolate Memphis, earliest city of the world; face about, and you behold the edge of the land of Goshen; two or three miles down the Nile, near the Embabeh end of the railway-bridge, Napoleon and his army, just a century ago, won the battle of the Pyramids over the Mameluke horde; and in a modern structure in the near foreground, the Egyptian Museum, rest the bodies of Seti and the great Rameses, while within a few paces of the spot from which you are viewing this matchless panorama sleeps the Roumelian warrior who by daring and bloodshed founded the dynasty now ruling Egypt. All this, and more, may be seen in an hour, if the blare of bugles, reverberated by the Mokattam Hills, does not inform you that the British soldier has decided it is time to close the gates of Saladin's stronghold, and you are awakened to the fact that your *table d'hôte* dinner begins in thirty minutes, and you must array yourself in conventional evening garb before you can partake thereof.

The suburbs have a double charm to students of the Bible. A visit to the Shubra road, the Corso of Cairo until fashion decreed the Ghizereh drive, at sunset, will illustrate the scriptural allusions to the sheep and the goats; and a pleasing picture may there be seen of the shepherd bearing in his arms a lamb or kid too feeble to keep pace with the herd. The scene might have been taken from an engraving in an old Bible. One will not proceed far without seeing devout Moslems engaged in eventide prayer on the housetops. The wine-skin of old was the same as that used now by the water-carrier, seen a hundred times a day in Cairo, enabling one to comprehend the simile of new wine in old bottles. Aged men about the mosques and bazaars are appareled to-day as they were in Abraham's time, carrying the same staves; and the scribe, with inkhorn and pens of reed in girdle, joins the throng in the Khan Halil to-day, and frowns upon the outcast Jew, as did the Pharisee upon the publican. A few minutes' walk from the hotels brings one face to face with the living Bible; a few minutes' drive in another direction may bring one face to face with the grotesque characters of a hotel costume ball, with *petits chevaux* for a diversion between dances. Cairo is paradoxical as well as fascinating.

In Fascinating Cairo

Walk eastward from your hotel, and in five minutes you are in the medley of East and West. At the post-office observe the mingling of nationalities. A German nurse-maid, leading the little son of a prosperous Frankish merchant, is inquiring for letters at the *poste restante* window, and a patriarchal sheik in silken caftan and turban is negotiating a money-order to send to some up-Nile village. With a swagger indicating a sense of importance, Tommy Atkins enters, pouch over shoulder, to get the dainty billets-doux for the smart regiment quartered at Abbassieh, and home letters for officers and men. Another window is surrounded by students from El-Azhar. One is expecting his monthly remittance from the family in Tunis, and his ten or twenty comrades take a keen interest in the operation of attaching the Arabic hieroglyphics to the several receipts demanded in case of a money-order or registered letter.

Over the way, ranged along the iron palings of the buildings of the Mixed Court, are the public letter-writers, gravely imperturbable, sitting at umbrella-shaded tables, prepared to write anything for illiterate applicants, in any language, for a piaster or two. One is preparing the soul-impassioned letter of Bianca to her Giovanni, back in Naples or Brindisi, assuring him that she has not ceased to love him, although separated by the turbulent Mediterranean for more than a month. At another table one of the professional scribes is inditing for Youssef Mohammed a bid for clearing a canal at Assiut, for which the government has invited tenders.

Present-Day Egypt

The contrasts presented by the people thronging the streets are amusing and bewildering. The European element—Greek, Italian, and French—is everywhere blended with the Oriental. Egyptian women swing along in blue gowns and black veils hanging loose, allowing the neck and line of cheek to be easily seen, while concealing the only part of the face scrupulously hidden by an Oriental woman —the mouth. Bedouins stalk about with lordly mien, wearing around their turbans the striped *kufieh* of their desert tribe. Coptic effendis, uncomfortable in the clerical-cut coat signifying governmental employment, scamper along on donkeyback conscious of their own importance, but as obsequious as slaves on encountering a person of higher official station. A clatter of hoofs of a cavalry guard draws every one to window or balcony to see his Highness the Khedive dash past, in open carriage, with aide-de-camp by his side, hurrying in from Koubbeh to conduct the day's affairs of state at Abdin Palace. Running footmen, with bare brown legs and embroidered jackets with flowing sleeves, carrying wands of authority, soon follow, commanding the populace to make way for the carriage of their master, perhaps a pasha making a call of ceremony, or the diplomatic representative of one of the great powers.

In the midst of this moving throng a camel-train comes noiselessly into the foreground, laden with rough building-stones slung in network sacks, contending with English dog-carts and bicycles for right of way. The camels never relax their super-

PUBLIC LETTER-WRITER (LETTER FROM BIANCA TO GIOVANNI).

In Fascinating Cairo

cilious expression, even when nibbling at beflowered Parisian bonnets on the heads of ladies seated in victorias in front of them. This, or a comic-opera-like medley fully as novel, may be seen any day from the veranda of Shepheard's or the new Savoy.

Equally heterogeneous is the jumble of humanity on tourist-hotel terraces. Princes of ruling European houses rub shoulders in friendly manner with sovereign visitors from the States. The Englishman, who never tires of informing the stranger of the benefits conferred on Egypt by the wholly disinterested British "occupation," is everywhere. Grand duchesses and society queens share tables with dressmakers from Paris and elsewhere, each sipping afternoon tea, not knowing, perhaps not caring, who or what her vis-à-vis may be. An Omdurman hero, modest and good-looking in civilian dress, is the cynosure for a few minutes of every feminine eye, and the recipient of courtly consideration from "Baehler," "Luigi," or "George,"—the managerial triumvirate of Cairo's hotels,—as the case may be. The Egyptologist, with long hair, excavating at Thebes or Sakkarah, with half the alphabet appended to his name, or the irrigation expert, rescuing from the desert a province of tillable soil, is eclipsed by the Mahdi's escaped prisoner. However, the inclination of this tea-drinking, gossiping—perhaps flirting—crowd is to forget cares and responsibilities, breathe the heavenly air, and watch indifferently the kaleidoscopic panorama of Egypt passing endlessly in the street. In a land of perpetual sunshine it is wonderful how

Present-Day Egypt

the willingness to do nothing grows on human beings who in other places must be employed to be happy.

An amusing feature of street life is the manner in which the huckstering of fowls is conducted. The fellah woman, paying duty at one of the octroi bureaus, comes into Cairo with a donkey loaded with baskets of hens, ducks, and geese, their heads standing out in every direction as if enjoying their outing. To sell a dozen fowls keeps the woman dickering all day. Her lord and master, maybe, is driving a flock of young turkeys through the crowded streets of the European quarter, singing the praises of his peeping, docile birds in a manner conveying a meaning only to the servant class. With a palm-branch he guides the flock wherever he wishes, keeping the birds clear of the traffic. The man loves to dicker, also, and has no appreciable regard for time. To effect the sale of a turkey requires a vast amount of palaver and much estimating of weight, in which numerous disinterested natives are invited to take part. Milk is sold in a manner too direct to admit of adulteration, for the cow is milked in front of the customer's door; but skeptical Egyptians hint that the cows are systematically plied with lukewarm water before setting out. A ridiculous custom is to have a small boy accompany the cows, carrying under his arm a stuffed calf, to make them submit willingly to the milking process. Badly moth-eaten, with stuffing of straw protruding from a dozen places, this calf is always in evidence. It is a custom, and in Egypt custom is unalterable; and, presumably, cows are not looked upon as possessing sufficient intellect to know a live from a dead calf, or to recognize their own.

Cairo presents the best exemplification of the confusion of tongues descending from the building of the tower of Babel that I know. Every language and patois of Europe, every shade of vernacular of Asia and Africa, may there be heard. It is humiliating to us of the Western world, who may have struggled the best part of a lifetime with a single foreign language, to find the Cairene able to speak fluently a dozen. The dragoman or the donkey-boy can exploit his vocation in a wonderful variety of tongues, although possibly unable to read his name in any. Ask your way in the street, and you must not be surprised if the information be given in a sentence made up of words from English, French, and Italian, perhaps with a Greek word thrown in. Polyglot as Cairo is, the medley of coinages is none the less confusing. Send your dragoman to the bazaars in quest of some article, and he may return with the astonishing information that it costs "one napoleon, half a sovereign, and eighteen piasters tariff." It calls for pencil, paper, and patience to compute the price of the article you are endeavoring to buy through your polynumismatic servant. And the piaster, the basis of computation, has a confusing value. The piaster "current" of small transactions is but half as much as the piaster "tariff" of high life; and this latter is only five cents in American money.

Present-Day Egypt

Cairenes are ever out of doors. Their religious calendar teems with ceremonious anniversaries, added to which are the numerous fantasias and fête-days required by their devotion to the khedive; and if things of their own are quiet, there being no wedding to be celebrated, or friend setting out on the pilgrimage to Mecca, or returning from the visit to the prophet's tomb, the native classes go to see the Greeks honor the name-day of their king, or the French colony commemorate the fall of the Bastille. With calendars ranging from the Hejira to the Gregorian, it is indeed an off day when nothing is being celebrated. Cairo has three fixed Sabbaths. Friday is that of the Mohammedan, Saturday of the Jew, and the succeeding day the Sunday of the Christian church. Being lunar, the Mohammedan year is eleven days shorter than our own. This makes it difficult for strangers to know just when a celebration is to occur, for the interesting function that one's friend witnessed in midwinter fifteen years ago, and told you that you must not fail to see, now falls in midsummer.

Every Moslem knows by his almanac when the fasting month of Ramadan should begin; but the crescent moon must first be seen by the imperial astronomer in Constantinople, and the fact be telegraphed to Cairo, before the citadel guns can announce to the Egyptian nation that the celebration of the ninth month of their year may officially begin. The streets then become thronged, the story-tellers at the cafés draw large audiences, and thousands of the faithful spend the night in the

In Fascinating Cairo

mosques. Ramadan is observed by the masses with fasting by day, for nothing passes their lips; even the cigarette is eschewed. But the instant the sun disappears below the horizon, feasting begins, and, with smoking and merrymaking, lasts well through the night. The mortality is very great when Ramadan comes in summer.

The occasion of a wedding is a favorite revel. Noisy processions, feasting of friends, and feeding of poor, last nearly a week. The wealthy pasha or bey gives a public character to his nuptials by having a military band and perhaps an escort of soldiers head the cortège bearing the bride to her new home. A bride elect of the middle class is dragged indefinitely about the streets, hidden within a closed carriage by Persian shawls drawn over the windows, and preceded usually by a clattering band producing the most penetrating of music from discordant instruments. A string of camels brings the furniture and gaudily painted boxes to her future husband's house, and for several nights the home of the happy pair is bright with lamps, and gay with thousands of red-and-green flags stretched across the street. A spectacular procession is that in which the happy woman is carried in a palanquin, borne by two camels, and surrounded by wild-looking fiends of the desert on other camels, who extract an unconscionable amount of noise from kettledrums. This is a survival of the Cairo of old, and if the procession be headed by half-naked mountebanks and swordsmen who frequently engage in mimic combat, and a group of dancing-girls, it attracts great crowds. To the bride, however, crouched for hours within the palanquin, swaying and rocking with the stride of the camels, the ordeal must be as joyless as a crossing of the English Channel in choppy weather to one yielding easily to *mal de mer*. The poor man feels justified in borrowing at ten, perhaps twenty, per cent. a month, the funds essential to a proper celebration of his marriage, even if it takes years to liberate himself from the toils of the Greek lending him the money.

In the month of Shawal occurs the impressive ceremony of despatching the holy carpet to Mecca, when streets are filled with soldiery, officials of state in gold-embroidered uniforms, and thousands upon thousands of the followers of the prophet. Every true believer, if possible, passes the day in the streets, and women and children appear in gay attire. The ceremonial is held in the great square under the citadel. Khedive and dignitaries are present in state to start formally the caravan bearing the sacred carpet, under military escort, on its journey to Arabia. The Egyptian troops in the capital, with bands playing, accompany the cavalcade to the outskirts of the city. A pyramidal wooden structure, covered with embroidered stuffs emblazoned in gold with quotations from the Koran, perched on the back of a camel of splendid proportions, contains the carpet. People press violently forward to touch the swinging drapery of the camel with their hands, which having done, they kiss with unmistakable fervor; and as the procession

MARRIAGE PROCESSION AND SABER DANCE, CAIRO.

In Fascinating Cairo

passes through the narrow streets, many women let down from latticed windows shawls or face-veils, to touch with them the sacred object. The pilgrimage takes place annually, and the carpet is placed on or near the sacred sanctuary in the temple at Mecca where rests the body of Mohammed. The caravan returns to Cairo with the carpet of the previous year. With the pomp attending its despatch, and its journey to and from Mecca, the carpet costs the Egyptian government fully fifty thousand dollars. An item of expense is the newly minted coins thrown to the multitude by the khedive when bidding the chief of the caravan to guard jealously his priceless charge.

The man who has been to Mecca is supremely happy, knowing that paradise will be his reward for a life devoted to the teachings of the Koran. Neighbors who have not made the pilgrimage look upon him as an exalted person, admitting that his religion is of a quality superior to their own. He may wear interwoven in his turban a strip of green cloth, the prophet's own color, proclaiming to all whom it may concern that its owner has prayed within the holy of holies, and is evermore to be given the title of hadji. These dignities and privileges are as nothing, in his opinion, compared with the right to announce pictorially from his housefront the salient features of the trip to the sacred city. This he does in his own way, with his own hands, and with perspective wholly wanting. If he went from Cairo to Suez by railway—which he did on a third-class ticket, probably—he describes the fact by portraying in indigo blue an impossible locomotive, drawing a train of impossible pink cars. A steamboat of marvelous design, with paddle-wheels revolving in a mass of fish, tells in purple how the trip from Suez to Djeddah was made. A train of green camels informs the uninitiated how the pious man journeyed from the Red Sea coast across the desert to Mecca. Huge lions, with round and almost human faces, in bright orange, tell of dangers in the desert march. But all ends happily, for the pictured story invariably concludes with the caravan halted before the prophet's tomb, with the good man prostrating himself in prayer thereat. Hadji Youssef Achmet knows no joy greater than sitting in his doorway beneath this mural proof of holiness, receiving the salaams of passers-by. Eternal peace is his. He knows this, and every Mussulman seeing him knows it as well.

The strangest of Cairo customs, perhaps, is the hiring of professional mourners, who, at a funeral, do the shrieking, howling, and garment-rending for the bereaved family. These black-shawled and barefooted objects are frequently to be seen, like birds of ill omen, squatting outside a house wherein a person is dying, awaiting the signal to begin their lamentations, which presumably vary in degree according to the stipulated payment. They follow the corpse to the cemetery, bewailing at the top of their voices and rending their scanty clothing. The place of interment reached, the wailing stops suddenly; the women enjoy a chat by themselves, possibly discuss the prospects of further business, and,

In Fascinating Cairo

if satisfied with the money given them by the relatives of the deceased, trot off homeward. Other forms of bereavement give them employment also. A score of these hags follow to the railway-station the squad of policemen taking a convict to prison. The women howl and curse, throw handfuls of dust over their heads, scream voluble and wide-embracing Arabic oaths at the authorities, and make the street almost unbearable with shrieks and lamentations. The train started for Tourah, the shrieking subsides, and they are ready for further professional engagements. The conscripting of young men for the army being profoundly dreaded, hired wailers accompany their weeping relatives when the unhappy lads are marched to the barracks.

The Cairene, never cultivating physical exertion, emerges from boyhood to sedate manhood before he is twenty, with tranquillity his chief characteristic. The middle-class man enjoys looking at dances, but never dances himself; he is fond of music, but never sings or plays. Everything athletic is foreign to his nature. He takes to sedentary amusements, and in shop or home will ponder long over a game of draughts or chess. If belonging to the class that goes to the café for diversion, he will watch for hours the antics of street hoodlums, or join in a game of interminable backgammon—which all Egyptians love—to decide who is to pay a few millièmes for the coffee or the smoke from the hubble-bubble. When he can sit for hours in front of the café, smoking the hubble-bubble, he realizes that he is doing the superlative of all that is grand,

and feels justified in giving it the character of a public spectacle. This is the conservative Egyptian, who sees nothing good in the movement Europeanizing his beloved Cairo.

Men of the wealthy classes are becoming daily less and less Oriental in appearance and habits. They wear clothes of Parisian make, pose before the photographer's camera, speak fluent French, dance with foreign ladies, flirt a little, and profess to think "five-o'clock tea" an institution reflecting the highest civilization. Each has his stall at the opera, and applauds at the right time. Between acts he calls on friends of the *haut ton* in their boxes, and perhaps recruits a coaching or river party for the following day. If the visitors are from abroad, the courteous native most likely will explain that as a lad he witnessed the premier production of "Aida" in that very theater, Verdi's opera being an item in the program arranged by Ismail for the edification of the Empress Eugénie and other distinguished guests attending the opening of the Suez Canal. If the visitors are from Alexandria only, the Cairo gentleman probably rings the changes on the contrasting temperature of the two cities, wondering how Alexandrians can stand the excessive humidity of the coast. The visitors retaliate by claiming that the superdryness of the capital affects their health, whereas in Alexandria they are always well. Thus the weather, in its humid aspect, is sadly overworked as a topic of small talk in the country having the best and driest climate in the world. If this ac-

In Fascinating Cairo

complished Egyptian would remove his inevitable tarboosh, in shape and shade of red the latest thing from Stamboul, he might to all intents and purposes pass for a European. But he never will, for he is as devoted to the religion of Islam as the man praying five times a day in mosque or street. His Europeanizing is but superficial, and in his heart, perhaps, he abhors all infidels.

The ladies of the rich man's household likewise know French, and affect gowns and ornaments from Paris and Vienna. Custom compels them to view the opera from screened boxes, and they are never included in coaching or river parties. They wear the gauziest of veils—exceedingly thin if their faces are beautiful—when driven from palace to palace in European-built carriages. If opportunity offers, they are not averse to peering from behind their carriage curtains at passing Europeans, revealing glimpses of their faces, and possibly the fact that they are smoking dainty cigarettes. Europeans are inclined to believe that Egyptian ladies admire European customs and perhaps wish to emerge from the veiled seclusion of the East. This is not the fact, for their adherence to the tenets of Mohammedanism is still rigid, and they look pityingly upon foreign women, so little valued by their lords as to be permitted to roam over the world with faces exposed to any man's admiration.

There is something profoundly impressive in the devotion of the Mohammedan to his religion. It governs his actions, pervades his thoughts, conversation, business dealings, and conduct of every-day life. He reads his Koran faithfully, for it lays down his standard of ethics, and is the foundation of his code of laws. See him at prayer, in the mosque, field, or busy street, addressing his supplications to Allah, through his prophet, face turned to Mecca: his faith is complete and his sincerity unquestionable. He cares not how the onlooker may regard him. The fellah on the canal-bank utters the same fervent, heartfelt prayer as the pasha prostrate upon his silken rug within the Mehemet Ali mosque. The cardinal requirement of the Koran, that food and riches must be shared with the unfortunate, is literally obeyed. The Mohammedan has no cant or hypocrisy in his nature. He is tolerant of all religions, but looks with horror upon the unbeliever. It is the good Mohammedan of whom I write—and there are many such; not the fanatic, liable by excitement to become a frenzied demon.

The provision of the Koran permitting four wives has become more honored in the breach by Cairenes than in the observance. Few Egyptians in public life have now more than one wife. Khedive Tewfik gave his influence to the monogamic idea; and the present khedive, although not taking a wife from the elevated class from which his mother came, is following his father's example. The middle class is gradually following the matrimonial precept of its superiors. Possibly its men found polygamy not particularly conducive to domestic tranquillity, in the absence of sufficient means to maintain several establishments. The

In Fascinating Cairo

common people, however, adhere to a plurality of wives, resenting what they look upon as a movement to abridge the Koranic custom and privilege.

The formality of divorce is much simpler than that of marriage. Among those not burdened with estates and personal belongings it is as easy and direct as the dismissal of a servant. The words "Woman, I divorce thee," uttered three times in the presence of witnesses, if attended by the return of the trifling sum that formed her dower, are as binding as the final decree of any court in the world. The restitution of dower sometimes leads to complications, but it is necessary to render the husband's words effectual.

Woman's position in the Egyptian capital is materially benefiting by the movement looking toward the education of native girls. Twenty years ago native ladies regarded education as the learning of sufficient French or Italian to read novels or follow the plot of the opera. The past few years have developed a desire among upper-class women to have their daughters educated with as much care as boys are, and an important adjunct to the household, consequently, is the European governess, most often English. A sister of the khedive, the Princess Khadija, is an active agent in improving the educational status of poor girls.

Most women visitors to Cairo are curious to see the interior of a harem. But this, as Europeans understand it, no longer exists in Egypt. Every native house, however, has its harem division, set apart for women, as the salamlik is for men—nothing more. In this department reside the wife or wives and children of the master, with the addition, perhaps, of his mother. In this case her rule is probably absolute. It is she who chooses instructresses for the children, orders the affairs of the household, and even prescribes the fabrics, fashions, and adornments of the women, who are simply the wives of his Excellency the Pasha. It is mother-in-law rule, literally. The windows of the harem usually overlook a courtyard or rear street, and are screened with mushrabeah lattices, penetrable only by the gaze of a person within. To minister to the wants of the women's division, a small army of servants—shiny black "slaves" from Nubia and Berber, and possibly a fair Circassian or two, imported from Constantinople—is essential. "Slavery" of this sort is scarcely bondage. It is the law of Egypt that manumission can be had for the asking, with little circumlocution or delay. These servitors are kindly treated, value their home, and shrink from any movement toward legal freedom. Except to the master and sons of the house, the harem is closed to all men, but women friends come and go freely. The tall, high-cheek-boned black men guarding the entrance to the harem, in these progressive days in Egypt possessing no suggestion of the houri scene of the stage, are trained from childhood to keep unauthorized persons from intruding, and have a highly developed aversion to sight-seers.

The howling dervish of Cairo is more or less a fraud. Go any Friday afternoon in the season—

In Fascinating Cairo

his religious fervor finds expression only during the tourist season—to the little mosque on the Nile bank midway between Kasr el-Ain and Old Cairo, and witness the weekly *zik'r* of these fiends. Sitting in a circle on the stone floor of a high-vaulted room are the dervishes, twenty or thirty in number. Their bearded leader, spectacled, and grave under his green turban, squats on a mat in the center. Standing outside the circle is a smooth and oily-faced old man, with a simple reed flute, flanked by others with large tom-toms. Clustered along two sides of the room are tourists, costumed in a way that would delight an arranger of up-to-date melodrama of the spectacular variety. Ladies, having misgivings as to what the entertainment is to be, seem to wish to sit behind the men, until the hotel dragomans having the visit in charge assure them that it is to be "very nice—very nice, yes! Mrs. Vanderbilt of Chicago she come last week, yes!"

A hush of silence falls over dervishes and tourists, and the leader mumbles a prayer. The circle of performers break into response; first in quiet, measured tones, then faster, faster, faster. Their bodies sway in perfect unison as, now growing vociferous, they affirm the creed of Islam. Faster, faster go the bodies, and the wild chant of "Allah la Ilaha," in perfect cadence, is becoming a volume like that of Niagara. The leader raises a warning hand, and the hush that follows instantly is broken only by the cooing of doves resting on the ledges of the windows in the dome. Then, low and mysterious, comes again the mumble of the leader. The dervishes spring to their feet. Off go robes and turbans, their stringy locks falling nearly to their hips. One of the howlers, placing his hand to the side of his mouth, strikes up a falsetto note that rises above the barbaric roar of the tom-toms and flute, plaintive, penetrating. Faster and faster swing heads and bodies; the air is filled with swishing hair; heads come perilously near striking the floor, or leaving their shoulders in the backward swing. Every dervish is frantic, beside himself with the ebullition of fervor, as he repeats in hisses the sacred exclamation, "Heû, heû. heû, heû, heû, heû, heû." On, on they go, until their mental intoxication is complete, and with staring eyes and frothing mouths two or three sink exhausted to the floor. Admirers break into the circle and lovingly carry into the air the dervishes who have "gone *melbûs*." The performance of the howling dervishes is over, and the coins given gladly by the spectators to get away from the mosque amount to enough to keep the howlers until the succeeding Friday. It is something to see — once. The motives of the whirling dervishes, like those of their howling brethren, are open to suspicion.

Another widely described institution, satisfying most spectators with a single view, is the dancing of the Ghawâzi girls, to be witnessed at a dozen Cairo theaters and cafés. The Chicago Midway, and certain places of amusement in Paris, by means of elaborations, have given this exhibition undeserved prominence. A performance wherein

A HOWLING DERVISH.

In Fascinating Cairo

the feet are seldom lifted from the floor can be termed "dancing" only by courtesy; but as an illustration of what the muscles of the body may be trained to do, the *danse du ventre* is in a way remarkable. The Ghawâzi, bred from childhood to their calling, are deemed essential at every form of Egyptian merrymaking, prince and fellah alike employing them. These women form a class, with headquarters at Keneh in Upper Egypt, and by thirty have generally managed to wriggle themselves into a competency. They are not necessarily immoral, but are not respected, the habitual exposure of the face, if nothing more, placing them beyond the pale.

Ophthalmia is the curse of the native in Cairo. Of six people of the poorer class perhaps only two will have fair sight; and of the rest, one will be blind, one can see from but one eye, and two will have otherwise defective vision. Few Egyptians have perfect eyesight, and the superstitious dread of falling under the baneful influence of the "evil eye" is responsible for this condition. Poor children go for years practically unwashed, the parents' theory being that if their children are made attractive they are almost certain to be stricken by the evil eye. Their unclean faces attract hordes of insects, never brushed away by their idolizing mothers, for that would be unlucky. During the summer months especially, children's eyes are almost hidden by pestiferous flies, and a race of people with imperfect vision is the result. Even educated Egyptians have the superstition to some extent, and men and women of high degree wear rings of silver wire to protect them from the evil eye. Cairo would be a rich field for the exercise of a little practical philanthropy based on the employment of soap, water, and scrubbing-brush; but it would come into conflict with the religion, which makes of the blind man a person to be revered, and affords him an almost priestly occupation.

Strange to relate, Cairo is being adorned with statues, like cities in the Christian world. In his determination to make his capital a triumph of artistic beauty, Ismail courageously ordered a French sculptor, thirty years or more ago, to model a few figures of Egyptian military worthies. The faithful in Alexandria had permitted a colossal effigy in bronze of Mehemet Ali to be raised in the public square, although a tenet of the Koran was violated thereby. Another statue, perpetuating the military exploits of the second viceroy of Egypt, Ibrahim Pasha, had been erected in the Place of the Opera in Cairo, without provoking an outbreak among strict followers of the Koran. The bronze lions guarding the Nile bridge were likewise accepted without protest. Ismail believed it would awaken the martial spirit of his subjects if every public square in Cairo could have its bronze presentment of a departed hero or notable; and if it amused him to turn the old city of the califs into a statuary gallery, who was to say nay? I suspect that Ismail must have seen the artistic side of the sculptured sentiment of the Campo Santo in Genoa.

In Fascinating Cairo

He was resolved, at all events, to erect images of distinguished Egyptians all over Cairo, and Frenchmen were employed to make them. Two were delivered before the national exchequer was seized with financial cramp and further supplies countermanded. For lack of money, perhaps, or the discovery that it was forbidden by the religion of Islam to fashion the image of man, the statues were given a resting-place in a shed. Two or three years ago they were excavated from the dust of a quarter of a century, and, under the guidance of British engineers, were placed upright on granite pedestals in the new quarter of the city; and natives, squatting on their haunches in the squares thus embellished, find in them a subject for never-ending chatter. They have forgotten that Ismail had the figures made, and place the responsibility of the bronzes at the door of the *Inglēsy*.

Had Ismail not lost his throne, and the money-lenders of Europe been content to let him have as much cash as he wanted, Cairo would to-day be more beautiful. It was his dream to make an Eastern Paris of his desert capital. The French metropolis, he argued, could be reproduced, if the financial agents of Paris and London did not object. A considerable part of the money borrowed was spent by Ismail at Gizeh, nearly opposite the spot where tradition claims that Moses was found in the bulrushes. Gardens like the Tuileries extended from the Nile nearly to the edge of the Libyan Desert; dozens of lath-and-plaster structures, with walls painted in a style suggesting solidity, went

Present-Day Egypt

up as by magic, in the fulfilment of his building passion; and many are the stories told of the magnificence of everything he did.

Electric tram-cars now rush boisterously through the streets of Cairo, filled with people who never understood the "go fever" until the advent of the street-railway, two or three years ago; and the Egyptians' best friend, the donkey, has been cast out from the capital by the trolley-car. The Egyptians take so kindly to tram-car riding that one wonders if their ancestors, who developed astronomy and mathematics as sciences and begot culture, knew the secret of the electric current. The patrons of the tram-cars are soldiers, Levantines, small merchants and clerks, turbaned sheiks, Bedouins, and simple fellaheen in town on business—and perhaps this business is chiefly to have a ride on the cars. In every direction—to Bulak, the citadel, Abbassieh, through the Ismaileh quarter, even to the site of ancient Fostat—the cars run, their occupants looking pityingly upon wayfarers employing nature's locomotion or the humble donkey or stalking camel. The people have learned the intricacies of "transfers" and "round trips," and their satisfaction over the street traction enterprise, doing more than all other agencies to obliterate the Cairo of old, seems sublime.

There is something painfully incongruous in the idea of being carried by trolley to the Sphinx and Pyramids. But the line enables the visitor who has first driven in state to Gizeh to go again and again at a cost of a few piasters. The authorities con-

TYPES OF MALE AND FEMALE BEDOUINS.

In Fascinating Cairo

trolling public affairs were not so short-sighted when giving the concession for the Pyramids railway as newspaper readers may have believed. The line in no way mars the superb beauty of the embowered causeway leading from the Nile to Mena House, for it is a goodly distance to the southward of the carriageway. If the foreigners directing the tramway company failed to make money from the start, it was due for a year or more to their being called upon almost daily to pay for a life extinguished or a body maimed by their modern cars of Juggernaut.

CHAPTER II

IN FASCINATING CAIRO (*Continued*)

A PROOF of the claim that Cairo is being Europeanized at an uncalled-for pace is suggested by innumerable shop-signs of cigarette-makers, announcing that they are "Purveyors to His Highness the Khedive," when that potentate is known to use tobacco in no form; another is the ostentatious advertisement of a barbering establishment that its keeper is "Hair-dresser to the Right Honorable Diplomatic Agent of Great Britain, by Appointment," when it is seen that the gentleman referred to has little need for tonsorial attentions. If these petty dishonesties fail to convince one that the Egyptian capital is adopting European ways and customs, the "Want to go shootin' t'-day?" or the "Want anyt'ing?"—the latter covering a multitude of sins,—that will be whispered in the stranger's ear by native vagabonds a dozen times in the course of a stroll in the Sharia Kamel or the Esbekieh Gardens, surely will; and the side-spring "Congress" boots, made of questionable leather, and the ulsters and other English clothes of impossible check or plaid, disfiguring the windows and fronts of shops in the Mouski, will painfully accentuate the fact.

In Fascinating Cairo

The bazaars, however, show no sign of European intrusion, and are to-day as Oriental as when Lane wrote his "Modern Egyptians." The bazaars of Damascus, possibly, are more correctly Eastern, but not so those of Constantinople and Smyrna. John Bull invades the bazaars of Cairo only as a sight-seer and purchaser, wearing sun-helmet and pugree, however chilling the wintry weather. He usually thinks the prices dear, and parts with his coins only after hours of dickering, and does not forget his bakshish. The bazaars are the only places in Egypt where the tourist receives bakshish. Elsewhere he gives it, or could give it, every minute of the day. Americans, on the other hand, regard the prices as cheap, and buy, buy, buy. It amuses them to sip the shopkeeper's excellent coffee and smoke his perfumed cigarettes. This hospitality partaken of, they buy more embroidered jackets, gauze scarfs, and inlaid weapons. Both British and American pay more than the things are worth, of course; but the Transatlantic purchaser has a balance of time to his credit.

It is novel to buy silk fabrics by weight rather than by measurement. The slipper bazaar, with the sun shut out by projecting lattices and awnings, is a subdued blend of red and yellow. Black leather is seldom seen there. The crude art of the brass-workers' lane, where serious-faced youths embellish finger-basins and coffee-trays with designs conceived by their forefathers when perspective was not valued, is popular. The carpet and rug bazaar

Present-Day Egypt

is a busy mart, where values are high and the sellers understand human nature. Turn to the right, turn to the left, go where you will, the shops appeal to some taste or fancy you possess. The jewelry bazaar, with its anklets and nose-rings of leaden-looking silver or brassy gold, has no temptation for the American, however.

The dingy passage where scents are dealt in is a nest of cheats who can sell a phial of common perfumed oil for genuine attar or essence without compunction. The tent bazaar, in which truly artistic appliqué awnings and hangings are wrought without visible pattern by men and boys, is always inviting. Two or three of these needlemen, perhaps, were sent to Chicago during the World's Fair; but a hundred will tell you they have been in Chicago, each producing dog-eared business cards or a stray coin of Uncle Sam's minting in substantiation of the statement. They are agreed that the exposition was a grand "fantasia," but most of them witnessed it vicariously. "Anteekas" are offered for sale in nearly every shop of every department of the vast labyrinth. The scarab, especially, is pushed into your face on every hand, and whether you give a piaster or a dozen coins of gold, you will have the same uncertainty as to the genuineness of the sacred beetle. The Red Sea turquoise, gummed to a bit of reed, is likewise omnipresent; it is beautiful to look at, but may change color in a week.

The throng of people in the bazaars is a study in humanity, as entertaining, perhaps, as the contents

In Fascinating Cairo

of the shops. Rotund women, enveloped in the unbecoming black-silk *habbeh*, displaying feet and ankles clad in magenta stockings and white slippers, seem to go out of their way to jostle Europeans, until driven off by one's dragoman. Donkeys, even camels, laden with merchandise, force their way through passages scarcely wide enough for two persons walking abreast. These, and persistent beggars and offensively dirty children, are the drawbacks to one's enjoyment here. But the bazaars are interesting, withal.

On the way back through the Mouski a half-hour may profitably be passed in viewing the fabrication at Hatoun's or Parvis's of the mushrabeah work, to be utilized in artistic screens and tables. Primitive indeed is the method of turning the myriad bits of wood for the mushrabeah, on tiny lathes revolved by hand, while the chisel is held by the bare feet of the operator, generally a lad, who guides the tool with the other hand.

The Mouski used to be all that an Oriental street of shops should be, but the past dozen years have seen a great change in its character. There no longer is matting overhead, affording protection from the parching sun in summer. In its place swinging signs indicate the presence of modern establishments, including a "British Bar," where all and sundry are cordially invited to try the American drinks compounded by La Belle Violette, "just arrived from Chicago." There are jewelers' shops that would attract notice in the Avenue de l'Opéra in Paris, the windows of which are filled with diamonds and other precious stones of a size suggesting that the kilo had supplanted the karat as a standard of weight. Places where ready-made clothing is sold, with unmistakable Hebraic names over the doors, have a remarkable similarity to Bowery stores.

Sandwiched between great magazines where "Prix Fixe" cards are conspicuously displayed may yet be found the *dokkan* of old. This is but a recess in the wall, with *mastabah*, or seat, of its proprietor on a level with the floor of the diminutive shop. On this the Arab trader, in flowing robe and turban, spends the day, bargaining at times in a leisurely way, now and then dozing, with his rosary of sandalwood beads ever between his fingers. When he goes out he hangs a network curtain before the shelves where his silken stuffs, spices, or embroideries are stored. Egyptians respect the netted veil, and, returned from his errand, or prayer in the mosque, the merchant resumes his seat on the mastabah, knowing that his stock has not been rifled during his absence. The water-seller's cry of "Oh, may God compensate thee," may attract this merchant, descended from the times of Abraham and Joseph. If so, he exchanges a millième for a draught from the earthen jar, returns to his meditations, and dreams of vanishing Cairo of Haussmannized avenues, and great emporia with plate-glass windows filled with ridiculous papier-mâché figures, in a few years destined to metamorphose the city of the califs. The Mouski, unlike the bazaars, is being Europeanized at a rate sad-

In Fascinating Cairo

dening to one who loves the Cairo of Ismail and Tewfik.

Habitués have their favorite mosques, as they have their favorite singers at the opera or horses on the Ghizereh race-course. With a city covering twelve or more square miles and having a sky-line effect of a forest of domes and minarets, there is sufficient variety of places of worship to suit any taste. Diminutive Kait Bey, in the midst of the Tombs of the Mamelukes, is deservedly sketched and photographed scores of times every day. The unfinished mosque of Rafai, under the citadel, contains the body of spendthrift Ismail, who ordered its construction, but is otherwise unimportant. The gem of the Mohammedan artistic world, admitted by good judges, is the venerable and bathhaun mosque of Sultan Hassan, close to the Rafai structure, always spoken of by the faithful as "the superb." For architectural beauty this Saracenic pile surpasses the Byzantine St. Sophia at Constantinople. Its vast circular dome, springing from a square tower, with corner pendentives of marvelous design, is a liberal education in architecture, although fashioned more than five hundred years ago. The Sultan Hassan mosque is one of the eral artistic structures known to travelers e the tale is told that the designer was put to or his hands cut off by his appreciative master to prevent a repetition of his artistic triumph.

The pencil-like minarets of the Mehemet Ali mosque, visible long before one reaches Cairo, are

Present-Day Egypt

as beautiful as the Hassan dome is wonderful. This mosque, with its alabaster walls and rich carpets, is attractive in its way, but comparatively new, and consequently clean. Connoisseurs shake their heads, however, when debating any pretension to its being "good art." The mosque of Amr, in Old Cairo, is the oldest in Egypt, its foundation having been laid in the year 643 of our calendar; and Ahmed Ibn Tulûn is the oldest in Cairo proper, having been built in 879. This latter is said to be a copy of the Kaaba at Mecca. Only in Coptic churches does the visitor discover pictorial representations of sacred scenes and personages. The Mohammedan on occasion takes the spoils of war to his house of worship, but never the presentment of human form.

Strange to state, Cairo has no obelisk, nor has Alexandria. New York possesses the last of these relics, probably; London and Paris have each a fine one, while Rome and Constantinople have many. One cannot behold these reminders of the greatness of ancient Egypt, in the cities mentioned, without a feeling of pity for Cairo, where rest the Rameses, but whose nearest obelisk is on the plain of Heliopolis, six miles away. Most tourists drive out to see it, planning their excursion to include a visit to the ostrich-farm close by, and also to catch a glimpse of the Virgin's tree en route.

Early in my residence in the Nile metropolis I evolved a project for removing to Cairo the superb obelisk standing near the river's bank at Luxor, and if possible having the expense defrayed by a few

WOOD-WORKERS.

In Fascinating Cairo

wealthy compatriots finding health and recreation under Egyptian skies. First I sought the opinion of a New-Yorker, proprietor of a great newspaper, on the subject. Accustomed to seeing the pros and cons of a question at a glance, with natural shrewdness tempered by much diplomatic experience, he foresaw in a minute more obstacles to the project than I had discovered in a month's consideration of the scheme. The engineering problems of bringing a monolith seventy-five feet long and weighing two hundred and twelve tons several hundred miles down the Nile, and reërecting it in Abdin Square, had chiefly interested me. My New York friend predicted an avalanche of reproach from the whole civilized world, that would surely be started directly the matter was made public. "It will not do at all," he said, in summing up. A Chicago friend, on the other hand, pronounced the scheme a good one. "Put me down for five hundred dollars toward the expense; and I can get a dozen more Chicagoans to give the same," he added.

In time I was forced to admit that the archæologists of France, Italy, England, and perhaps the United States, having provided their own countries with obelisks, would assail the suggestion to give dear old Cairo just one of the massive shafts that were indigenous to Egypt; and I saw enough in the opinion of the astute New-Yorker to cool my ardor and cause me to abandon the plan that sentiment had suggested. But I cannot help thinking that the capital of Egypt is entitled to an obelisk. How graceful the act if some great city, in which the

Present-Day Egypt

transplanted granite of Assuan is yielding to the ravages of climate, would return to the country of the Pharaohs one of the priceless monuments of which it has been deprived!

No picture of Cairo that does not include the soldier can be considered complete, for the military aspect of the city is in almost aggressive evidence. When there is no campaign calling the troops to the Sudan, from six to nine thousand men are quartered in the capital. Nile palaces, khedival apartments in the citadel, and straggling pink barracks at Abbassieh, shelter English regiments; while tucked in everywhere, even extending miles out of Cairo to the canvas city on the desert road to Suez, are Egyptian soldiers of all degrees of color and of every class. And what a variety of costumes! There are Arab lancers in uniforms of light blue, almost esthetic in shade; members of the camel corps and Sudanese infantry regiments of the blackest of black men, wearing kaki costumes of the color of the desert; and men of other arms of the military establishment, in the smartest of white clothes.

By company or regiment, soldiers are so frequently marched through the streets that the visitor might believe Cairo to be a vast military camp. Martial music is the adjunct of every function and every anniversary, religious and festive. Drum and fife corps, full military bands, some of them mounted, parade daily, playing frequently the beautiful khedival hymn. It is a part of the scheme of administration to keep the soldier in evi-

In Fascinating Cairo

dence, impressing the simple native with the importance of the army, in which he must serve, however reluctant. The obverse of this display is the recompense of the soldier—five cents a day for five years. Egyptian soldiers are well disciplined and make a fine appearance on parade. Their comrades recruited from the region south of Assuan, forming the so-called Sudanese regiments, are fearless fighters, but lack the smartness of appearance essential to reviews and dress-parades. The superior officers of the khedival army are Englishmen, "loaned" by the British War Office, and paid by the Egyptian government twice as much as their services under the British flag would bring. A captain in his regiment in England is a colonel in Egypt, and a lieutenant is a captain or major.

It hardly required the victory of the Anglo-Egyptian expedition, in 1898, to prove General Kitchener, sirdar (commander-in-chief) of the Egyptian army, to be a remarkable man and a great soldier. Those familiar with the official life of recent years in Egypt knew this. Their attention was drawn to him by the expedition against the Mahdi, when the hope of Gordon's release from beleaguered Khartum was enlisting the sympathies of the world. Disastrous as the expedition was, Kitchener emerged from the campaign with an established reputation as a soldier of infinite resource, vigor, and brilliant strategy, which, combined with his knowledge of the customs and dialects of the Sudan, stamped him as England's best

Present-Day Egypt

desert fighter. In command of the mounted troops at the battle of Toski, in 1889, young Kitchener headed off the great dervish general, Njumi, who had annihilated Hicks's army, and who despised Egyptian soldiers, compelling him to stand, fight, and be crushed. Rapidly ascending the grades thereafter, Kitchener in a few years found himself the sirdar of the khedival army.

To Kitchener belongs the credit of organizing and training the new army, recruited from the fellaheen of the country. To build up an effective force from the same peasants who had fled before the Mahdist warriors, who stopped in their flight to kneel on the ground and stretch forth their necks to the sword, was a task calculated to dishearten an ordinary man; but to Kitchener and his assistants this obstacle only quickened their determination to attain success. To accomplish the end crowning their efforts required almost a reconstruction of the Egyptian nature. Had Kitchener and his aides not triumphed in this, the Egyptian army could never have driven back its old-time foes from Firket, from Dongola, from Berber, and finally from Omdurman itself. Yet the heroes of Omdurman were the brothers of the cravens who made the name Tel-el-Kebir a synonym for all that is cowardly. And only sixteen years had intervened between the two battles! After the routing of the Khalifa's army no fair-minded person can criticize the fighting capacity of the son of the Nile, when well led. It used to be the fashion to sneer at him as a warrior, and not without reason. Even now

In Fascinating Cairo

he is not a perfect soldier; but Spartan virtues must not be looked for from a nation of Helots.

General Lord Kitchener, sirdar of the Egyptian army and governor-general of the Sudan, is yet several years on the right side of fifty, is every inch a soldier, and only a soldier, and has the proverbial dash and courage of the Irishman. He went to Egypt resolved to win his spurs in a field where others had failed, and never for an instant allowed his courage to falter or his energies to be diverted to other channels. He has, indeed, added his name to the list of great military leaders of the nineteenth century.

The British army of occupation, which is independent of the Egyptian army, is in Egypt on financial terms liberal to the Egyptians, for the khedival government pays only the difference between the cost of home and foreign service, being less than half a million dollars yearly for the forty-five hundred men composing this contingent. Usually about three thousand Britishers are kept in Cairo; but, on occasions when there has been friction between the khedive and the British administrators, these have been countermarched so ingeniously as to give the impression that ten times as many redcoats were there. The English officers lend much to a winter's gaiety. Courageous fellows, trained to conquer, no season is complete that does not add to their conquests those of the ball-room. "Scarlet fever" is in the atmosphere of Cairo breathed by the girl visitor, but is seldom serious or lasting.

Present-Day Egypt

The diurnal procession of young women to the Nile bank just before the going down of the sun, to obtain the water required for the evening and early morning in their homes, presents a beautiful picture of womanly grace. These Rebeccas hold themselves erect and walk with superlative grace and majesty. If a promenading Fifth Avenue girl could exhibit half the naturalness she would be the envy of every spectator. Egyptian girls begin early to perform their share of the work of the home, and at seven or eight years commence to carry half-filled water-jars, and at twelve think nothing of balancing a full half-hundredweight on their heads, walking leisurely homeward, chatting with neighbors bent on the same mission, and discussing the gossip of the neighborhood with unconcealed relish. For thousands of years their ancestors did the same; but they carried the water-jars represented in biblical pictures. The present generation, discarding these, prefers the square two-gallon tins in which Standard Oil has come to Egypt. They are lighter than the pottery jars, and if the modern Rebecca becomes excited in discussion, the petroleum tin never breaks in its fall.

Every petroleum tin coming to Egypt finds a use in the daily life of the people. The "slates" of school-boys are but sides of oil tins, on which they write their sums and quotations from the Koran with reed pens. The petroleum tins from America supply tinsmiths of the bazaars with material from which they fashion lantern-frames, household utensils, ornaments, and even bird-cages and traveling-

In Fascinating Cairo

boxes for the peasantry. Not a scrap is wasted. To discover that dates purchased at up-Nile landings are packed in boxes on the bottoms of which are impressed such legends as "Best American," "Standard," and "95 Degrees Pure," may be startling to fastidious tourists.

The great school of the Mohammedan world is one of Cairo's important sights; but few travelers are aware of its interest, and not one in a hundred visits it. The Pyramids, the Sphinx, and the Nile are too absorbing for tourists to remember that in the same wondrous city exists the largest and oldest university in the world—El-Azhar, meaning "the splendid." Constantinople may be regarded as the official head of the great religion of Islam, but Cairo for nine hundred years has been the educational center, and if one wishes to attain the summit of Mussulman learning he must attend the classes of this collegiate establishment. Unless one be familiar with Arabic and knows where to look among musty books and manuscripts in the Egyptian Library, it is very difficult to get reliable information regarding this wonderful mosque-college.

The claim of possessing the oldest university has often been made for Oxford, Paris, or Bologna, but the founding of their ancient seats of learning is legendary as to dates, while the records of El-Azhar are clear from the year 975. Whether it is really a "university" in our meaning can be more appropriately questioned. It is widely different from Harvard and Yale, but wise men of the East have ever termed it a university.

Present-Day Egypt

Years ago it was difficult and disagreeable to view the interior of this great school that draws scholars from the remotest lands where the Koran is read. Now the formalities are simple and easily complied with, and the presence of strangers is scarcely noticed. From the hotel quarter it is but a fifteen-minute drive to El-Azhar. One passes through that marvelous street of shops, the Mouski, and turning off, forces his way through the narrow lane known as the "Street of the Booksellers," where Arab workmen are binding curious-looking volumes, seated cross-legged on the floor of tiny box-like shops, and with a surging conglomeration of humanity, camels, and braying donkeys passing not two feet away. This brings one to the "Barbers' Gate," about which are always to be seen students having their heads so closely shaved as to leave no suggestion of hair.

The structure, too often restored to leave any indication of the original building, surrounds a large open court with arcades on every side. The lofty minarets are fine examples of Eastern art. The pavement is of marble, much worn in places, and everywhere polished by constant use. There are seven entrances, each with a name as singular as that where the barbers congregate. El-Azhar is so surrounded by houses that very little can be seen of it externally, and the building is almost destitute of architectural embellishment.

The enormous square court is bordered with porticos, each divided into various compartments for the separate use of students of different nations.

In Fascinating Cairo

One, for example, is for those who come from Algeria, another for those from Morocco, one for Indians, one for Nubians, one for Turks, and so on. There is a compartment even for students from the holy city of Mecca, where the prophet Mohammed is buried, and there are divisions for scholars representing different sections of Egypt.

There is a department for blind pupils, as well, for whom special instructors and funds are provided. It is a strange fact that these unfortunates are peculiarly turbulent and fanatical. If they believe their rights invaded, or their food not good, they give way to fury and attack any one within reach. If aware that an "unbelieving Christian" is looking at them, their resentment becomes offensively apparent.

Followers of the prophet hold different views in regard to their theology, as do different denominations of Christians. There are four great orthodox sects of Mohammedans,—Shafeites, Malekites, Hanefites, and Hambalites,—and all are represented in El-Azhar. An American would think it a queer place of learning, for nowhere is there a desk or a chair, and masters and pupils appear to go about everything backward. Before they cross the threshold in entering the place they remove their shoes, but always keep their heads covered; and all books read from right to left, the first leaf being, according to our way of thinking, the last.

There are more than ten thousand scholars and two hundred and twenty-five masters, and the period of instruction may be indefinitely extended, even for a lifetime; but from three to six years is the usual course. One may see old and grizzled men there, as well as children of four years. The institution is so richly endowed and owns such valuable property—for few true Mohammedans of fortune die without leaving something to El-Azhar of Cairo—that no scholar is compelled to pay anything, although many, from choice, contribute to the expenses.

The masters get no pay, but receive liberal allowances of food. Those of certain degree once a week draw several hundred loaves of bread,—a traditional custom,—and these loaves presumably find their way into outside shops and are sold. A master usually teaches in odd hours at private houses, reads the Koran at weddings and funerals, copies books, or holds a petty office of a religious character to which a small salary is attached. Wealthy students voluntarily help the masters to live. The head master, known as the Sheik El-Azhar, is chosen from the faculty for his superior knowledge and holiness, and in the eyes of the faithful occupies a position not many degrees less than that of the khedive.

Some of the sheiks are men of marvelous learning, but independence of thought is never found among them. Progressiveness is discouraged as a dangerous tendency. Masters and pupils learn only what may be found in books centuries old, and religion pervades every branch of study. Students who come from abroad toil for years to learn the Arabic grammar, after which they take up re-

In Fascinating Cairo

ligious science, with the Koran as text-book. Then follows jurisprudence, religious and secular. Literature, syntax, philosophy, prosody, logic, and intricacies of the Koranic teaching as directed to an upright life, round out the course.

In lieu of a professor occupying a "chair" of any high-sounding "ology," he may be said to hold such and such a pillar, for when lecturing he sits on a sheepskin rug at the base of a stone column, with his students squatted in a half-circle before him. Nearly three hundred marble pillars support the roof of the porticos and such portions of El-Azhar as are not open to the sky, and each is a "classroom" for some particular subject. Pupils listen with rapt attention, taking part in the discussion of a theme so intently as to be oblivious of the presence of Christian spectators. A lecture finished, they respectfully kiss the hand of their instructor and hasten to another class to become absorbed in further study.

Equality seems to be characteristic of the university. Outward evidences of superiority and position are unimportant, for the son of the pasha or bey, in robes of silk, sits side by side with peasant youths clothed scantily in coarse cotton. Occasionally a green turban is seen, indicating that its wearer has made a pilgrimage to the holy city, or that his family is believed to be descended from the prophet. Rich and poor alike perform at stated intervals the purifying ablutions at the fountains within the inclosure, and all prostrate themselves in prayer many times a day. This they do when-

Present-Day Egypt

ever the spirit moves them, although at fixed hours all pray in unison, with heads invariably turned toward the "Kibla," the niche in the largest assembly-room, indicating the direction of Mecca.

A thousand or two youths actually live within the walls of El-Azhar. They partake of their simple meals when the spirit moves them. Their food is exceedingly plain and inexpensive. A bowl of lentil soup, a flat loaf or cake of bread, and a handful of garlic or perhaps dates, are enough to attract a group of school-fellows, over which they discuss affairs and joke as youths do elsewhere. To needy students nine hundred loaves of bread are distributed each day.

The great quadrangle presents a picture to be rivaled nowhere in the world. Singly and in groups, students sit on their skin rugs, earnestly toiling over lessons. No matter how scorching the sun's rays, if the impulse seizes them they stretch at full length on the pavement, enveloped in their long outer garments, and tranquilly sleep. Pupils and professors step over and around them, always respecting their slumber. Cats without number, that seem to belong to the place, hobnob with the boys upon terms of perfect harmony; but dogs, being "unclean" by Koranic teaching, are never permitted by the doorkeepers to enter the sacred precinct. Sellers of bread and water pass freely among the studying thousands, always careful not to disturb sleepers, and here and there students may be seen mending their garments, perhaps washing and drying them in the sun.

In Fascinating Cairo

Juvenile pupils are taught little but the Koran. Day after day their masters beat it into them, not infrequently aided by a palm-branch, the Oriental equivalent of the birch. The youngsters sway back and forth and sidewise in concert when reciting. The sheik, perhaps, knows less about the printed page than the boys, but to him the Koran is so familiar that he is able to detect the slightest error of his class. On his part "reading" is a feat of memory, and should a professor of higher grade refer him to the book, he would most likely claim to be suffering from weak eyes, and request a student-teacher to read for him. The urchins are as industrious as beavers. When far enough advanced to write, favorite quotations from the Koran, such as, "There is no God but God, and Mohammed is his prophet," and "I testify that Mohammed is God's apostle," are given them for exercises.

An Azhar student is always under the supervision of the school authority. In roaming about the streets of Cairo, should he misbehave, the police could only detain him until an official be summoned from El-Azhar to take him into custody. This system of proctorship is in fact the same as at the English universities of Oxford and Cambridge. Because an Azhar scholar has immunity from military service, it is suspected that many young men are enrolled as students for no other purpose than to escape the life of a soldier—to most Mohammedans an undesirable calling.

In the school year there is no definite recess; but during the month of Ramadan and on the occasion of the several religious feasts there are holidays, amounting in the aggregate to the long summer vacation so dear to the western-world boy. El-Azhar students are up with the sun for the first prayer of the day. By midday their work in the university is finished. Apparently Azhar youths have few amusements or recreations. Base-ball, foot-ball, cane-rushes, and boat-racing have yet to be brought to their consideration. They have, of course, their diversions, but what they may be is a mystery to the onlooker. A singular tradition associated with this renowned seat of learning is that, although practically without roof, no bird, not even the inquisitive sparrow, ever ventures within.

The Egyptian Museum, still in its youth as a national institution, contains a unique collection of antiquities, ranking with the world's important treasures. It was Mariette's marvelous energy and persistence that awakened Egyptians to the propriety of preserving the souvenirs of their great ancestors. His efforts first bore fruit in the museum at Bulak, and the promulgation of a decree establishing governmental control of antiquities. Up to that time Egypt had been prolific ground for European museums, and for half a century scarcely a vessel sailed from Alexandria that carried nothing for the British Museum or the Louvre. The Rosetta Stone, even, revealing the secret of the hieroglyphs of the ancient Egyptians, that had been forgotten for fourteen centuries, was allowed to be removed from the country where it unques-

THE ROSETTA STONE.

In Fascinating Cairo

tionably belonged, to become an exhibit of the British Museum.

The fame of the Bulak collection became world-wide with the transfer from Dêr el-Bahari of the mummies of Rameses the Great and many of his royal predecessors and successors. The storing of these priceless objects in the trumpery Bulak buildings, small and inflammable, awakened the government to the need for better quarters. Then the collection was moved across the Nile to the palace of Gizeh. There, in a few years, it grew with such rapidity, through the frequent finds of valuable sarcophagi, statues, papyri, and stelæ, that a popular demand for a fire-proof structure arose, and in 1897 the khedive laid with much ceremony the corner-stone of a great building near Kasr el-Nil, in Cairo, where the bodies of the kings, the antiquities, the wonderful jewelry unearthed a few years since at Dashur,—equal in design and finish to anything a Tiffany of to-day can fashion,—and all the marvelous articles, will be deposited, there to remain, it is hoped, forever. The building will be a fitting monument to the labors of Mariette, Maspéro, Grébaut, the two Brugsches, and De Morgan.

There is no more interesting ceremony in Cairo than the annual cutting of the Khalig, in the early days of August. When the Nile begins to rise, its height is daily chanted through the streets, until it reaches sixteen cubits on the ancient Nilometer at the southern end of the island of Roda. This mark reached, the Khalig el-Masri, the old canal that flows through the heart of Cairo, is opened. Up to this time it is dry, and, full or empty, it is little more than a sanitary abomination in these days; but in former times, when the Nile was high enough to flow down its bed, it was taken by the people as proof that the yearly flood was coming, and that the kindly fruits of the earth would quickly follow.

The head of the Khalig, on the road to Old Cairo, is closed by an earthwork embankment weeks before the function. As the festival draws near, elaborate preparations are made for its celebration; tents with innumerable lamps are erected on one side of the canal, while the opposite bank is lined with frames for fireworks. All the notables of the capital, civic, religious, and military, in gorgeous uniforms and canonicals, attend the festivity. The khedive, or a minister representing him, is there, as are the Sheik ul Islam (the highest dignitary of the Mohammedan faith), the Sheik el Bekri, and the acknowledged descendant of the prophet, the Sheik es Sadat. El-Azhar is represented by its learned priests and scribes, the Egyptian government by cabinet officers and secretaries, and foreign powers by their diplomatic and consular officials. The sirdar and his staff, judges from the international and native courts, and a sprinkling of functionaries from governmental departments and bureaus, complete the picturesque and heterogeneous gathering.

Egyptian regiments are turned out, salutes are fired, and by eight o'clock in the evening, when the ceremony officially commences, there may be twenty or thirty thousand spectators massed on

In Fascinating Cairo

land and river. An inclosure is reserved for harem carriages, packed with closely veiled women, who can see but little of the entertainment. Out on the Nile, opposite the canal's mouth, is moored the hulk of a vessel, ablaze with lamps and fireworks, which is claimed to be emblematic of the time when the republic of Venice sent an envoy to witness the ceremony. The excitement increases with every discharge of fireworks or arrival of a grandee, and the populace shouts and dances itself into a frenzy of delight. Meanwhile scores of copper-skinned Egyptians are shoulder-deep in the Nile, cutting away the embankment with their mattocks, while bands play and the sky is zigzagged with rockets. The officials go home by midnight, but the common people keep up their merriment until morning. By seven o'clock most of the high functionaries have returned. Then the Sheik ul Islam solemnly thanks the Almighty, Allah the All-powerful, the All-merciful. He implores his blessing on the flood, and at a signal the bank is cut, the waters rush in, and hundreds of men and boys plunge into the torrent to scramble for the bright piasters thrown by the khedive's representative and the religious luminaries. It is claimed that the daily records of the Nilometer for a thousand years are preserved in the archives of Cairo.

The Shubra Palace and grounds, now deserted and decaying, but once the home of viceregal splendor and voluptuousness, are worth all the trouble required to secure permission to visit them. Shubra was the favorite residence of Mehemet Ali, from whom it descended to Halim Pasha, his son, but for many years has been the subject of acrimonious litigation among members of the khedival family, the magnificent place remaining unoccupied since Prince Hassan's demise. The umbrageous Shubra avenue, two miles in length, connecting Cairo and the palace, was beloved by generations of gay people, until the oval Ghizereh drive became the Rotten Row of the Egyptian capital. From that moment the decline of the Shubra drive was rapid, until in these days it attracts very few Cairenes. The palace has that look of absenteeism so suggestive of lawsuits, and the fine villas lining the roadway from Cairo are in great part tenantless as well.

Standing close to the Nile, with the Pyramids in plain view, the palace seems worthy of occupancy. Its situation is not rivaled by any other princely home in the country, surely; but it is probably permanently dismantled. The gardens are still magnificent, rich with tropical plants and trees, and very extensive. The gem of the place is the wonderful kiosk, hidden from sight by groves of orange-, sycamore-, and lebbek-trees. It is a curious structure, covering an acre or more, and was once resplendent with decorations of the Italian Renaissance school. These are now peeling off, the silken hangings of the corner rooms almost fall into shreds from their own weight, the tortoise-shell-inlaid billiard-cues are succumbing to the warping hand of time, and the fresco-portraits of Mehemet Ali and Ibrahim are almost unrecognizable.

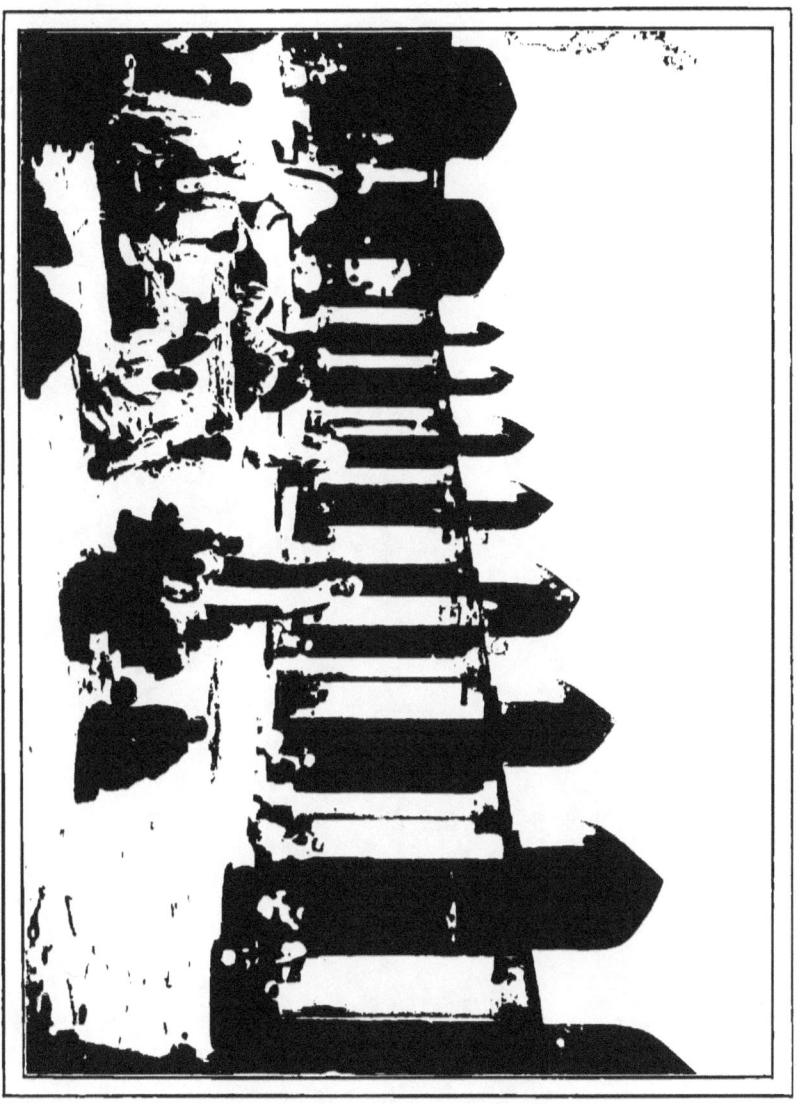

COURT OF EL-AZHAR, CAIRO.

In Fascinating Cairo

This kiosk was a favorite plaything of Mehemet Ali, and its walls have screened from the knowledge of the world many orgies of the Eastern sort, in which fair women played important parts. A special pastime of the great despot, affording him the keenest enjoyment, was to collect together the ladies of the harem, perhaps a hundred at once, divide them into boating parties, and have them paddled into the middle of the lakelet within the kiosk. Then, at his signal, the eunuchs would overturn the boats, precipitating the lovely freight, screaming and scrambling, into the water, while their lord and master was convulsed with delight and laughter. It amused the viceroy more than any *pas* of his odalisks.

The name "Egyptian cigarette," applied to the article established as an adjunct to fashionable and club life, is, strictly speaking, a misnomer, for no tobacco is grown in the country; in fact, cultivation of the plant has been since 1890 forbidden by khedival decree. "Cigarettes made in Egypt" would be the truthful description. Practically all the tobacco comes from Turkey, where it is shipped chiefly from Kavala, Latakia, and Yenidje. The paper comes from Austria and Italy, and the major part of the labor employed is Greek, except for common cigarettes, which are made by native workmen. The manufacture is very largely in the hands of Greeks, and so deeply founded is the belief that Europe and America will buy only Egyptian cigarettes made by a Greek firm that several Cairo manufactories are carried on under trade-names invented or borrowed in pursuance of this strange notion.

The tobacco used is not adulterated in any way, it is claimed, but is skilfully blended to acquire the desired strength and flavor. The best leaves are used for export orders, the common grades being consumed in Egypt, where nearly every man, woman, and child is a constant smoker of cigarettes. Custom-house returns show that of the tobacco entering the country only about one third is exported in manufactured form, thus indicating the enormous home consumption, and giving a suggestion of the quantity leaving Egypt in the baggage of travelers. Machinery is not employed in any way, except for cutting the tobacco, and it is said that the workmen wield sufficient power to render the adoption of machinery for making cigarettes a step too dangerous to be contemplated. The trade is centered in Cairo, where there are nearly a hundred export establishments.

The Egyptian cigarette has such an enviable position among the luxuries of the world that it is difficult to believe that this flourishing trade is of very recent growth; but it is, in fact, one of the many indirect advantages accruing to the country from the impetus imparted by the invasion of foreign enterprise.

The Cairo-made cigarette is valued above all others manufactured in Egypt. The same tobacco may be used and as skilful workmen employed in other places, but nowhere else is the same delicacy of flavor achieved. It is claimed by experts that

THE SPHINX.

In Fascinating Cairo

the cause of the superiority of the Cairo cigarette over that of Alexandria or Port Saïd is the super-dry climate of the capital, which is better adapted to the fabrication of cigarettes than is the humid atmosphere of the sea-coast. The constant flow of tourists has been the chief means of spreading the taste for the Egyptian cigarette, acquired in the land of the Nile, and its delicate aroma is familiar, in consequence, not only in America and England, but in far corners of the earth. All tobacco entering Egypt pays a duty equal to one dollar per kilogram, and a drawback equal to fifty cents a kilogram is allowed on cigarettes sent out of the country.

CHAPTER III

ALEXANDRIA, SEAT OF EGYPTIAN COMMERCE

ALEXANDRIA is a city with a past, truly; but renowned as it was in the world's early history for intellectual development and political position, I regard its present-day aspect, as the one great mart of the southern coast of the Mediterranean and entrepôt of a nation's commerce, to be more important still. Cairo looks old, but comparatively is not; Alexandria has the appearance of newness, but was twelve hundred years old before the first stone of Cairo was laid. This is paradoxical by suggestion.

The approach to Alexandria from the sea is not prepossessing, and the steamer is within ten miles or so of the harbor before any portion of the low-lying coast can be discerned. The object first seen on the horizon, looking like a distant sail, proves to be the Phare, the direct descendant of the earliest lighthouse in the world. Pompey's Pillar next comes into view on the left, followed by the dome of Ras-el-Teen Palace, Napoleon's windmills at Mex, and the rising ground beyond Ramleh. By this time the coast-line is uplifted, and Alexandria is in sight.

In half an hour the Arab pilot is on board, the

Alexandria, Seat of Commerce

vessel rounds the great breakwater, and the traveler is actually in Egypt—the new Egypt. The motley scene meeting the eye on getting ashore vividly indicates the transition that is in progress from the half-barbarism of the East to the civilization of the West, and in its contrasts—its wealth and its squalor, its busy new life rising like a tide over its old conservatism—the newcomer has a fair symbol of the actual Egypt. Modern methods of procedure enable you to pass the custom-house with little loss of time, system having taken the place of bakshish as an accelerating agent. The drive to the hotel, the Khedival or Abbat's, takes one first through narrow native streets and alleys, then into the vast public square of Mehemet Ali, with Italianate structures of imposing size on every side, then through streets of modern shops, and your first drive in the city of Alexander and Cleopatra is at an end. The sapphire sky, balmy atmosphere, and palm-trees overtopping the houses, tell you that you are in Egypt; but the buildings, the shops and their wares, suggest a city in Italy or southern France—perhaps Naples, possibly Marseilles.

The people in the streets and their chatter affirm that you are over the threshold of the Orient, however. There are Arabs, Turks, Syrians, Copts, Nubians, Greeks, Jews, Armenians, Albanians, Levantines, Italians, Maltese, French, many English, some Austrians—in fact, a variety of humanity, from which a perfect congress of nations might be drafted. The appearance of the people removes any doubt of the whereabouts of the traveler, for it

Present-Day Egypt

is only in Alexandria that this endless variety may be found. Cairo, like Washington, is official and administrative in all its attributes—everything, perhaps, but commercial; Alexandria, on the other hand, is as exclusively commercial as Liverpool.

In the selection of the site to which the great Macedonian was to give his name, Alexander proved himself to possess the unerring instinct of engineering genius. A less able man might have chosen the natural harbor of one of the Nile's mouths. But Alexander evidently was aware of the current sweeping the whole northern shore of Africa from west to east, and his foresight told him that a harbor to serve as a port for his projected Eastern dominions must be west of the several mouths of the great river, to be safe from the accumulation of the alluvial soil ever sweeping into the Mediterranean. It was this soil-laden wash that choked the old Pelusiac harbor beyond Port Saïd, and that to-day, in spite of bars and breakwaters, makes the task of keeping the entrance to the Suez Canal open for ships of deep draft a difficult one. Hence the wisdom of Alexander the Great, and the foundation of Alexandria in the year 332 B. C.

The diminutive island of Pharos must have been employed as a shelter for shipping in Alexander's reign, and the first of his lieutenants to wear the crown of Egypt, Ptolemy Soter, constructed thereon the Pharos tower, famed in history as the father of lighthouses. It is recorded that this tower was nearly six hundred feet high, and that on its top

WATER ENTRANCE OF RAS-EL-TEEN PALACE, ALEXANDRIA.

Alexandria, Seat of Commerce

beacon-fires were burned by night as a guide and warning to mariners. This pile of masonry, of greater proportions than the Washington Monument, reared when the world was young, naturally was included in the list of wonderful structures; it was termed the seventh wonder of the earth. Ptolemy Soter likewise connected Pharos with the city by the Heptastadium causeway, bringing the island within easier reach, and dividing the intervening space into two harbors. The action of seacurrents for centuries has supplemented building operations from time to time, and the causeway has so long been a feature of the city that few dwellers in modern Alexandria are aware of its artificial origin.

Ptolemy Soter was also responsible for making Alexandria a seat of learning, and for the creation of the world-famous library and museum. He brought there many of the wise men of Europe, and through his efforts Alexandria for years occupied the leading place in literature, philosophy, and science. His son and successor, Ptolemy Philadelphus, continued the wise policy, and Ptolemy Euergetes made his reign famous for the encouragement given to learning. This king brought to Alexandria, among other great personages, Aristophanes of Byzantium, who became keeper of the library. When the Romans laid siege to the city in Cæsar's time, both library and museum were ruthlessly burned. As a foundation for a second library, Antony presented Cleopatra with the Pergamenian manuscripts, two hundred thousand in number. The collection grew rapidly. Copies of

Present-Day Egypt

works of importance were made at public expense, and it is stated that every book that came into the city was seized and kept, a copy only being handed to the owner. Scholars from many lands made Alexandria their abiding-place, to enjoy the benefits of the priceless books and parchments. Strabo and Euclid studied there. When the fanatical calif Omar overran Egypt, in the seventh century, he proclaimed that, as the Koran contained everything that man should know, other books had no right to exist. Consequently he decreed that the second great library to bring renown to Alexandria should forthwith be destroyed. It is recorded that seven hundred thousand manuscripts and volumes in all languages were apportioned to the city's four thousand public bathing establishments, with which the fires of these were fed for six months. This was, indeed, the most crushing blow ever inflicted on literature.

Ruled now by Persian, now by Roman, now by Greek, and enervated by vice and luxury, and with the loss of population and prestige that preceded the stagnation and decay spreading over the centuries from Cleopatra to Mehemet Ali, Alexandria's varying welfare could not be detailed within the limits of a sketchy chapter. The death-blow to its fortunes was the discovery, in 1497, of the passage round the Cape of Good Hope, which changed the direction of the commerce of the East.

The Alexandria that visitors see dates only from the beginning of the nineteenth century, with the advent of Mehemet Ali. Taking the leaderless

Alexandria, Seat of Commerce

soldiers of the shattered Turkish supremacy in Egypt, who had retired with sulky scorn from Alexandria to a quarter of their own, on what once was the island of Pharos, Mehemet Ali united them with his Albanian troops, and found he had then the unbreakable backbone of an army of fighters, few in number, it is true, but sufficiently powerful with his cunning to overthrow the Mamelukes ruling at Cairo. The fearless Rumelian then organized the Egyptian people,—Arabs and Nilots,—and by sheer genius welded into something approaching a nationality these discordant elements. The renaissance of Egypt and the revival of Alexandria's fortunes date, consequently, from the coming of Mehemet Ali. He loved the city and made it his capital.

His master mind recognizing the need of connecting the seaport with the Nile, this autocrat traced a line fifty miles long on a map, and two hundred and fifty thousand fellaheen, working without pay or food from their dictator, in a year scooped out of the sand with their hands the trench known as the Mahmudiyeh Canal. Thirty thousand of the peasants died before the canal was completed, but it brought fresh water and a nation's commerce to Alexandria.

As viceroy, Mehemet Ali sought to make Alexandria great in trade. To this end, before providing palaces, he improved the harbor and erected warehouses, docks, a dry-dock, and an arsenal. To accomplish these things, and to develop irrigation in the Delta, he had the assistance of Linant Pasha

Present-Day Egypt

and other brilliant engineers, recruited in France. Although some of Mehemet Ali's successors have been woefully inert, all, with the exception of the first Abbas, have done something toward upbuilding Alexandria. The population has developed until, in the present year, it is computed to be three hundred and twenty-five thousand. Ismail had a superstitious fear that he was destined to die in Alexandria, and consequently passed little time there. The most conspicuous modern Egyptian buried in this commercial capital, where Archimedes conceived his most useful inventions, and where St. Mark preached the gospel, is Viceroy Saïd.

To-day Alexandria has broad avenues, theaters, clubs, and many other features, good and bad, of a flourishing city in Europe, and better-paved streets than most European towns. Ten or fifteen years since, the condition of the streets left so much to be desired that the leading export merchants took the matter in hand, and agreed to pay to the municipality a small fee on each bale of cotton and sack of grain or sugar shipped by them. The aggregate in a few years was sufficient to give every important thoroughfare a paving of stone blocks, and from the handsome residue a fire-boat and other needed adjuncts were donated to the city. All this was accomplished without taxing the people.

In these times the harbor exhibits almost as great a variety of foreign flags as the crowd on the quays represents nationalities. More than

PLACE MEHEMET ALI, ALEXANDRIA.

Alexandria, Seat of Commerce

twenty regular lines of steamers ply to and from Alexandria; visiting men-of-war and yachts lie for weeks at a time in the harbor, and the life and movement are those of a great international seaport.

The harbor is protected by a sea-wall nearly two miles in length, constructed of more than twenty-six thousand square blocks of concrete, each weighing twenty-two tons, and is perfectly lighted. The well-protected haven, of a depth of twenty to sixty feet, and an area of eighteen hundred acres, thus formed, is supplemented by an inner port of perhaps one fourth the size. The harbor dues are considerable, but these, combined with the income of the country's railways and telegraphs, were pledged to European creditors demanding security when the national treasury had been depleted by Ismail's wild extravagance.

Could the bronze statue of the founder of the dynasty, appareled in the Turkish costume of his time, and astride a horse of superb proportions, in the Place Mehemet Ali, be endowed with life, the Great Initiator might see endless processions of cotton-laden vehicles moving toward the docks. If such a return to life were possible, his mind might revert to the time when a friendly botanist found growing wild in a Cairene garden a few plants whose blossoms developed into fiber-filled bolls, which, the savant advised the viceroy, might be cultivated in Egypt on a large scale with great profit. This was the origin of cotton-culture there, representing in shipments from Alexandria now

Present-Day Egypt

nearly a million bales in a season, and from this incident sprang the nation's principal industry. When civil war raged in the United States, and English mills were compelled to find fiber elsewhere for their looms, Egyptian cotton sold at a dollar a pound. In two years Alexandria waxed rich in consequence, and its wealth found expression in streets of Italianate business buildings and residences. Those that were smashed to atoms by the British bombardment in 1882 were replaced by larger and handsomer structures, still in the Italian style of architecture.

One feature of the massacre of Europeans on that memorable July 11, 1882, and of the subsequent sacking of the city, was peculiarly significant. The grand square of Mehemet Ali was wrecked from end to end, and its sidewalks ran with blood. But one thing was respected by the brutal mob, sparing no one, nothing, save this. Imperious Mehemet Ali sat there throughout all the strife on his Arab horse. The crowd suffered no one to molest it. Had it been an effigy of Ismail instead, it would have been destroyed by the fanatical, degraded ruffians at the outset of their orgy of blood.

Apart from the splendid monolith miscalled Pompey's Pillar, and the catacombs, dating from the time of Constantine, of which there are remains of rare architectural symmetry, nothing exists in Alexandria to reward the search of the traveler with a fondness for antiquities. The pillar, erected in honor of Diocletian, and having nothing to do

Alexandria, Seat of Commerce

with Pompey, is of the familiar red granite of Assuan. Some investigators believe that this Corinthian column was once an obelisk, and that it was rounded to its present form by the Romans, and, further, that its situation marks the site of the famous Serapeum. It is known to have been erected in the third century after Christ, to commemorate the capture of the city by the Emperor Diocletian, after the rebellion of Achilleus. The statue which must have adorned its summit long since disappeared, leaving no trace to tell us whom it represented. The column's shadow falls to-day upon a dreary Arab cemetery—pathetic symbol of the buried glories of the metropolis it once graced.

The two obelisks which Cleopatra or Cæsar removed from the Temple of the Sun at Heliopolis to adorn the Cæsarium were lost to Alexandria in Ismail's time. One, after lying prone for centuries where it fell, is in London; the other in New York.

To the south of Alexandria lies the extensive but shallow sheet of water known as Lake Mareotis. It covers what was once a fertile plain, possessing a lake upon which Alexandria depended for fresh water. In 1801, when a British force was conducting an operation before the city, then in the hands of Bonaparte's troops, it was deemed a good strategic expedient to cut off Alexandria's supply of fresh water. To accomplish this the English severed at Mex the neck of land separating the lake from the Mediterranean, thereby admitting the sea and flooding a hundred thousand acres of cultivable soil, sacrificing many lives, and ruining forty villages—and the climate of Alexandria. It was a wicked act, hardly justified by the needs of warfare. It is a curious example of the irony of fate that monster English pumps and a staff of English engineers—paid for by the Egyptian government—are given constant employment to-day in keeping the salt water of Lake Mareotis within bounds, for no engineering resource can now prevent the percolation of the sea to the lower level of Mareotis. Engineering skill can only keep the water from overflowing still more valuable territory. A million and a half tons of water are pumped back into the Mediterranean every twenty-four hours.

Ramleh is the only residential suburb of Alexandria. It is easier to make the assertion than to describe the limits of the place. It has many titular subdivisions, but generically Ramleh may be said to stretch along the entire sea-front from Alexandria to Abukir Bay, a dozen miles away. "Ramleh" is the native word for sand, and in this instance is applied with signal appropriateness. In summer all that portion of Cairo's officialdom unable to manage European leave of absence betakes itself *en masse* to the hotels and villas of the Alexandrian suburb, there to keep cool and incidentally assail the humid atmosphere by invidious comparison. Hundreds of Alexandria's business men reside throughout the year at Ramleh. Judges of the international courts, consuls, functionaries of every degree, bourse operators, and Jewish and Greek money magnates, find there peaceful repose.

NATIVE WOMAN AND CHILD.

Alexandria, Seat of Commerce

A primitive line of railway, owned by Englishmen and very profitable, sets down passengers at several stations. Mustapha Pasha station accommodates the British soldiers housed in the old khedival palace, and St. Stephano station is the objective point of the *haut ton* going to spend an evening at the casino, or have a cooling swim in the Mediterranean. When Alexandrians desire to celebrate, singly or collectively, they go to the Ramleh casino, and do it well. Pashas and others having no need for observing regularity of hours in town drive back and forth on the splendid road patronized by his Highness the Khedive when he passes to and fro between Montazah and Ras-el-Teen Palace.

Besides being very convenient, this Egyptian Long Branch is exceedingly pleasant at all times. The blue sea, stretching to the horizon, is ever soothing to exhausted nerves, and in summer bears a refreshing inshore breeze with commendable regularity. In the mad race to get away from Egypt in the early summer, hundreds of people go farther and fare worse than if contenting themselves with the easily attainable comforts of Ramleh.

Abukir possesses resources of interest amply rewarding a visit to this place where history has been made, not to inspect the insignificant village, but to view the bay where one of the greatest of naval engagements was contested. The semicircular bay is surrounded by obsolete forts and earthworks, many of whose guns are dismantled, and all of a type long ago discarded. A pleasant half-day may be passed about these forts, with lunch-basket

Present-Day Egypt

at hand, viewing the scene of the battle of the Nile, and picturing in the mind's eye Lord Nelson's brilliant manœuvers, by which thirteen doughty French ships of the line were destroyed.

There is a distinct admixture of Greek blood in the people of Alexandria, observable in many countenances, and the Greek colony is the largest of foreign origin dwelling in the great seaport. A considerable share of its financial and commercial business is conducted by Greeks, and innumerable names seen over shop doors recall the nomenclature of the classics familiar to every student. Some of the palatial homes of the city and its suburbs are those of Greek bankers and merchants, and there is an intimate intercourse between Alexandria and Athens. Love of the home country is a characteristic of these transplanted people, whose patriotism finds frequent expression in gifts to Athenian institutions and causes. It is a boast of many Greeks in Alexandria that their ancestors have dwelt in Egypt since the days of Cleopatra; that their countrymen were there before the advent of the Arabs, and have been there uninterruptedly longer than the people of any other nation.

One can scarcely walk the historic streets of Alexandria without his thoughts dwelling at times upon the splendid woman who once ruled Egypt from that place, whose beauty enslaved all that beheld it, and caused the bravest generals to forsake the conquering missions that brought them from Rome, and let themselves be conquered by the irresistible charm of Cleopatra. Mere presence in

Alexandria, Seat of Commerce

the city once her capital marshals in memory all that one has read or seen depicted on stage or canvas of the fascinating queen, and more than one visitor aimlessly strolls the streets pondering the problem of her nationality, and asking himself whether the tale of her death from the bite of an asp had its origin, like the William Tell narrative, in a popular work of an early romancist. The name haunts one everywhere. Even pleasure-boats in the harbor and cafés in important thoroughfares record the name of Egypt's last queen, and cigarettes served with after-dinner coffee are called in her honor as well.

Tarrying travelers discuss Cleopatra with each other, and with those whom they meet, as if she had been of a recent century. Guide-books assure them that she was but thirty-nine when she died by her own hand, that the tragedy preceded the Christian era by only thirty years, and that Alexandria was alike the city of her nativity and her entombment.

There are Alexandrians sufficiently cultured to entitle their opinions to credence on most subjects, who insist that Cleopatra was a beauty of dusky face; some go so far as to insist that she was undeniably a Nubian, and point to the bas-reliefs of the temple of Hathor, at Denderah, in substantiation of their opinion. But no cultured Greek will enter the lists in a debate jeopardizing for an instant the nationality of the great goddess of beauty, for he knows with as much certainty as he does the name of the present King of Greece that Cleopatra was the purest of pure Greek, a Ptolemy,

Present-Day Egypt

and that her complexion was as fair as that of any Athenian belle to-day. The erudite Greek gets out his Plutarch—the best-known historian coeval with Cleopatra, and who must have seen her or talked with those knowing her—and points to chapters leaving as little doubt of the purity of her Greek blood as of her charm of person and conversation.

The Denderah sculptures when analyzed, the erudite champion maintains with every show of reason, portray a face whose outline and characteristics are unmistakably Greek. Were the temple of Denderah not situated near the Nubian frontier, no logical examiner could ever have found a suggestion in the portraits that the queen was negroid. The shape of the nose proves to the contrary, and the bust of Cleopatra in the Capitol at Rome supports the assertion. Furthermore, the Egyptian sculptors did not attempt to idealize. They sculptured with honest fidelity the faces they saw. In these up-Nile portraits the consummate mistress of the art of fascination wears a winning smile, but the figure of the queen is distorted.

Painters, poets, novelists, writers of dramas, and actresses seem ever to have had in mind the idea that Cleopatra was a half-caste, in whom the charms of Europe and Africa were combined, a woman who ruled the world with the intellect of a thinker directing the arts of an odalisk. It requires little investigation, on the contrary, to learn that the great queen was, as her name suggests, a Greek of the Greeks, of pure and illustrious descent, and not an African. Gérôme, Picou, Alma-Tadema,

CLEOPATRA (FROM THE TEMPLE OF DENDERAH)

Alexandria, Seat of Commerce

Cabanel, Sichel, Grolleau, and other artists have exercised as much license in portraying the beautiful woman as Shakspere and less renowned poets have in describing her.

The means employed by the baffled queen—too proud to return to Rome after Antony's self-destruction, to be exhibited in the festival celebrating the triumph of Octavianus—to produce death unfortunately cannot be as directly dealt with as the question of her descent. In Alexandrian suburbs to-day are groves of fig-trees, whose fruit, arranged in flat baskets and covered with fig-leaves, is sold by the roadside by native lads, as it might have been in the time of Cleopatra. An occasional lizard, basking in the warm sunshine on the sand, which scurries away when footsteps approach, may have suggested the asp story to a writer of long ago, constructing a romantic epic or play. The theory of the poisonous reptile conveyed to the unhappy queen in a basket of figs is improbable. Cleopatra was too experienced in Eastern ways not to have understood the secret of poisons and have them at hand. The brother-husband, sharing with her the throne, had died from poison years before, under circumstances that indicated his murderess; and, besides, a woman of her vanity would choose death from one of the destroying drugs known to her, rather than from the poison of the asp, disfiguring in its agency of destruction.

Many thousands of Mohammedans of the lower social grades in Alexandria, and for that matter throughout Lower Egypt, are slaves to the hashish

Present-Day Egypt

habit. There is a law rigidly forbidding the importation of this noxious product of Indian hemp, and the government employs every means for keeping it out of Egypt. Hundreds of miles of littoral to the west and east of Alexandria, that, were it not for hashish smuggling, would seldom be watched, are systematically patrolled by coast-guardsmen, and every foot of the Suez Canal is similarly under surveillance; while port authorities at Alexandria, Rosetta, Damietta, and Port Saïd expend more energy in endeavoring to prevent the secret landing of hashish than all other articles declared by Egyptian law to be contraband.

Notwithstanding these precautions, the cunning of the smugglers enables them to run the forbidden article across from islands of the Grecian Archipelago, and land it in Egypt with a certainty permitting the demand for the compound to be regularly supplied. It is manufactured in many out-of-the-way places in the eastern Mediterranean, and its excessive value, once within reach of its devotees in Egypt, is enough to compensate those concerned in the trade for the occasional confiscation of a shipment. Many of the devices practised for getting it into the country are ingenious in the extreme. A visit to the little museum connected with the Alexandrian custom-house proves this. One may there see innocent-looking trunks and bulging piano-legs, the one with false bottoms and the other with capacious cavities, that were filled with hashish when investigated by the custom-house examiners. These are perhaps the simplest

Alexandria, Seat of Commerce

tricks resorted to by shippers of the illicit article. Many others more difficult to detect are to be seen in the curious collection.

By means of confederates on the lookout, many a rubber bag and water-tight box of hashish finds its way ashore, on the Mediterranean beach or in the Suez Canal, nearly every night. The authorities cannot cope with the cunning of the aliens waxing fat from the Egyptian slaves to hashish. I have been assured that in both Alexandria and Cairo the cafés and other establishments where a smoke of hashish may be had number hundreds. The Koran strictly forbidding the use of liquors and wines, the mind of lower-class Mohammedans has seized the intoxicating hemp compound as an alternative. It is more debasing and injurious than strong drink, physicians claim, and often leads to insanity or idiocy. Alexandria, with its native population living in intimate relations with the offscourings of every Mediterranean land, has for generations been the headquarters of the use of hashish.

CHAPTER IV

PARADOXICAL BUT EFFECTIVE ADMINISTRATION

AMONG the nations of the earth Egypt stands unique in history, and in unusual and paradoxical conditions. Mysterious and fascinating as it was to Strabo and Herodotus, so it is to the observer to-day, and especially to the winter visitor who endeavors in a brief season to fathom its wealth of archæological wonders and its scheme of political administration. This last is nearly as difficult to understand as are the hieroglyphs of the monuments, for it has no equivalent in ancient or modern times.

Nominally a province of the Ottoman empire, Egypt is autonomous, subject only to a yearly tribute to the Sultan of about three million five hundred thousand dollars. The title of its ruler means sovereign, or king, without qualification or limitation; yet the country is in large measure administered by Great Britain, standing in the capacity of trustee for creditors of her own and of several other nationalities as well. This trusteeship is voluntary on England's part, and is forced upon the khedival government.

The situation might not inaptly be compared

Paradoxical Administration

to one by which a farm is worked on shares by an important creditor, with both mortgagor and mortgagee reaping substantial benefit by the arrangement, and the farm yearly made more valuable. This simile describes but one of the conditions contributing to the involved Egyptian situation. Another partnership is represented by the International Debt Commission, in which Egypt has six partners—France, Germany, Russia, Austria, and Italy, as well as Great Britain. Each of these countries has a delegate at Cairo to watch the cash-box and collect from time to time a share of the country's receipts, in excess of actual running expenses, proportionate to the amount of Egyptian bonds held by his countrypeople. In this partnership Egypt would be described in legal phraseology as the "party of the first part," the six foreign commissioners combining in the "party of the second part."

Then comes a third copartnership, the International Courts, in which Egypt figures but triflingly. Thirteen European powers and the United States of America have complete jurisdiction in these tribunals in actions involving property rights in which a European or American may be interested with other aliens or with Egyptians. In these "mixed" courts a foreigner can bring to the bar the Egyptian government, or its titular head, in an action involving property or monetary interest.

If these conditions fail to complete a predicament remarkable in its complications, the ancient capitulations of Ottoman rulers, by which fourteen foreign governments, including the United States, have almost sovereign rights in Egypt, independent of local authority, will surely do so. The concessions of the Sublime Porte give to these nations as full control of their subjects or citizens as if in their own lands. The Egyptian government itself has no stronger control over its subjects. Thus an American, an Englishman, or a Frenchman, who can be proceeded against in property matters only in the international courts, can be apprehended and tried for a criminal offense solely by the consular authority of his government resident in Egypt.

It would tax the capacity of the proverbial Philadelphia lawyer to understand the capitulations sufficiently to be able to impart their exact significance. I have known many wiseacres who could explain the legal status of the Debt Commission, give a comprehensible epitome of the jurisdiction of the mixed courts, or define the diplomatic niceties of difference between "occupation" and "protectorate"; but not one in a thousand can describe the Ottoman capitulations, beyond telling you that they date from this or that century, and more or less vaguely deal with the rights and privileges of Christians living within the Turkish realm.

I am not claiming a knowledge superior to that of other seekers for light who take the time to explore official works on treaties and wade through dozens of massive volumes on Oriental law. It is not difficult to learn that the first capitulation given by the Turkish empire to the United States of

Paradoxical Administration

America was accepted by Congress and the President in 1832; but this sort of international treaty antedates America's discovery.

The intercourse of the Christian world with the Mohammedan is not founded upon the law of nations. International law, as professed by the nations of Christendom, is the offspring of the communion of ideas subsisting between them, and is based upon a common origin and an almost identical religious faith. Between the peoples of Islam and those of Europe and America there exists no such communion of ideas and principles from which a true international law could spring. Inasmuch as the propagation of Islam is the chief aim of all Moslems, perpetual warfare against Christians and other unbelievers, to convert them or subject them to the payment of tribute, was regarded as the most sacred duty of the Mohammedan. From his point of view the whole world is divided into two parts—the house of Islam, and the conglomerate mass of unbelievers. Yet the Moslem felt that perpetual war with the infidel was not possible, and that conventions should be made for the advantage of both.

Commerce, the source of wealth and the means of satisfying some of the most imperative needs of mankind, could not be carried on without deviating from the severity of the maxims that were professed. Either the destruction of one of the two peoples must have ensued, or else these maxims must be departed from, the Moslems saw. But a subterfuge was resorted to to escape the severe conditions, whereby a conflict with the doctrine of the law in its full vigor might be avoided, and the doctrine itself left intact. Treaty measures were thought of. But it would never do to call them treaties. The representative on earth of the prophet could never treat a Christian ruler as an equal. The sultans considered themselves the only sovereigns of the earth; all others deserved nothing but pity and toleration. Treaties could be entered into only with their equals, they argued. To their inferiors only grants and favors were possible.

So the word "capitulation," meaning letter of privilege, was brought into use. No reciprocal obligation was constituted by a capitulation, as it was meant to be a purely gratuitous concession and favor granted to Christians, by virtue of which they were to be tolerated upon the soil of Islam.

The need for this concession on the part of the Mussulmans was commerce, as I have said. Had not the ships of the western world come to their eastern shores to exchange with them the products of the Levant, these products would have had no outlet, and the producing country a limited source of wealth; and had not the merchant of Europe been able to establish his domicile in the land of the Moslem, his ships would never have approached Turkish shores. Some of the capitulations with the Italian republics were dated as early as 1150. In an early capitulation with France the Sultan called himself "the Sultan of glorious sultans, Emperor of powerful emperors, distributor of crowns to those seated upon thrones, the Shadow of God upon earth, the asylum of justice, the fount of

Paradoxical Administration

happiness," and much more in the same vein. In response to a memorial from the Queen of England, many years ago, that sovereign was described by the Sultan of Turkey as one praying for certain privileges for her merchants. In bestowing the prayed-for concession, the document from the Sultan described him thus modestly: "The King of kings, the Prince of emperors of every age, the dispenser of crowns to monarchs, who, by divine grace, assistance, will, benevolence," etc.

But these dispensations, notwithstanding their grandiloquence, have the force and character of treaties, and guarantee to the stranger within the Sultan's gates, whether in Turkey proper or in Egypt, full and complete immunity from laws governing native dwellers in those lands. Inviolability of domicile, freedom from taxation of every sort, and immunity from arrest for crime and misdemeanors, are but items in the general promise not to molest the alien. These treaties, it will readily be seen, give to the nations possessing them almost every privilege of extraterritoriality, and are guarded with jealous watchfulness.

The capitulations occasioned so much confusion of jurisdiction in Egypt, where many Christian nationalities were represented, that Nubar Pasha called the attention of Ismail to the necessity for reform, and himself drew up a project which was communicated to all the governments maintaining representatives in Egypt.

As a result, an international commission assembled in 1869, under the presidency of Nubar, who was minister of foreign affairs, and united in a report recommending the scheme. This was signed by the representatives of the United States, Austria, Germany, England, France, Russia, and Italy. At subsequent conventions Belgium, Spain, Holland, Greece, Portugal, Denmark, and Sweden-Norway approved the plan. On June 28, 1875, Khedive Ismail inaugurated the court at Alexandria, although it was not until February 1, 1876, that the new system of jurisprudence was actually launched.

The procedure is practically that of France, the Code Napoléon, modified to suit the circumstances of a country where local customs and religious obligations must be respected. The jurisdiction is stated in this extract from the code itself:

"The new tribunals shall have cognizance of all controversies in matters civil or commercial between natives and foreigners, or between foreigners of different nationalities. Apart from questions touching the *statut personnel* [questions of wills, successions, heirship, and the like, which are regulated by the laws of the country of the individual], they shall have cognizance of all questions touching real estate between all persons, even though they belong to the same [foreign] nationality."

It is of good augury for the national progress that the tribunals years ago won the confidence of both natives and foreigners, and that the government bows to their authority. Europe needed no better proof of their efficacy than when Ismail and the government itself were brought before the Court

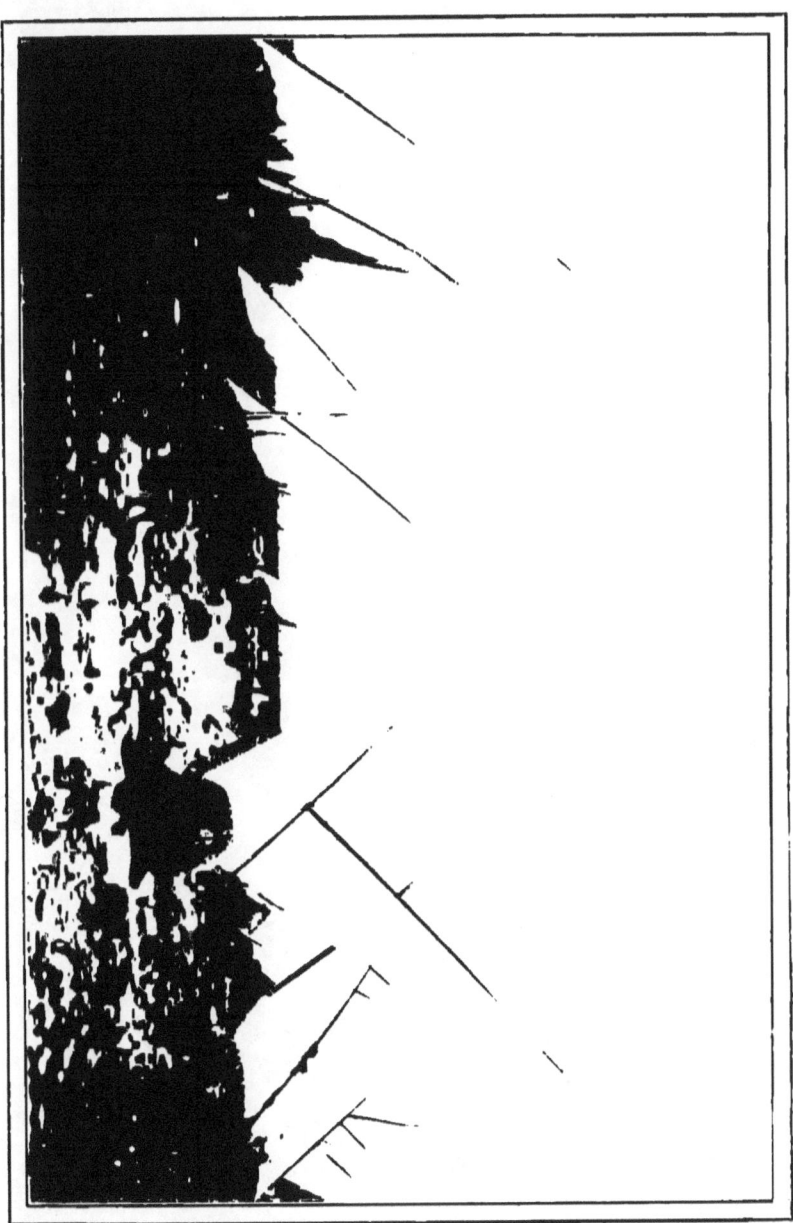

AFTER PASSING DRAWBRIDGE, CAIRO.

Paradoxical Administration

of Appeal as defendants, when failing to meet obligations to foreign creditors.

The practice is common for a native having an important suit to assign his interest to a foreign friend, in order to give the international courts jurisdiction of his cause, thus securing intelligent and fair consideration. A few years since, when some of the powers were dilatory in giving their adhesion to the extension of the courts,—for every five years there is a formal renewal,—something like a panic occurred among the commercial community.

Courts of first instance are located at Cairo, Alexandria, and Mansurah, and the Court of Appeal is at Alexandria. The minimum pecuniary limit of appeal is four hundred dollars. Three languages are recognized in pleadings and documents,—French, Italian, and Arabic,—and it is probable that English will shortly be added to the list. The foreign counselors of the appellate court, nine in number, receive a yearly salary of nine thousand two hundred and fifty dollars each, and their four native colleagues half as much. For the three lower courts twenty-seven foreign judges are employed, each receiving a salary of seven thousand dollars, their fourteen native coadjutors receiving half as much. Five judges—three foreign and two native—sit at a time. The United States, like other great powers, has one representative in the upper and two in the lower courts. While the tribunals were not intended to be profit-earners, their receipts for years have been considerably in excess of expenses. Not since the courts were created has the United States been represented by abler judges than at present. Judges Keiley, Tuck, and Batcheller reflect credit alike on their profession and the government that selected them.

Inasmuch as the jurisdiction of the international courts has extended since the reconquest of the Sudan, the Egyptian government is agitating the matter of sending judges on circuit to Assuan, Suakim, and other places, if they can be prevailed upon to travel such distances.

The exclusion of the English language from these courts has for years been an obvious anomaly, particularly so when it is learned that more than one half of the trade of the country is with Great Britain and her colonies, and that nearly one half the tonnage entering Alexandria harbor is British. International jealousy has made it difficult to change in any measure the organic scheme of the courts, and until now Great Britain has feared to press the question of admitting the English language. A change is inevitable.

To take the census in Egypt it is necessary for the Egyptian government first to assure the representatives of the powers that its agents will only knock at the foreigner's door and *request* the desired information. Under no provocation will the inquisitor enter the domicile, except upon the invitation of its occupant. Giovanni, the Italian subject, who opens an innocent roulette game in his back room for revenue, has no more to fear from the police of Egypt than from the police of Patagonia,

Paradoxical Administration

for the simple reason that his domicile is a legal atom of Italy set down on Egyptian territory. His consul alone possesses the right to cause his arrest and to inflict imprisonment or fine. The son of Malta, should he take the life of an Egyptian, as he sometimes does, can be tried and punished only by the consular authority of Great Britain. The Greek skipper can sail fearlessly into Alexandria with a cargo of hashish, and the local police can say nothing to him. If he is unwise enough to attempt to land the contraband article while the eyes of the Egyptian government are upon him, the police can seize and destroy the hashish, but the smuggler can be reached only through the Greek diplomatic agent and consul-general. This makes it necessary for the skipper to get his merchandise ashore when the police are not looking.

Emanating from the same source as the firman upon which is based the khedival authority, and being generally much older than Egyptian autonomy, the capitulations were in no degree abrogated or amended when Ismail induced the Sublime Porte to confer upon his family the privileges of entailed rulership. As a consequence, there is at times much vexatious friction and conflict of authority between the Egyptian administration and the governments enjoying these capitulations. Cairo can have no system of modern drainage because some of the European governments refuse to give their consent to sanitary officials to enter the houses of their subjects.

The highest Egyptian officials, when discharging

the duties of their positions, sometimes forget the existence of the capitulations. A few years ago a French newspaper published in Cairo was so severe in its criticisms of the local government that a khedival minister felt that the journal could be suppressed under a law found in the statute-book regulating what newspapers could and could not print. The press censor explained to him that his duty was clear, and with a posse of policemen he forcibly closed the office of the offending publication. This was the only bit of good luck the editor had ever experienced. He laid the case before the representative of the French government, who, it being in the midst of the holiday period, happened to be a very young man of inferior secretarial rank. But he was the visible representative of his nation, nevertheless, and alone enjoyed the power to mete out punishment to the French editor. The minister, recognizing the blunder he had made, promptly set to work to repair the damage. Dressed in the full uniform of his high office, he proceeded to the French diplomatic agency and formally apologized to the young diplomatist; the flag of France was saluted by twenty-one guns from the citadel, and the editor was given one hundred thousand dollars of the Egyptian taxpayers' money for the injury he had suffered through the too summary method by which he had been apprehended for a flagrant offense against an administration at that time a good friend of France.

The minister was Nubar Pasha, who died in 1899, and from the incident I have detailed he is said to

Paradoxical Administration

have formed an aversion for journalists amounting almost to detestation. On the occasion of his being made prime minister by Khedive Abbas, I went to his ministry to extend the congratulations and good wishes usual to the event. As I was coming away, a group of correspondents of Continental and English papers called to present their congratulations, and incidentally to discover if he had any news to be communicated to the European world. Nubar shook the hand of each almost effusively before saying: "Gentlemen, I am glad to see you, and appreciate your kindness; but while I am premier there will be no news—none whatever."

The Egypt of the map shows upward of four hundred thousand square miles, an area seven times as great as New England, twice that of France, and more than three times that of the British Isles. But the practical Egypt—that which sustains life by vegetation, and the government by taxation—is not nearly as large as the States of Massachusetts and Connecticut together, or of Belgium alone. The ribbon-like strip of cultivable land bordering the Nile and forming the Delta between Cairo and the Mediterranean comprises ten thousand five hundred square miles of fertile soil, and makes, strictly speaking, an elongated oasis in the North African desert.

The Egypt thus sketched stretches from Wady-Halfa (second cataract), 21° 53" north latitude, to the Mediterranean Sea, 31° 35" north latitude. The breadth is limited by the Libyan and Arabian chains of hills on either bank of the Nile, and

Present-Day Egypt

varies from five eighths of a mile to fourteen miles. The name "Egypt" is of Greek origin. According to Brugsch, it is corrupted from the hieroglyphic *Ha-ka-pta*, that is, "House of the Worship of Ptah," the Creator of the world. The name in vogue among the ancient Egyptians was Chemi, meaning "Black Country," derived from the color of the Nile mud. Among the Hebrews Egypt was called Masar, the Mizraim of the Bible; and the Arabs of to-day call it Masr, which name applies especially to Cairo, the capital. The Turks call the country Gipt, which is evidently an abbreviation of the Greek *Aigyptos*.

Ten or twelve years ago Egypt was insolvent. To-day she is easy with prosperity. The position of the fellaheen is constantly improving. The corvée is abolished, and the people have no more compulsory labor, except to keep the Nile within bounds at high flood, for which they are paid. Slavery is forbidden by khedival decree, land-taxes are gradually being reduced, and extortion and corruption seem to have been stamped out. Egypt sells cereals enough to pay for the imported articles necessary to maintain her simple standard of life.

The population of Egypt is a theme that has interested more than one generation of observers and writers. Under the Ptolemies we are asked to believe that the country had 20,000,000 people; but it is fairly authentic that Napoleon found only 2,500,000 when he went there in 1798. At that time they had long been ground down into hopeless degradation and poverty to pander to the luxury

THE NILE AND NORTHEASTERN AFRICA.

Paradoxical Administration

and vice of a few haughty masters. Oriental voluptuousness had reigned in the palaces, while beggary and wretchedness dwelt in the mud hovels of the defrauded and degraded people.

In 1846, under Mehemet Ali, the population was estimated at only 4,500,000. The census of 1882, which was a most imperfect one, showed over 6,750,000; and that of 1897, to be considered as fairly accurate, as it was made under British supervision, indicated a total population between Wady-Halfa and the Mediterranean of 9,750,000. Of this total, 50.8 per cent. were males, and 49.2 per cent. females. After deductions for women, children under seven years, and desert Bedouins, it was calculated that 12 per cent. of the males could read and write, the remainder being entirely illiterate. The native Egyptians numbered 9,008,000, to which were to be added 40,000 originally from other parts of the Ottoman empire, and 574,000 Bedouins. Of these last only 89,000 were really nomads, the remainder being described as semi-sedentary. Of foreign residents there were 112,500, of whom the Greeks were the most numerous, with 38,000; then came the Italians, 24,500; British (including 6500 Maltese and 5000 of the army of occupation), 19,500; French (including 4000 Algerians and Tunisians), 14,000; Austrians, 7000; Russians, 1400; Germans, 1300; and the remainder divided among ten different nationalities, the United States being represented by less than 200 missionaries and naturalized citizens.

The classification according to religions showed

Present-Day Egypt

nearly 9,000,000 Mohammedans, 730,000 Christians, and 25,000 Israelites. The Christians included the Coptic race, numbering about 608,000, of whom only a small proportion professed the Roman Catholic or Protestant faith. Cairo was found to contain 570,000 inhabitants; Alexandria, 320,000; Tanta (the largest town in the interior of the Delta), 57,000; Zagazig and Mansurah, 35,000 each; Port Saïd, 42,000; Suez, 17,000; and Ismailia, nearly 7000. From the figures dealing with the last three towns it may be inferred that over 50,000 persons derive their living from the Suez Canal. The largest town in Upper Egypt, Assiut, had 42,000, Keneh ranking next with 24,000. The total number of centers of population, comprising towns, villages, farms, settlements, and Bedouin encampments, was found to be 18,129.

The rapid increase in recent years in the population is explained in great measure by the prosperity of the country, which had drawn a large number of discontented people from the Mahdi's territory south of Wady-Halfa. A decided lessening of mortality, resulting from the introduction of rigorous hygienic measures, has likewise had its effect. There has been a marked decrease in child mortality of late years.

With the cultivated area estimated to be ten thousand five hundred square miles, Egypt's population has increased in density to the enormous figure of 928 to the square mile,[1] being thus greater

[1] To make this statement credible to those who may look to other countries for comparisons, it must be explained that in Egypt prac-

Paradoxical Administration

than any country in Europe. Belgium has a density of 540 to the square mile, while Great Britain has a home population of only 315, Germany 224, and France 186.

Since the year 1886 the finances of Egypt have improved to an extent emphasizing the nation's emergence from practical bankruptcy to an enviable condition of credit to be found in the history of but few countries. So marked was the improvement that in 1890 the government was in a position to carry into effect a conversion of the whole of its external debt, thereby scaling the rate of interest in some instances nearly half. Although Egypt's burden of interest has thus been greatly decreased, yet the country has still to find nearly nineteen million dollars for the yearly interest charges. The present bonded debt, approximately stated, with the current premium quoted on European bourses on the several classes of obligations, is as follows:

Guaranteed loan,	3 %	(quoted 5 premium)	$ 42,442,000
Privileged debt,	3½%	(quoted 2¾ premium)	142,854,000
Unified debt,	4 %	(quoted 7 premium)	272,037,000
Domains loan,	4¼%	(quoted 5 premium)	19,418,000
Daira Sanieh loan,	4 %	(quoted 1¼ premium)	32,191,000
		Total bonded debt,	$508,942,000

tically every acre of the soil not belonging to the desert is under cultivation, producing one, oftentimes two, and occasionally three crops a year. There are no waste lands, forests, or mountains. Were not almost every foot of the soil utilized, it would not be possible for 928 persons to the square mile to be supported. And, further, it should be borne in mind that the official census fixing Egypt's population at 9,750,000 included many Bedouin tribes and other desert-dwellers, and was further swollen by the inclusion of many Nubians who had left their southern provinces and crossed the frontier into Egypt.

Present-Day Egypt

This burden, applying to a community purely agricultural, where manual labor is worth from fifteen to twenty cents a day, and to a tillable area estimated at ten thousand five hundred square miles, is almost overpowering. It means a per capita debt of $52.20, accepting the late official census to be correct. The count of 1882 showed the indebtedness to be $72.70, but the last census aids England's desire to make a statistical showing of progress. The too liberal inclusion of desert-dwellers and Sudanese in the statement of population has little real bearing upon the condition of the agricultural native. But, accepting the pro rata debt as $52.20, that obligation of the Nilot is more than the present or half a dozen generations can discharge. Even the Turk or the Greek does not owe as much. Frenchmen and Englishmen owe considerably more than the Egyptians, but their resources and earning capacity are incomparably greater, and their creditors are their own countrypeople. The public debt of the United States, recently emerged from a costly foreign war, shows a per capita obligation of only about $19.

Egyptian securities ruled very low in the year of the Arabi rebellion, and the year following, in which occurred the fiasco in the Sudan. "Unifieds" for a time were quoted at $46\frac{1}{2}$, and an average price for months for nearly every class of Egyptian securities was 50, meaning that prudent investors would give only half its face value for the bonded debt of Egypt. It has never been possible to determine the nationality of holders of Egyptian

Paradoxical Administration

securities. Interest coupons are presented in London, Paris, Berlin, and Cairo, and naturally at the place where exchange is highest, or where income taxes can best be escaped. It is believed, however, that Britishers own half of them.

Discouragements of every sort beset the work of regeneration entered upon, by Tewfik Pasha and the Englishmen electing to labor with him, following the events of 1882. For years it was a neck-and-neck race with bankruptcy. Indemnification of Alexandrians whose property was destroyed by reason of the bombardment and sacking, the military disaster resulting in the loss of the Sudan, and other inevitable expenditures, swelled the national debt by nearly forty million dollars in excess of what it was when the British went to the country. Recuperation was brought about by checking waste and dishonesty, developing the soil, and adding to the cultivable territory by scientific irrigation. The reduction by half of railroad, postal, and telegraph rates proved the wisdom of legislating for the earning classes, by doubling the service and augmenting the income. The salt monopoly, as well, was rendered more profitable by the sweeping reduction in the price of that commodity.

Changes of any sort are made with difficulty, because of the unique conditions detailed in this chapter. The public cash-box guarded by representatives of six European governments, and treaty privileges possessed by fourteen powers, some of which are not in sympathy with the present control of affairs by England, make progress difficult. The

Present-Day Egypt

restoration of Egypt to admitted prosperity, consequently, at a period when shrinkage in prices of cotton, sugar, and grain has been very great, must be regarded as a conspicuous triumph. Khedive Abbas and his co-workers have much to accomplish still; but system and economy being now established on a secure basis, the attainment to permanent success cannot be difficult.

A striking feature of the governmental management of railways in Egypt is that only forty-three per cent. of the gross receipts are applied to operating expenses. Native labor, moderate speed of ordinary trains, and a rainless and frostless climate make this possible. The state lines carry now upward of ten million passengers in a year, and the receipts from all sources are not far from nine million dollars annually. By reason of the important reduction of fares, previously spoken of, the number of passengers has been doubled in a few years. All-rail travel from the Mediterranean to the first cataract of the Nile has been possible for nearly a year. From Luxor southward the railway is narrow-gage, harmonizing with the lines building in the Sudan for military purposes.

The rapid augmentation of winter travel to the Nile is helping the lot of the Egyptian materially. In an average year the pleasure- and health-seekers, approaching eight thousand in number, distribute fully five million dollars in the country, and it is estimated that in a good season half this sum is left behind by Americans.

As in all countries where the gulf between the

THE PYRAMIDS, SEEN FROM NATIVE VILLAGE.

Paradoxical Administration

masses and the upper class is wide, the desire for petty office-holding is one of the crying evils of Egypt. It is estimated that two per cent. of the able-bodied men serve the government in some capacity, and to secure public employ is the dream of nearly every youth not satisfied to become a farmer. Nepotism formerly had full play, and it is now difficult to make the people understand that merit and capacity should place one in the public service, rather than favor. Ministries and public offices appear to be overcrowded with subordinates of every conceivable nationality. The responsible heads of departments are generally English, but the clerks are French, Italian, Syrian, and Egyptian, with a liberal sprinkling of British subjects. Functionaries of the Egyptian government are surprisingly overpaid or underpaid, their salaries being strangely out of proportion. Cabinet officers are paid fifteen thousand dollars a year, and undersecretaries seventy-five hundred dollars—twice what Washington officials of the same grade receive. But many of the hardest-worked accountants and translators are rewarded with salaries barely sufficient to provide the necessaries of life. The departments and bureaus of the government are open only in the forenoon, and the official day's work never exceeds five hours, and nearly every week has a religious or other anniversary that is treated as a holiday. In that halcyon period known as "the good old days" there were more civil servants in Egypt than in Great Britain, with five times the population. Many abuses have been abolished, but thorough reform has yet to be accomplished in the public service of Egypt to place it on a footing by which it might be compared with public employment in either the United States or Great Britain.

The "international" aspect of Egypt is an expensive luxury, and contributes in no small measure to the demands upon the public treasury. The International Debt Commission, for illustration, brings to Cairo delegates of the powers which are the country's creditors. Each is paid a salary of ten thousand dollars by the khedival government for looking after the interests of his countrymen fortunate enough to own Egyptian bonds, which can be sold anywhere at a substantial premium, and which, very likely, were purchased at a price far below their par value. Having no voice whatever in fixing the rate of interest, or the proportion going to the different countries, it might occur to the strict reformer that a competent, trustworthy accountant could perform the service of these six officials, with a great saving to the toiling masses of Egypt. But the countries interested would no more be able to agree on the nationality of such an accountant than were the same powers in deciding the question of nationality of the governor of Crete after the Greco-Turkish war.

The railway system of less than fifteen hundred miles is managed by three princely paid men, acting for England, France, and Egypt. In Europe or America a single competent man would do it all, for a fraction of the pay, and most likely find time hanging heavily on his hands and want more to do.

Paradoxical Administration

Similarly, the spirit of internationalism dominates the Daira Sanieh, the State Domains, and other divisions of the government, aggregating a mighty draft on the exchequer. But the customs and post-office departments, each with a single head, are models of perfection. The postal service, managed by Saba Pasha, seems to be faultless.

The purchasing power, held to be indicative of a nation's pecuniary condition, has advanced with other statistics dealing with the country's welfare. In 1882 the imports were valued at $32,127,650; in 1890, $40,409,635, and in 1896, $45,750,000. Exports for the same years—cotton, cotton-seed, sugar, and grain—were valued at $54,977,850, $59,373,490, and $66,000,000, respectively. More than half of the foreign commerce is with Great Britain. The cotton crop, wholly exported, produces in the neighborhood of $50,000,000 a year. Of this the United States buys about $4,000,000 worth. The tonnage arrivals at the port of Alexandria have nearly doubled since 1882, and in a normal year are slightly in excess of two million tons. The port receipts are as high as $7,000,000 in a year.

To carry on the government requires about $53,000,000 a year. It used to be more in the free-and-easy times when budget-making was the merest guesswork, and deficiencies could be explained in the convenient phrase, "insufficiency of receipts." The heaviest outlay is for interest on the bonded indebtedness, $18,850,000; while the annual tribute to the Sultan (signed away by that monarch to European bankers) consumes $3,365,200 more.

Present-Day Egypt

The khedive, khedival family, and palace expenses, coming under the head of "civil list," call for $1,159,000. In ordinary times the army and military police cost $2,390,000, and civil and military pensions $2,150,000 more.

Nearly half of the sum required to carry on the Egyptian government is produced by direct taxation on land. The other half is made up by indirect taxation, from the following sources: customs receipts (eight per cent. on imports and one per cent. on exports), tax on date-trees, tobacco tax, municipal octroi on food and merchandise, stamp duties, receipts from railways, post-offices, telegraphs, lighthouses, and courts of justice. The sale of salt and natron gives a yearly revenue of nearly $8,000,000.

A reform of the greatest importance, to become effective in the immediate future, is the adjustment of inequalities in the land-tax. By the old scheme of estimating values many anomalies were countenanced, as well as many injustices. It was not unusual to find land renting at thirty or thirty-five dollars an acre paying the government only two and a half dollars in taxes. In Ismail's time there was no rule for the collection of taxes, and the minions of the government went prepared to take from the farmer every penny his crops had produced, and then flog him into borrowing at heavy usury any additional sum the rapacious collector chose to demand. Not until Khedive Tewfik's reign was a receipt of any kind given the peasant to show that he had paid his taxes and that no

AN OFFICIAL GROUP IN GROUNDS OF THE UNITED STATES DIPLOMATIC AGENCY

Paradoxical Administration

more was due for the current year. Simple as was the giving of such a receipt, nothing more potent for alleviating the position of the fellaheen was ever inaugurated. It was a reform benefiting every tiller of the soil, and was in operation before "the coming of the English."

The scheme of taxation in force for some years has been arbitrary and inequitable. A definite tax has been prescribed for certain districts, which only a portion of the land was capable of paying. The reform in hand has been to create a schedule based upon rental values, that each acre may be assessed commensurately with its producing capacity. The total taxation of the country is not to be increased under the new system, the movement being intended to relieve the small proprietor, who will pay less per acre, while the pasha landlord, once powerful enough to have his thousands of acres assessed at whatever he chose to pay, will be called upon to contribute to the public expenses by a proportionately higher estimate of land values. These glaring inequalities were brought into prominence by the decreasing prices of crops, and relief was imperatively necessary.

The land-tax has ever been the millstone about the neck of the Egyptian, sapping his energies and stunting his intellectual growth. The ancestors of the peasant now toiling from long before sunrise until after sunset, nearly every day in the year, have been tillers of the soil and drawers of water since the world began; and their incessant toil has produced but little—for them. It will surprise

Present-Day Egypt

American farmers and British agriculturists to know that some of their brethren of the Nile pay a land-tax of eight dollars per acre annually, and that the average tax of the country approximates four dollars to the acre. The heaviest tax is on the choice lands of the Delta, possessing such exceptional richness that five hundredweight or more of cotton per acre is produced each year with comparative certainty.

To-day's prosperity of the fellah of Egypt, permitting him to have a few dollars after the adjustment of accounts following the sale of his crops, occasionally to augment his vegetable diet by a dish of meat, and to seek recreation at his beloved religious fairs, is of recent origin and slow growth: it began with the introduction of tax receipts, and has been nurtured at intervals by trifling reductions in taxation, as the area has been added to by irrigation at a rate in excess of the government's pecuniary needs. Being humanely treated, the present-day Egyptian realizes that he is a human being; and it is the opinion of those capable of judging that more has been done in the last fifteen years for his well-being than in all the rest of the century. The humane work was inaugurated under Tewfik Pasha, and the administration headed by Khedive Abbas is carrying it forward with intelligent perseverance.

The country's obligations to European creditors are sufficiently menacing and burdensome to compel the small farmer to keep out of the clutches of the Greek or Syrian money-lender at his gates, if

Paradoxical Administration

he can. Nevertheless, the strictly home indebtedness secured by farm mortgages is greater than it should be. Some critics insist that this is certain proof that the boasted prosperity of the country is fictitious, and exhibit statistics to support their argument. Critics friendly to English rule array figures calculated to show that the aggregate domestic mortgage indebtedness is very small, less than forty million dollars, and that it is the proprietors of fifty acres and upward who have pledged their farms; and, further, that they have done this only to be able to buy more land, being confident of an appreciation of values. It is a fact, I believe, that the proportion of petty holders borrowing by mortgage is small, and they are the people whose welfare first deserves consideration.

The recent expansion of the cultivable area being chiefly in Upper Egypt and portions of the Nile valley where the fertility cannot be compared to that of Lower Egypt, there has been a corresponding decrease in the average value of the acre. When I investigated the subject five years ago, I arrived at the conclusion that $115 was a fair estimate of the value of productive Egypt, acre for acre. Now, when the character of the newly acquired extensions is considered, it is my judgment that the average value of the 6,720,000 acres has fallen to $105. Readers of mathematical mind, discovering that the foreign bonded indebtedness on every acre of productive soil averages $75.74, and adding $8 for home mortgage burden (to my mind estimated at too low a sum), find that but little

Present-Day Egypt

equity remains to the Egyptian, who for more than six thousand years has been the most industrious and light-hearted of husbandmen. Plainly stated, it means a margin of only $21.26 an acre. And his energy must not flag for generations to come, lest his fellow-creature in enlightened Europe be in arrears over his interest on "Egyptians." Blessed be Allah!

In Viscount Cromer the British government has one of its ablest administrators, and as forceful and far-seeing a man as England's group of aggressive empire-builders can show. A Baring, of the banking family, he graduated from the British army into the foreign civil service, where his administrative genius was manifested years ago by his good work in India, and the fact accepted by all political parties in Parliament that he was a man to be trusted. As England's representative in the dual financial control of Egypt, in the years immediately precedent to the "occupation" of the country by Great Britain, his tact and honesty contributed greatly to preserving the apparent *entente cordiale* with France, really chafing under the gradual impairment of prestige in the land of the Nile. The dual control ended, Major Baring was elevated to the position of diplomatic agent and consul-general in Egypt, and given almost plenary power, not only in carrying into effect instructions and suggestions from London, but in shaping Britain's policy in the Nile valley and Delta. The effective manner in which he has handled Egyptian affairs has made him his nation's credi-

VISCOUNT CROMER, BRITISH DIPLOMATIC AGENT
AND CONSUL-GENERAL.

Paradoxical Administration

tor; and the honors bestowed upon him—knighthood first, then a barony and peerage, and finally the viscountship—but inadequately discharge the debt that his government owes him. So determined is he to carry his administration of Egypt to a triumphant termination that an offer of the viceroyship of India, or a cabinet position in London, has awakened no desire to leave Cairo.

Lord Cromer is *de facto* ruler of Egypt, the visible but unclassified representative of the majesty of Great Britain, with almost unlimited power and authority. *De jure* he is Britain's diplomatic representative,—nothing more,—and his exequatur issues from the Sublime Porte in exactly the same form as that of the representative of any other government at the court of the khedive. This is but one of the paradoxes incident to present-day Egypt. Possessing little aptitude for accepted formulæ of diplomacy, perhaps, Lord Cromer makes a thoroughly reliable doyen of the diplomatic corps, which he is because his appointment antedates that of any of his colleagues. He cares nothing for display, detests shams, is a keen judge of men, and selects his assistants with such discernment that his judgment seldom errs. Devoid of a sense of humor, and unimaginative, Lord Cromer analyzes with great care a question in which the interests of others are concerned; and, an opinion formed, his conclusion is bound to prevail. Viscount Cromer is a man of marvelous industry. He reads Homer, learns a language,—even Turkish,—and plays tennis or whist with the same energy, and with the same object—to win. Since the demise of Lady Cromer he toils harder than ever. In conversation one feels that he is more preoccupied with what he intends to say than with his manner of expressing it. This is but a sketchy description of an interesting man and his character; but it is sufficient, possibly, to explain the success of England's rule in Egypt.

CHAPTER V

THE EXPANSION OF PRODUCTIVE EGYPT BY IRRIGATION

THE most interesting page in the modern history of Egypt is that which records the development of scientific irrigation.

Coincident with the preparation of this volume for publication, one of the most stupendous engineering feats ever undertaken by man is being executed on the Egyptian frontier, having for its purpose the ponding back into Nubia of a body of water perhaps a hundred and fifty miles long, crossing the tropic of Cancer, and extending southward nearly to Korosko,—a goodly step on the journey to Abu-Simbel and Wady-Halfa,—by means of a great dam across the Nile at Assuan. The Pyramids and the Sphinx have borne testimony through the centuries to the grandeur and power of execution which dwelt within the Nile valley; and what more fitting now than that the same valley should be the theater of a gigantic engineering exploit, audacious perhaps, but certain of success, and ministering to man's necessities, rather than to his vanity?

As a wholesale rearrangement of nature's surface the project outranks anything hitherto attempted by engineering skill; and as a building achievement the scheme is on a scale worthy of a Rameses or a Pharaoh. To create in the midst of the African desert a lake having possibly three times the superficial area of Lake Geneva in Switzerland, and control it with scientific precision, so that the impounded flood may be turned into distant channels at will, is a comprehensive undertaking. But the engineers claim that their plans can be carried out to the letter; they have estimated the exact cost of the dam, computed almost to the gallon the volume of water that will be imprisoned, and figured the necessary resistance to be provided at every point of the masonry. In Cairo, the experts of the ministries of public works and finance, likewise, have calculated to a nicety the sum from taxation that will come into the public treasury through the country's augmented productiveness.

Subordinate to the great dam, a smaller one, not unlike the barrage at the apex of the Delta, ten miles to the north of Cairo, is to be made at Assiut. Its function will be to give sufficient head to the river to force the water into the system of irrigation canals that veins hundreds of thousands of acres between Assiut and Cairo. The completion of the Cairo barrage so developed cotton-culture as to add to the public revenue of the country at least ten million dollars annually. It may safely be concluded that the Assuan reservoir is but one of a series which will in time be constructed southward to Berber, Khartum, and perhaps the Victoria Nyanza. The reëstablishment of khedival author-

Expansion by Irrigation

ity at Khartum practically determined this, as it means that in time the Sudan provinces will be important grain-exporters.

The agricultural industry that will be chiefly benefited by the Assuan reservoir and the tributary weir at Assiut is cane-culture. With Cuba's productiveness greatly impaired as a result of the prolonged strife in the island, the opening years of the twentieth century are considered propitious for doubling or trebling Egypt's output of raw sugar. The Nile cane is of such exceptional quality that much European capital has been invested in its cultivation, while crushing-factories have gone up on the river's banks as if by magic.

No subject is receiving wider attention at this time than that of territorial expansion. Great Britain, as well as France, Germany, and Russia, is yearly pressing forward its domain in Africa or Asia, preceded by the soldier or explorer; and the fortunes of war have carried the Stars and Stripes oversea, and brought numerous islands as well as an Asiatic archipelago under administrative guidance from Washington.

But the triumph of practical science, such as irrigation, bearing no relation to the sword or diplomacy, which turns a single acre of desert sand into a productive field, must be a thousandfold more valuable to the world than the victory of arms that merely changes a frontier or deprives a defeated nation of a single foot of soil: it is the victory of peace; it is creation. As a method of making territory, it is one over which statesmen can never differ.

Present-Day Egypt

Old Egypt is now so fairly in step with the march of progress as to be attracting the attention of the civilized world. Irrigation is the lever of this progress—the irrigation of definite science, rather than of chance or guesswork; and the move to harness the Nile and compel it to surrender its magical richness to the soil is a project that will be watched by millions of students of utilitarianism. Stated simply, it means the increase of the country's productive capacity by twenty-five per cent., bringing, as it will, considerable stretches of desert soil within the limits of cultivation, while vast sections of land already arable will be rendered capable of producing two, if not three, crops in the year, by having "summer water" supplied to the thirsting ground.

As shown in another chapter, the Egypt of the map contains more than four hundred thousand square miles, an expanse seven times as great as New England; but the practical Egypt—that which produces crops and sustains life—is considerably less than the States of Massachusetts and Connecticut united. This is the ribbon-like strip of alluvial land bordering the Nile, a few miles wide on each side, and measuring not more than ten thousand five hundred square miles. The extension planned, and to be completed in the next six or eight years, wholly by irrigation, is no less magnificent in conception than the rescuing from the Libyan and Arabian deserts of twenty-five hundred square miles, or twice the area of Rhode Island. This will be exploitation in its truest sense, and its accom-

GENERAL VIEW OF THE FIRST CATARACT, LOOKING SOUTH FROM ASSUAN.

Expansion by Irrigation

plishment will be a verification of the ancient saying that "Egypt is the Nile, and the Nile is Egypt."

As an object-lesson, this Egyptian enterprise should have no more interested observers than in America, especially in Colorado, Nevada, California, and other States of the West, where the irrigation expert is succeeding the railway-builder as a developer.

British contractors have agreed that the dam that is to "hold up" the historic river on which Cleopatra floated in her gilded barge, and on which Moses was cradled, will be completed by July 1, 1903. It will be built of granite ashler, much of which will be quarried from the Assuan side of the river, coming from the ledges that furnished the obelisks that now stand in Central Park in New York, and on London's Thames Embankment, and in the Place de la Concorde in Paris. It will be seventy-six feet high in places, and with its approaches nearly a mile and a quarter long. The difference in water-level above and below the dam will be forty-six feet; and the top of the structure, thirty or forty feet in width, will give bridge facilities to pedestrians, camel-trains, and other traffic of the region. It may interest arithmeticians to know that it is estimated that a thousand million tons of water can be stored in the reservoir.

The laying of the foundation-block, of syenite granite and weighing several tons, was an impressive function. Queen Victoria's third son, his Royal Highness the Duke of Connaught, performed the office with rule, level, mallet, and silver trowel, surrounded by many distinguished personages, including his amiable duchess; Fakhry Pasha, Egyptian minister of public works; Mr. John Aird, member of the British Parliament, who is the chief contractor for the work; and representatives of several branches of the Anglo-Egyptian administration. A guard of honor was furnished by Egyptian troops. The following inscription is chiseled on the face of the stone:

H. H. Abbas Hilmi, Khedive.

This Foundation-Stone
was laid by
H. R. H. The Duke of Connaught,
12th February, 1899.

H. E. Hussein Fakhry Pasha,
Minister of Public Works.

After the laying of the stone, the Duke of Connaught sent the following telegram to the khedive, which he wrote on the stone itself: "Having this moment completed the laying of the foundation-stone of the great dam here at the request of your Highness, I telegraph my warmest congratulations on the occasion of Bairam. Arthur." A telegram was likewise sent to the Queen, informing her Majesty that the great work had been formally commenced. The official party subsequently proceeded across the cataract to take refreshments, and see natives swim the rapids. The following day the duke and duchess continued their voyage

Expansion by Irrigation

to Wady-Halfa, and later to Omdurman and Khartum.

The contractors present what looks like a moderate bill. They are to receive eight hundred thousand dollars a year for thirty years, aggregating about twenty-four million dollars. As an incentive for them to live up to their agreement, the first payment by the Egyptian government is not to be made until the work is completed and accepted. The credit is a long one, certainly, and its present actuarial value cannot be much in excess of ten million dollars. The ability of Egypt to make such a favorable contract, by which she apparently takes little risk, and is to pay away each year only a portion of the sum the reservoir brings to her exchequer, reflects the enviable position of her national credit. The transaction may further be taken as an earnest of Great Britain's intention to retain indefinitely her grasp upon the land of the Pharaohs. English engineers and surveyors and a horde of native laborers have for months been at work at Assuan. A single order for three million barrels of cement is being filled from Europe.

For years Sir William Garstin, Mr. Willcocks, and other English engineers in the khedival service have strenuously advocated the creation of one or more reservoirs that would give perennial irrigation to Egypt. Experts of other nations have been called into consultation, and all admitted the feasibility of the project, but they were not at first in accord as to the location of the principal dam. They were agreed that the natural advantages of the Assuan site, with its bed of syenite granite beneath the river, the conformation of the surrounding country, and the inexhaustible supply of stone near by, offered advantages approached by no other location.

A situation thirty miles south, at Kalabsheh, was favored by some; but the structure proposed, necessarily resting on a foundation of crumbly sandstone, could not be regarded as permanent or as safe as if it rested on a foundation of granite. The Silsila Gate, fifty miles north of Assuan, having the same underlying sandstone, was rejected as a site on the ground of insecurity. A dam there, besides, would submerge the temple at Kom-Ombos, as well as a good part of the town of Assuan. Hence all the engineers in the end favored damming the Nile at the first cataract, at a point about four miles south of Assuan, and not far from the island of Philæ. There nature has been lavish in providing hills of solid rock on each side of the river that will stand the ravages of the elements as long as the world lasts.

Little time was wasted in the preparation of the original plans for the dam. But the officials having the matter in charge, intent only on the utilitarian aspect of the problem, brought about their heads, four or five years ago, a wide-spread outburst of indignation, when it was announced that the treasured ruins of Philæ would be submerged for months at a time, were their recommendations carried into effect. Meetings were held by learned societies everywhere to protest against any desecra-

LOG-SWIMMING DOWN THE ASSUAN CATARACT.

Expansion by Irrigation

tion of Philæ, and their memorials besieged the Egyptian government for months. From every country in Europe, from the United States, and from the centers of learning in the East, antiquarians, Egyptologists, archæologists, and literary people generally, joined in vigorous protest. The late Sir Frederick Leighton, president of England's Royal Academy, did not hesitate to say that "any tampering with Philæ would be a lasting blot on the British occupation of Egypt." This stinging remark brought the subject into the realm of British politics, and did as much as all the protests to cause the too practical plans of the English engineers to be held in abeyance until a modified project, conciliating archæological interests with engineering necessities, could be devised.

To silence their critics, if possible, the engineers proposed many makeshift plans, some of which displayed surprising ingenuity. Sir Benjamin Baker, of Manchester Canal fame, favored the raising of the island, as a whole, some twelve feet, and offered to do it for a million dollars, guaranteeing its safe accomplishment. Another gravely proposed that the temple of Isis, pylons and all, be moved to a neighboring and higher island and re-erected, and submitted a proposal for the contract. Still another recommended building a caisson of masonry around the island, that would protect it from flood, but make it necessary to descend a flight of stairs to view the buildings, themselves so artistic that people travel great distances to admire them.

Present-Day Egypt

The proposal to remove Philæ stone by stone was too fantastic even for the pen of a Jules Verne. An American writer suggested that if Philæ's wondrous structures were to be disturbed at all, they should be floated six hundred miles down the Nile and reërected in Cairo. This, the writer urged, would bring to the doors of the tourists' hotels one of Egypt's greatest attractions, and carry business enterprise to its utmost extent. This bit of sarcasm had its effect.

The publicity given to these absurd proposals caused scholarly Europe and America again to protest against the threatened vandalism, and a torrent of newspaper invective was hurled at Britain's rule of Egyptian affairs, which threatened to destroy one of the world's most precious gems in order that European holders of Egyptian bonds might be more certain of their interest and security. The reservoir project was now in danger of drifting into European politics, and it was wisely concluded in Cairo and London to let the matter drop from public notice for a few years.

"What is a useless temple," asked engineers, "in comparison with a work involving the welfare of millions of human beings?" "Are sordid commercial motives," replied archæologists, "to override everything artistic in the world, and is a priceless monument of antiquity to be lost to civilization that a few more fellaheen, already prosperous, may grow more cotton and sugar and grain?" "Why must the Philistine come to Philæ at all?" inquired sentimentalists everywhere.

Expansion by Irrigation

With these conflicting claims to reconcile, the engineers were compelled to weigh the pros and cons of their project in every aspect before again testing public opinion. That they succeeded in their task is shown by the general approval of their modified scheme, by which the dam is to be but two thirds as high as at first proposed. A head of forty-six feet of water satisfies the engineers, and does not alarm the archæologists; for, although submerging portions of the island, it leaves the temple, pylons, and prized sculptures fairly above water-level.

When the builders have finished their labors, visitors to Upper Egypt can never realize the present beauty of Philæ. The Isis temple, the chapel of Hathor, the Diocletian portal, one of the legendary graves of Osiris, the well-preserved pavilion called "Pharaoh's Bed,"—the designer of which was no stranger to Greek art, and within whose walls thousands of tourists have partaken of their midday luncheon,—will all be there, like jewels wrenched from glorious settings. The structures will rise from a placid lake, deprived of the graceful elevation and artistic symmetry that add much to their fame.

Confessedly Philæ will be impaired artistically, for it is safe to assume that the zealous engineers understate the extent of the submergence. A scientific English observer, who studied the subject at close quarters,—from the island itself,—says: "The four great pylons will, of course, stand up out of the new lake, but its waters will rise to their floors. The splendid Nilometer will be utterly swallowed up. The colonnade of the temple of Nectanebo will be under water most of the year, and I fear the structures at its ends will tumble into the reservoir, as there are already cracks in the foundation-walls."

It is not the native population that deplores the disappearance of the antique and the picturesque, for the modern Egyptian has no appreciation for the ancient or his works. To his feelings the magnitude of the Pyramids and the mystery of the Sphinx make no appeal. The only value of the priceless antiquities of the Nile valley to the fellah or Bedouin is to bring in piasters. The ruthless hands that stripped the pyramid of Cheops of its outer casing to deck a mosque in Cairo would not spare Karnak or Philæ. After all, Philæ's remains, noble as they are, appear comparatively young beside many of the monuments of this hoary land. They do not, it is said, go as far back as 300 B. C. Pharaoh's Bed was really built in Roman times, though, presumably, by native architects.

Standing without meaning upon a wide stretch of mirroring water, Philæ will completely lose its character, and can no longer be the stately sentinel guarding the natural boundary between Nubia and Egypt. The artist's dahabiyeh, drawn well up on the strand beneath Pharaoh's Bed, can never again give a touch of color to the scene. Nor can the patriarchal sheik of the cataract load his clumsy boats at the point of the island with tourists sufficiently courageous to "shoot the rapids" on the

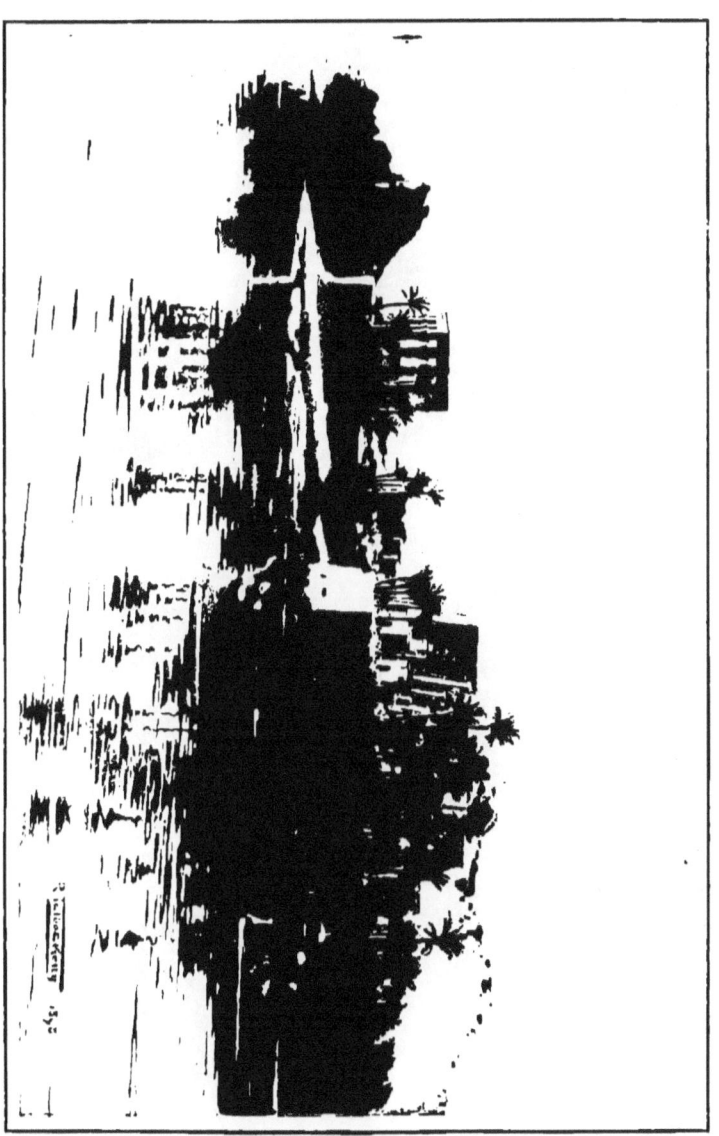

PHILÆ AS IT IS.

Expansion by Irrigation

way back to their steamers or hotel at Assuan. The making of the dam will force the nude population of the region to prosecute their amphibious pursuits elsewhere—most likely in eddying rapids farther down-stream. But the daring soul who has "shot" what will remain of the cataract will, as of old, be landed on the bank at Assuan to the resounding "Heep, heep, hooray! Zank you, zank you!" of his crew of black rowers, whom he will liberally bakshish while yet believing himself a hero.

The American sun-seeker or English milord, making the voyage to Wady-Halfa by his own dahabiyeh, will no longer have his craft hauled up the Assuan cataract by a hundred shrieking Arabs and Berberins, for most likely it will be taken up the rapids and through the locks by electricity generated by the rushing Nile itself. Indeed, a practical Britisher is in the field for utilizing the cataract's force for electrically lighting Assuan and propelling irrigating machinery for a hundred miles or more down-stream, to the possible relief of the familiar shadoof and creaking sakieh.

The Assuan structure will differ in several respects from any great dam hitherto built. In the first place, none for impounding water has ever been made on any river approaching the size of the Nile; and, in the second place, it is to be both dam and waterway, a conjunction exceedingly difficult to effect. To confine Father Nile in flood-time would be hopeless, and therefore the river must be allowed to run unimpeded through the dam

Present-Day Egypt

during several months of the year. As soon as the flood subsides, but while the discharge is still greater than can be at once used for irrigation, the water will be retained for use during the parching summer months. For this purpose the structure will be divided into a large number of piers, with openings that can be closed at will by gates.

Each pier must be capable of supporting its own weight and the pressure of water against the adjoining sluice-gates, and the piers must be able to pass the torrent without damage. At times the velocity of the escaping flood-water will be very great; consequently the piers are to be enormously massive. The locks for steamers and other craft navigating the Nile will be on the west side.

It being the particles of soil contributed to the river by the wash of the mountains and hills in Abyssinia that enrich the fields, the dam will be so designed that the water released daily, during low Nile, will be drawn from near the bottom of the reservoir. Egyptian farmers prize the "red water," which is vastly richer in fertilizing value than clear water can be. In the autumn, after the silt-laden water has passed off, the sluice-gates will be closed gradually until the reservoir is full, which, with normal conditions, will be in January and February. From April to the end of August, when the Nile runs low, and the demand for water for the crops is at its highest, the gates will be systematically opened, and the summer supply of the river supplemented by the water, which, had it not been stored, would have flowed uselessly into the Medi-

Expansion by Irrigation

terranean. Thus Middle Egypt and the Delta will secure more or less perennial irrigation.

The Nile, the only river of Egypt, has a length of 4062 miles, and is thus exceeded only by the Mississippi, having a length of 4112 miles. At Cairo the river is eleven hundred yards in breadth. After the confluence of the Blue and White Niles at Khartum, it receives but one tributary, the Atbara. In Egypt proper the great river has no affluent and is contributed to in no way. The most important of the outlets of the Nile is Joseph's Canal (the Bahr Youssef), that leaves the river near Girgeh, and for two hundred and twenty miles follows along the foot of the Libyan chain of hills, finally entering the Fayum and fertilizing this fruitful oasis, its own creation, in numerous ramifications. In the Delta the most important canal is the Mahmudiyeh, built by Mehemet Ali in 1823. It connects the Rosetta arm with the harbor of Alexandria.

At Assuan the Nile is three hundred and thirty feet above the level of the Mediterranean. From Assuan to Cairo the fall is a trifle under five inches in the mile, and from Cairo to the sea the fall averages nearly an inch to the mile.

To equalize the distribution of the Nile water among cultivators, the whole country devoted to agriculture is divided by low earthwork dams into large fields, to which the water is conducted by canals. Lands that cannot be reached by the overflow of the canals have to be mechanically irrigated. To do this the small proprietor lifts the water from

Present-Day Egypt

the river or canal with the primitive shadoof operated by hand, but the important landowner in these days employs cattle or steam-power.

It was determined by the explorations of Speke, Grant, and Baker that the rainfall of the equatorial region of Africa supplies the Victoria and Albert lakes, and that the overflow of these gives sufficient volume to support the Nile throughout its northward course of thirty degrees of latitude, crossing arid sands and burning deserts, until it reaches the Mediterranean.

It might at first sight appear that the discovery of the Nile's sources had completely solved the mystery of ages, and proved the fertility of Egypt to be dependent upon the rainfall of the equator concentrated in the Victoria Nyanza and Albert Nyanza; but the exploration of the Nile tributaries of Abyssinia divides the Nile system into two parts, and unravels the entire mystery of the river by assigning to each its share in ministering to the prosperity of Egypt.

The lake sources maintain the life of Egypt by supplying a stream throughout all seasons that has sufficient volume to support the exhaustion of evaporation and absorption; but this stream unaided could never overflow its banks, and Egypt, deprived of the annual inundation, would be forced to exist with the cultivation of the circumscribed area immediately bordering the great river.

The two great affluents of Abyssinia are the Blue Nile and the Atbara (called by the natives Bahr-al-Aswad, or the Black Nile), which, although

PROBABLE APPEARANCE OF THE CATARACT ON THE COMPLETION OF THE DAM.

Expansion by Irrigation

streams of unusual grandeur during the period of Abyssinian rains, from the middle of June until September, are reduced to insignificance during the dry months. Then, the water-supply from Abyssinia having ceased, Egypt is forced to depend solely upon the equatorial lakes and the affluents of the White Nile until the rainy season shall have again flooded the two great Abyssinian arteries. That flood occurs about the 20th of June, and the rush of water pouring down the Blue Nile and the Atbara into the main channel inundates Egypt, and is the cause of its magical fertility. Not only is the inundation the effect of the Abyssinian rains, but the deposit of mud that has formed the Delta, and which is annually precipitated by the rising waters, is also due to the Abyssinian streams, chiefly to the Atbara, which carries a larger proportion of soil than any other tributary of the Nile. Therefore to the Atbara,—spanned by an American-built railroad-bridge, by the way,—above all other rivers, must the wealth and fertility of Egypt be attributed. In writing of his Nile explorations, Baker employed this happy description: "The equatorial lakes *feed* Egypt, but the Abyssinian rivers *cause the inundation.*"

There is a fascination in the unchangeable features of the Nile region. There are the Pyramids and Sphinx that have defied time; the sandy deserts through which Moses led his people, and the watering-places where their flocks were led to drink. There is no change in these; and the poor people who dwell in Nubia and Upper Egypt on the banks of the melancholy river rolling toward the sea in the cloudless glare of a tropical sun, to-day as thousands of years ago, snatch every sand-bank from the receding stream, and plant melons, beans, and other articles of their simple diet. Not an inch of available soil is lost; and day by day, as the stream decreases in spring and summer, fresh rows of vegetables are sown upon the newly acquired land.

In Middle and Lower Egypt, the soil, created by the deposits of the great river and ever fertilized by it, is perhaps the richest in the world, and is tilled with such ease and certain results as cannot fail to excite the envy of the traveling American. The Egyptian peasant is by instinct at once farmer and irrigation expert. With the rudest of wooden plows, a mattock, and a well-sweep water-hoisting shadoof, his labors are blessed with a success impossible to tillers of the soil elsewhere.

From ages before the beginnings of history down to the reign of Mehemet Ali, all Egypt followed but one rule of cultivation. The land was saturated in the flood season with the fertilizing waters of the great river, and when the flood abated the seed was sown in the ooze, and the result was a single harvest of great abundance. Mehemet Ali revolutionized this system in the Delta. He introduced the cultivation of cotton and sugar, and the system of perennial irrigation which these highly profitable crops require.

Nature made the Delta; all that man did was to construct the canals that distribute the water.

Expansion by Irrigation

It has been computed that more than half of the Nile, with its priceless sediment, pours into the Mediterranean. In other words, water and soil enough to create many Egypts run to waste. Much of this loss will always be inevitable, naturally. Napoleon had no sooner seen the Nile at Cairo than he suggested a dam to hold back the surplus waters and irrigate a larger area. Lord Nelson and General Abercrombie cut short Napoleon's plans for administering Egypt; but his scheme for irrigating the Delta had been published, and forty years later, in 1837, the construction of the great barrage near Cairo, at the point where the Rosetta and Damietta branches of the Nile bifurcate and their arms inclose the Delta, was begun from plans by Mougel Bey, a Frenchman. It took twenty-four years to construct it, and then it was not a success, for the first time it was tried the force of the dammed-up water was too great for the masonry, which really rested on a foundation of mud.

I overheard an amusing conversation one day at the barrage. The engineer in charge was explaining the importance of the structure to a British tourist, who apparently never permitted his patriotic ardor to slumber when away from home. "Yes, it's a great work," said he, "and these foreigners ought to better appreciate what we are doing for their good. This thing has put them on their feet financially, sure enough; but I don't believe they feel any gratitude for our having built it." "I beg your pardon," replied the gentle representative of the khedival government, "but it was designed and built by French engineers." "Was it?" ejaculated the visitor in sun-helmet and pugree. "I did n't know that. Well, anyway, they have to get an Englishman to take care of it!" "I beg your pardon again," was the polite response of Liuener Bey, D. P. W.; "I have the honor of being a native-born American citizen." The contretemps was of short duration, and as the touring Albion took his leave he remarked, with a twinkle in his eye: "I 'm going back to Shepheard's before some one tells me that Frenchmen built those Pyramids over there."

It was the countrymen of the gentleman of the sun-helmet, however, that made the barrage safe and effective. Its failure could not properly be laid at the door of Mougel, nevertheless, for Mehemet Ali furnished him little or no support in the way of intelligent labor. It is probable that the foundations intended by so talented a man as Mougel would have been properly laid had skilled workmen been employed; but he was allowed only half-starved fellaheen, receiving no pay. When the work was delayed, extra thousands of natives would be pressed into service, only to spoil what had already been done, it is told. Millions of tons of stone and gravel were thrown into the river, and on this unreliable basis was piled the vast dike of masonry, pierced by one hundred and twenty arches. Mehemet Ali died before it was finished, and his successors carried the work forward in the most desultory manner, until, in 1861, it was declared completed. Two years later the structure

TOURIST-BOAT LEAVING SHELAL FOR THE CATARACT.

Expansion by Irrigation

would have been swept away had not the sluices been quickly raised. From 1863 until it was taken in hand by Sir Colin Moncrieff and Mr. Willcocks in 1884, it was called upon to perform but a fraction of the duty for which it was planned. By reason of Moncrieff's genius, the dam was in a few years rendered safe, and much of the prosperity of the Delta in these times is due to his triumph.

If tradition be correct, Mougel Bey's quick wit saved the Gizeh Pyramids from destruction. When he went to Mehemet Ali to be told where the stones for the barrage were to come from, the viceroy said: "You have those great useless heaps of stone; use them up, every block if need be, for the purpose." The engineer, knowing what odium would attach to his name if he agreed to this proposition, asked for a few days to make calculations. His autocratic master would give but one day. When the engineer again appeared he said the cost of transporting the stone from the Pyramids would be greater than to quarry it anew in the hills. "Then let the Pyramids stay, and quarry new stone," said the tyrant, and the monuments were saved.

The added irrigation resulting from the Assuan reservoir, it has been computed, will permanently benefit Egypt fully one hundred million dollars. A direct annual return to the revenue of two million dollars—more than twice the sum to be paid each year to the firm building the dam—from sale of water and taxation on lands that will be rendered fruitful is promised. The government will further realize considerable sums from the sale of reclaimed public lands, and indirect revenues traceable to the country's augmented producing capacity. The customs and railways are certain to show large increases, and the reservoir will thus add considerably to the security behind Egyptian bonds of all classes.

The British diplomatic agent in Egypt, Lord Cromer, has recently had something to say on the financial aspects of the reservoir measure, as at first sight it might appear a somewhat hazardous undertaking to increase the liabilities of the Egyptian treasury while development of the Sudan is only entered upon. It is Lord Cromer's belief that the expenditure of capital to improve the water-supply, thereby increasing the revenue, affords the best and most certain way out of the pecuniary difficulties attending the reoccupation of the Sudan. As regards the views of the native population concerning the Assuan reservoir, he informed his government that he had never before known a measure to be received with such unanimous approbation; and Lord Cromer knows, for the new Egypt is largely his creation.

There is a legend that the yearly flooding of the Nile is caused by the tears shed by Isis over the tomb of Osiris, and the question has for uncounted centuries been asked as a type of impossibility, "Can man arrest the tears of Isis as they flow?" Joseph of Israel did it, at Pharaoh's command, by constructing a reservoir and canals, which fertilized the Fayum province, and gave to the Nile an

Expansion by Irrigation

equable flow. It was Joseph who conceived the idea of turning the surplus waters of high Nile into that vast depression in the desert to the southwest of the Fayum, creating thereby the Lake Mœris of ancient history.

A delving American, Mr. Cope Whitehouse, capable of intelligently exploring both the desert and moldy manuscripts and maps in Italian libraries, showed the khedive's engineers a few years ago how again to store the flood of the Nile in the same desert depression—or that part of it known as the Wady-Rayan—by utilizing Joseph's Canal, which leaves the Nile at Assiut and conveys the water of life to the Fayum. But the Englishmen guiding the Egyptian chariot of state having no wish to divide honors with Joseph, however worthy as an irrigationist, nor with Mr. Whitehouse, the latter was formally thanked for his scholarly suggestion, decorated by the khedive as a Grand Commander of the Medjidieh—and the Englishmen proceeded with their studies preliminary to the Assuan dam.

To comprehend the importance of present-day irrigation in Egypt, it must be borne in mind that the country owes its fertility solely to the Nile. Its agriculture, even the country's existence, depends on irrigation, for Egypt is practically rainless. Wherever the Nile water can be regularly supplied to the soil, the most bountiful crops follow, which, like cotton and sugar, command high prices because of their excellence. Indeed, with a reliable supply of water, farming in the Nile country can be pursued with more certainty of success than in any other country that I have knowledge of.

The present census gives to the practical Egypt a population averaging nine hundred and twenty-eight to the square mile of tillable soil—a density far in excess of any European state, and not to be equaled outside of Asiatic countries. The provision of sustenance for so many mouths depends on the marvelous fertility of the soil, and that again wholly on the mud and water of the Nile. In going by rail southward from Cairo, or from Ismailia to Cairo, one sees hundreds of striking illustrations of this truth. Side by side one passes rich fields that are under perennial cultivation, and close by sandy wastes that never grow a blade of grass. The sterile expanse may be only a foot or two above the luxuriant soil, but water never reaches it, and that is enough.

It will no doubt surprise most readers of this volume to learn that a fair estimate of the value of Egypt's ten thousand five hundred square miles of cultivable territory is $105 an acre. It is a fact, as well, that the foreign bonded indebtedness—naturally based upon the intrinsic value of the country—averages $75.74 per acre, while the per capita proportion of the external debt burden is no less than $52.20. The average land-tax of Egypt is something in excess of $4 per acre. These vital statistics are repeated here to reflect in its fullest importance what the building of the great dam at Assuan means to the people of Egypt. In the circumstances, the world can well afford to permit the

NATIVES HAULING A BOAT UP THE "GREAT GATE."

Expansion by Irrigation

artistic beauty of the island of Philæ to be slightly impaired, if necessary.

It is appropriate here to quote from a book written more than thirty-five years ago by Sir Samuel Baker. After descending the great river from source to mouth, he wrote: "The Nile might be so controlled that the enormous volume of water that now rushes uselessly into the Mediterranean might be led through the deserts to transform them into cotton-fields that would render England in.....

..... area to the Delta, the soil thus rescued from the desert is usually planted with cotton. An average year's crop is now equal to one million one hundred thousand bales of five hundred pounds each, and all this is sold in foreign markets at a price two cents per pound in excess of quotations for good American upland cotton. It is its fiber, nearly an inch and a half long, that gives Egyptian cotton its peculiar value. Great as the price is, this is not the only advantage possessed by the fellah cotton-grower over the planter of our Southern States; for the magical fecundity of the Nile soil permits the harvesting of a crop averaging five hundredweight to the acre. This is twice what American planters get from an acre, and the Nilot is exempt from certain disastrous elements ever menacing his American rival. The Egyptian has no dread of frost, and no labor question to deal with.

Present-Day Egypt

If the assistance of the women and children of his family proves insufficient, the needed additional labor may be secured at the rate of fifteen or eighteen cents a day for each man. In the unlikely event of having to sell his cotton at the same price as the American, even then he could make a profit. His prosperity is assured so long as the Southern planter accepts the opinion that long-fiber cotton can be grown only on the Nile, and that European manufacturers will always be content to use the American common staple.

Egyptian cotton has become a necessity, not only in Europe but in the United States as well, and it brings to Egypt, for staple and seed, nearly fifty-five million dollars per year, which sum is sufficient to pay the interest on her enormous foreign debt, carry on the government, and, when there are no military operations up the Nile, leave something in the treasury. The United States is buying a hundred thousand bales of Egyptian cotton annually, and its consumption by New England spindles increases by leaps and bounds.

In the provinces of Dongola and Berber huge tracts are now open to the growing of breadstuffs; and the Nile basin promises, as in the days of the Pharaohs, to be in the near future one of the granaries of the world. This will permit Lower Egypt to be devoted to cotton-culture, and the crop's area may be made to include the Fayum, and extended south of Cairo fifty miles or more.

It is a conservative estimate that by 1905 Egypt will produce a million and a third bales of cotton;

Expansion by Irrigation

and the same hypothesis regarding agricultural development in Dongola and neighboring provinces, by which they are to feed the entire country, likewise gives over to sugar-growing the Nile valley from Beni Suef to Assuan. Cane-culture has been developed there with amazing rapidity. As with cotton, Egyptian sugar is of superior quality. It now brings nearly ten million dollars per year to Egypt, and it may surprise American readers to be told that the United States has for some time been a liberal buyer of Nile-grown sugar.

At many points between Assiut and Assuan important crushing-works have recently been erected by native or foreign capital, supplied with the most perfect machinery obtainable in Europe. The peasant farmer in Upper Egypt has, by means of enhanced irrigation, become a capitalist in a small way through the sugar crop, and the cane area will be doubled, if not trebled, in a very few years, and statisticians must hereafter take the Egyptian crop into account when dealing with the world's production.

Thus, Lower Egypt is destined to be devoted to cotton, Middle and Upper Egypt to sugar, while the provinces south of the first cataract will produce more than enough cereals to feed Egypt's population. All this is feasible and quickly accomplished, and no doubt has a place in England's elaborate scheme for exploiting the valley of the Nile.

CHAPTER VI

THE STORY OF THE SUEZ CANAL

VOCABULARIES of praise and censure have been well-nigh exhausted on Ismail Pasha and Ferdinand de Lesseps, whose deaths were chronicled, during my residence in Cairo, simply as items of news rather than events; but the nineteenth century is indebted to them for one of its greatest achievements, a work of incalculable value to the whole world, Egypt alone excepted. Their lives had run in channels strangely similar. Each had been a mighty personage, the cynosure of the world's gaze; and, in the case of each, death delayed until the man's importance had been forgotten in a slough of degradation, the one in exile, the other in the oblivion of mental decay.

That Egypt reaps no benefit from the international waterway crossing its domain, there uniting the Orient with the Occident, is an amazing statement, manifestly. And it is a sad fact that the Suez Canal, which has played a mighty political part with European nations, has made and unmade khedives, and by a strange fatality has passed from the control of the nation that built it to that of the country that fought its construction strenuously, is responsible for the mortgaging of the Egyptian people, body and soul, inasmuch as it inspired and developed to an inordinate degree the borrowing habit of two of their rulers. Prior to the giving of the canal concession in 1856, by Viceroy Saïd, Egypt had no debt whatever. Her credit was first pledged in Europe by Saïd Pasha, who, to add luster to his name, subscribed seventeen million dollars to the stock of the canal enterprise, although the undertaking was to cost Egypt nothing, and for ninety-nine years the country was to receive from it fifteen per cent. of the gross revenue. Saïd's vainglorious act laid the corner-stone of Egypt's new house of bondage.

Ismail, succeeding to the throne, lent himself readily to the seductive project. Learning how easy it was to get money simply by affixing his signature to an innocent-looking paper, thoughtfully prepared in Europe, thenceforth there was frequent exchange between the khedive and the money-capitals of Europe of these innocent-looking papers for gold. There were many investors in the canal scheme, of course; but it seemed as if Egypt was ever feeding the insatiable monster with money, and human life as well; for four fifths of the laborers who dug the vast ditch were drafted from the Egyptian peasantry, and so poorly cared for that thousands died. A day of reckoning came, however, when financial engagements could not be met; for Egypt was hypothecated to its utmost value, and the usurers of Europe made such bitter outcry that Ismail Pasha was forced by the Sultan, the actual sovereign of the country, to surrender his throne and go into exile. Foreseeing the crash, Ismail had sold his personal shares in the canal to the British government for twenty million dollars, and on these the Egyptian treasury faithfully paid England five per cent. interest for twenty years. This purchase illustrated Lord Beaconsfield's shrewdness, for by prompt action he prevented these shares from going to France. To-day they are worth more than four times what was paid for them, and secure to England the voting control in canal affairs. The stipulation in the concession that Egypt should receive fifteen per cent. of the tolls had also been marketed, Ismail pledging this consideration as security on which to borrow a few millions when the French company could raise no more money. Thus, having no maritime interests, and possessing not a share in the enterprise, no pecuniary benefit can accrue to the Egyptian people from the Suez Canal. And, further, it can be conjectured that, had Ismail not burdened his subjects with overwhelming indebtedness, thereby breeding discontent, there would have been no European interference with Egyptian finances, involving his dethronement; no Arabi rebellion, and no British army of occupation.

The idea of a water communication between the Mediterranean and the Red Sea is as old as history, and nearly every ruler of Egypt, from Seti, father of Rameses the Great, to Napoleon Bonaparte, gave attention to the problem, with varying degrees of success. Strabo asserted that Seti,

Story of the Suez Canal

fourteen centuries before the Christian era, cut a canal fifty-seven miles long, from Bubastis, near the present town of Zagazig, on the Pelusiac branch of the Nile, to Heroopolis, at the head of the Bitter Lakes, then forming the northern extremity of the Gulf of Suez. Eight hundred years later, says Herodotus, the second Necho gave his attention to canal-building, persevering in the task until one hundred and twenty thousand lives had been sacrificed, but abandoning the undertaking because the oracle he consulted told him that dire results would follow the completion of his labors, and Egypt be surrendered to barbarians—or, in other words, the making of a canal would so entangle the Egyptians with foreign interests that their safety would be imperiled. A century later came the Persian Darius, son of Hystaspes, who took up the work abandoned by Necho; but being assured by certain wise men that the land would be deluged, he gave up the task when near its completion. Traces of Necho's canal, so archæologists claim, are still distinguishable near the southern end of the Bitter Lakes. The project of Necho, as well as that of Darius, involved the transhipment of cargo at Heroopolis, and each was unsatisfactory for other reasons. To remedy these defects, Ptolemy Philadelphus, in B. C. 285, joined the Nile canal with the Heroopolite Gulf by means of locks, opening when a vessel wished to pass. The southern terminus of this waterway was at Arsinoë, near the Suez of to-day. The failure of Cleopatra's ships to escape through this canal into the Red Sea, two

Present-Day Egypt

centuries later, indicates that it had fallen into disuse and was most likely unnavigable. The Roman emperors Trajan and Hadrian aspired each in his time to make it possible for ships to go from one sea to another, but the desert sands finally obliterated their efforts to pierce the Suez Isthmus.

In the interval of centuries thus spanned, the Nile had almost deserted its Pelusiac branch, and Roman engineers, coming later, tapped the great river above its bifurcation, near the capital of the present day, and ran a new canal from that point to the old Bubastic canal, which they cleared and restored to use. But this system was only temporarily successful, and Amrou, the Arabian conqueror, found inter-sea navigation impossible, and himself essayed, with partial success, to solve the great problem. Then, after the sands of the Arabian desert had for centuries asserted their dominion, came the great Napoleon, to whom all things were possible. Shortly after he had conquered the ancient land of the Pharaohs, in 1798, his engineers were given the task of bringing the Mediterranean into communication with the Gulf of Suez. They studied the project assiduously, and estimating from their surveys, as others before them had done, that the Mediterranean was thirty feet below the level of the Red Sea, recommended a complicated scheme calling for sluices and locks. Napoleon's evacuation of Egypt in 1801 caused the work to be dropped while yet in embryo.

Mehemet Ali probably detected the dangers foreshadowed by the oracle of old when urged to con-

BRITISH TROOP-SHIP PASSING THROUGH SUEZ CANAL.

Story of the Suez Canal

struct a ship-canal across his territory. This soldier who had founded a dynasty by successive deeds of bravery, and had butchered three or four hundred Mamelukes whom he had asked to a feast, could not have been suspected of lacking in daring; but he never fully yielded to the blandishments of foreigners striving to get him interested in isthmian canalization. His sagacious intellect kept him from embarking therein, save in a tentative way. The discovery in 1830, by Lieutenant Waghorn, that the level of the two seas was nearly identical, failed even to impress the hard-headed viceroy. He commissioned Linant Pasha, however, to prepare a plan for a canal across the narrowest part of the isthmus, from Tihreh to Suez; but as this Frenchman accepted the survey of Bonaparte's engineers, and discredited the statement of Waghorn as to the level of the waters, the viceroy still withheld his confidence from the scheme. In 1846 he asked a board of engineers, comprising representatives of England, France, and Austria, to solve once for all the question of the sea-levels. These experts confirmed the judgment of the Englishman, Waghorn; but the British member of the board, the renowned Robert Stephenson, with his instinct for railway-making, persuaded Mehemet Ali to construct instead a railway from Cairo to Suez, in connection with the line from Alexandria. This was done, and it formed the connecting-link between Europe and the East, and brought great profit, and no political dangers, to Egypt.

In the meantime another mind was occupied

with the project. When Waghorn was carrying on his controversy, young Ferdinand de Lesseps was an attaché at the French consulate-general in Cairo, and there conceived the idea of accomplishing what had baffled Pharaohs, Ptolemies, and a Bonaparte. Rapid promotion in the diplomatic service in no way lessened his ambition some day to wed the Mediterranean to the Red Sea. For more than twenty years this was his constant dream, until, in 1854, once more in Egypt, facile, accomplished, impulsive, and convincing, he developed his plan to the viceroy, Saïd Pasha. On January 5, 1856, De Lesseps was given a concession to build the canal. With the coveted document in his pocket, he realized that his aspirations to be famous, some day to be " Le grand Français," were to be fulfilled; and incidentally he saw an effective way of crushing the Waghorn "overland route" from Alexandria to Suez, detested by Frenchmen because the creation of a Britisher.

Saïd lacked the superstitious caution of his grandfather, Mehemet Ali, and cared nothing for the opinion of an antiquated oracle, if he had ever heard of it. Paris was his Mecca; and, loving Frenchmen as he did, he saw a most agreeable way of making his own name immortal, and his country so prosperous that it would attain to a dazzling position in the family of nations—all by means of the canal, through the facile and convincing De Lesseps. The canal was not to cost Saïd or his people a single franc; on the contrary, fifteen per cent. of the revenue coming from its operation was

Story of the Suez Canal

to flow into the national purse; and at the end of only ninety-nine years the magnificent enterprise would belong to Egypt!

The concession gave M. de Lesseps, and "La Compagnie Universelle du Canal Maritime de Suez," to be created by him, the monopoly of operating a waterway to be constructed in a direct line across the isthmus, utilizing the chain of Bitter Lakes on the south, and intersecting on the north the vast marsh called Lake Menzaleh. In no sense was the arrangement a contract involving any obligation on Egypt, and it was stipulated that at the end of the period for which the concession was given everything was to revert to the Egyptian government, on payment of the actual value of improvements on the banks of the canal, as determined by arbitration. The concessionaries were also to build at their own cost a smaller canal from the Nile to the line of the ship-canal, primarily to supply the work-people with fresh water, and ultimately for commercial purposes. To prevent bringing to his country thousands of laborers, representing the flotsam and jetsam of southern Europe, and mercenaries of all shades, the viceroy exacted the right of furnishing native laborers if he chose, at a nominal expense to the company; and it was agreed by the latter that the fellaheen diggers would be fed and have all necessary medical and hospital facilities.

It was stipulated and reiterated that all these conditions, as well as the concession itself, should be valid only when the Sultan of Turkey, the suze-

Present-Day Egypt

rain of Egypt, should give his sanction thereto. De Lesseps and his associates were to arrange the matter at Constantinople, providing whatever incentive in the way of bakshish they might find necessary.

De Lesseps's initial endeavors to secure funds for his company were disappointing in the extreme. French capital in those days was averse to investment away from home; and, besides, the Suez scheme was a startling novelty, and traditions were against it. France had but recently emerged from the Crimean campaign, and for a time, at least, money was wanted at home. German bankers, close-fisted and unimaginative, saw nothing financially attractive in the Paris enterprise. England was opposed to it intuitively. London journals raised a howl against the French project that was to provide a short cut to India for any Tom, Dick, or Harry. As a consequence, Lombard Street said "No," emphatically, and made the fact known to all the world; and thereafter all possible difficulties were thrown in the way of the scheme by Lord Palmerston's ministry.

The sum that De Lesseps could raise among his friends was but a drop in the bucket. What he wanted was two hundred million francs. A sanguine engineer had assured him that this amount would be sufficient for ditch, buildings, machinery, and everything. Nothing had yet been done to secure the Constantinople approval, probably because there was no money. There was an unpromising drag to the whole matter. Something had to

Story of the Suez Canal

be done, and the man who had spent twenty-four years in meditation over the canal scheme saw that he alone must do it. To create the Suez Canal was to be a feat of financiering, not of engineering.

There was the easy-going Saïd, down in Egypt. Why not have a try at him? Saïd loved Frenchmen, and believed the Suez Canal was to make his name immortal. So the intrepid diplomat hurried to Cairo and saw the viceroy. "Certainly," was his reply to De Lesseps's appeal, and he actually loaned the money required for making the surveys and for exploiting the company throughout Europe—2,394,914 francs in all. Had the Egyptian viceroy said "No" as vigorously as had the London bankers, how different would the modern history of Egypt read, and how different would be the material condition of the people of Egypt!

Encouraged by his success with Saïd Pasha, De Lesseps thought the time propitious for getting from him another concession, cognate but subordinate to the great scheme. This was to connect the canal bringing fresh water from the Nile with another small canal running from Ismailia to the termini of the great ship-canal. The concession permitted De Lesseps and his associates to sell irrigation privileges from this special waterway; and wherever the magical water of Father Nile can be turned upon the desert, the sands thereof blossom like the rose.

In 1860 the Paris company of the long name was again without a copper in its cash-box, and in debt to an extent making the prospect almost hopeless.

Present-Day Egypt

For two years the subscription books had been open without attracting serious investors. Again did the resourceful De Lesseps think of the amiable pasha down in Egypt, and again was he appealed to for succor. Saïd was this time induced to subscribe for 177,662 shares out of the 400,000 representing the Suez company's total capitalization; and he further pledged himself to contribute in other ways to the construction of the canal—and this was the affair that originally was to cost Egypt not a piaster! The viceroy's magnificent subscription dazzled impressionable France, and for a time a torrent of gold flowed into the Paris offices of the Suez company. When it came time for Saïd to pay for the bonds he had so dramatically bespoken, however, he was forced to confess that he was suffering from financial cramp himself, and could supply no more cash. "No matter," said the members of the canal ring; "we can get the viceroy's promises to pay discounted in Europe." This they did, the obligations taking the form of treasury warrants, bearing ten per cent. interest, and payable in four yearly instalments. These obligations, with their interest, the whole a charge upon the Egyptian treasury, totaled 24,-705,734 francs! Was it to be wondered at that Egypt became a happy hunting-ground for financial sportsmen?

In 1863 the magnificent Ismail inherited the viceroyship from his deceased uncle. This placed a prince of immense fortune in control of Egypt, and the impecunious canal ring blessed the good

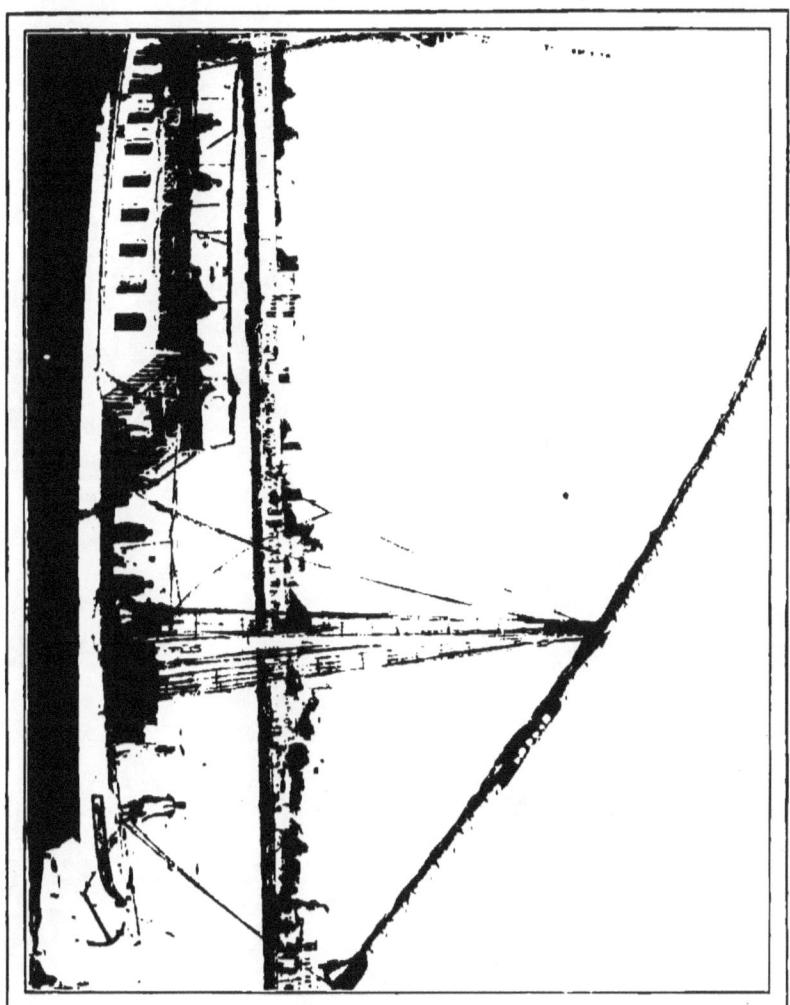

A DAHABIYEH ON THE NILE.

Story of the Suez Canal

luck that had given them another Oriental, who likewise loved Frenchmen, to fatten on. At their first interview with Ismail Pasha they made a point of their own generosity, assuring him that as one of the fresh-water canals appeared to them to be needless, they would surrender the special concession under which it was to have been constructed, on condition that the new viceroy would agree to complete the other minor canal at his own cost— but for the company's benefit. These suave tricksters certainly had formed a strange estimate of the character of the new ruler; and Ismail must have recognized the colossal impudence of the company's request, surely. Had he investigated, he, too, would have learned that the small canal in question could not possibly be constructed because of legal complications and rights of jurisdiction. But, not haunted by the ghosts of his astute relative, Mehemet Ali, and that other King of Egypt, Pharaoh Necho, he assented to the request of the Frenchmen, thereby putting practically another fifty million francs into the Suez company's coffers.

The digging of the vast ditch was now only a quarter completed. But the vigilant promoters of the enterprise recognized in Ismail a valued "friend," and to their minds an essential problem in connection with their work had been solved. Ismail now called himself khedive,[1] and was negotiating

[1] In 1866, in consideration of a large sum of money, Ismail obtained the sanction of the Sublime Porte to a new order of succession based on the law of primogeniture; and in 1867 he was raised to the rank of khedive. In 1873 Khedive Ismail obtained a new firman, confirming and extending his privileges in the matter of indepen-

at Stamboul for a firman that would change the order of inheritance in the ruling family, and had another card up his sleeve that he hoped would give him full sovereignty.

Time went on, and work on the canal proceeded with halting pace. Although the khedive ordered twenty-five thousand peasants every three months to the isthmus, canal-making by a process so primitive as the scooping of the sand with bare hands into palm-leaf baskets, to be carried up the steep bank and emptied, without mechanical assistance of any sort, was slow work. The taskmasters used the lash liberally, but forgot about the agreement to provide for the medical and sanitary welfare of the poor slaves. The food was wretched and insufficient; and the matter of the nominal compensation—well, that was something that did not concern the fellaheen, forced to labor in the corvée. Under the heat of summer the wretched Arabs perished by thousands, and Europe was properly indignant at the tales of suffering and inhumanity to be read in every newspaper.

Long viewing with distrust and disapproval the work that in time was to give the world an open sesame to their treasure-house in the East, English people were particularly loud in their outcry against the treatment of the poor Egyptians. John Bull's philanthropy and political interest were aroused to

dence of administration and judiciaries, right of concluding treaties of commerce with foreign governments, right of coining money, right of borrowing money, and permission to increase his army and navy. These were the provisions of autonomy, in consideration of which he was to pay an annual tribute to the Sultan of £681,538.

simultaneous action, the outcome being a spirited appeal to the Sublime Porte to have the barbarities stopped. The Sultan was entreated, it is also claimed, to give orders to have the work on the canal cease altogether. This he could do, for his Imperial Majesty had never confirmed the concession under which the canal was being built. For a reason not difficult to discern, M. de Lesseps had omitted to consult him, and the gentlemen forming his divan, on the momentous subject.

French diplomacy was called upon to nullify the effect of Great Britain's interference, the canal ring swarmed on the Bosporus—and the Sultan announced a happy compromise of the difficulty, by formally approving the concession of his vassal, on condition that the peasant should no longer be forced to do the digging; this was specifically forbidden. The Sultan even hinted at the propriety of employing machinery.

Here was a grievance of real magnitude, the De Lesseps cohort claimed; and they promptly announced their determination to hold the khedive responsible for the Sultan's action, although the imperial indorsement was an essential clause in the Saïd concession, and any legal tribunal would have said there was no breach of contract—for no contract existed, and the concession imposed no obligation or liability upon Egypt. French journals in the pay of the canal raised a furious outcry, and De Lesseps and his lieutenants beat their tom-toms with unceasing clamor, insisting that without fellah labor the canal could never be finished, and that ruin, ignominious ruin, consequently stared the enterprise in the face. It was an audacious plea; for at the time when their shrieks were loudest, infiltration from the sea and neighboring lakes had flooded the big trench to an extent that practically put at an end the need of an army of men, unless amphibious men could be found. The point had been reached where steam-dredges must be employed. Yet the canal company formulated a bill of damages of portentous amount, and politely requested the khedive to settle. Ismail protested, pointed to the stipulations of the concession, and pleaded for justice. Daily fomented by the French press, the dispute became the talk of Europe. Ismail set too high a value upon negotiations of a personal nature at Constantinople to dare appeal to the Sultan for a reconsideration of his canal decision, and had no desire to make ducks and drakes of his chances for securing absolute independence. So he preserved a serene exterior and awaited developments, being now heartily tired of the canal scheme and all connected with it.

Trusting to find a way of advantageously breaking the deadlock, De Lesseps again went to Cairo, and for weeks plied the khedive with arguments intended to convince him of his liability. The medium of arbitration, as a solvent of stubborn differences of opinion, was finally brought to his notice by the diplomatic De Lesseps; and Ismail was actually talked into consenting to let the Emperor of the French weigh the pros and cons of the situation, his decision to be final and binding. The influence compelling the khedive to accept Napoleon III as umpire in the dispute between himself and the French people—for the Suez Canal had now become almost a national affair—must have been something unusually potent, perhaps hypnotic. Ismail's abiding faith in Napoleon was sublime, and he was fashioning his own life in more ways than one upon that of the emperor; and, besides, Ismail was hoping to make Cairo a second Paris. The khedive should have remembered that M. de Lesseps was a favorite at the Tuileries, and that his kinship with the empress was recognized.

The emperor was willing to serve; and with amazing promptness he rendered a decision that must have shattered any remaining trust that Ismail had in humanity, for it gave the canal people even heavier damages than they had asked for, and opened the way for the presentation of a second claim by them. Looked at in any light, Napoleon's monstrous award becomes one of the strongest arguments against arbitration by a single person, possessing no legal education or judicial aptitude, that history reveals.

Napoleon decided that the provision relating to the supply of native labor was of the nature of a contract, and that Ismail was responsible for the consequences of its violation. For this the khedive was to pay the company thirty-eight million francs, which sum, coming at the very moment it was needed, enabled the company to purchase the labor-saving machinery now indispensable to completing the canal. Secondly, the emperor decided that the retrocession of the company's rights in the small fresh-water canal deprived them of large prospective profits through the renting of lands and providing irrigation therefor. The company's bookkeeper ingeniously figured expenditures of seven and a half million francs up to the time the concession was resigned, which, with interest, made a round ten million francs. Napoleon further gave his countrymen six million francs for the supposititious loss of water-tolls, and thirty million more for the assumed value of the lands that would have been rendered productive by the sweet-water canal, had it been made. This canal, it will be remembered, was not proceeded with because the concessionaries requested Ismail to take back the authorization for its construction; yet Emperor Napoleon compelled the khedive to pay forty-six million francs for allowing the concession to be canceled.

The entire award footed up eighty-four million francs, and so successful was the canal ring in this essay at financiering that some of its members grumbled because more items had not been included in the schedule of claims laid before the emperor for adjudication. They had actually forgotten to make a demand for the "value of the fish" in the canal that was never built. A supplementary bill was sent to Ismail, consequently; and when he demurred, arbitration was again suggested. He had taken his medicine without flinching in the first case, but had had enough arbitration

EGYPTIAN PROTOTYPE OF FERRIS WHEEL, HUNDREDS OF YEARS OLD.

Story of the Suez Canal

in that one dose to last the rest of his life. He preferred compromising a disputed claim, believing it would be cheaper and perhaps end the matter. "Take what you must, but give me a receipt in full," cried the unhappy khedive. The canal harpies got another forty million francs for the "fish" claim and other more or less specious allegations of loss, included in which payment were ten million francs for the repurchase of some lands sold to the company five years before by Saïd Pasha for a quarter of the sum.

The Egyptian treasury was empty, national progress was at a standstill, and Ismail's credit with the money-lenders was as shaky as his political position at Constantinople, before the canal leeches dropped their quarry. It is estimated by competent experts that the Suez Canal, directly and indirectly, cost Egypt close upon eighty-five million dollars, of which only twenty million dollars are represented in any manner in the capital stock of the now prosperous Compagnie Universelle du Canal Maritime de Suez: this was the personal holding of Ismail in the undertaking, which he practically surrendered to creditors a short time before his dethronement, the British government being the purchaser.

The banished khedive's legacy to his country was a debt of four hundred and fifty million dollars, probably not more than two thirds of which sum ever left the hands of the bankers' agents and negotiators in Europe. Docks and breakwaters at Alexandria and Suez, and a few hundred miles of railways and telegraphs, represented the more important benefits to his people; for steam-vessels of obsolete type, unwieldy yachts, a score or more of stucco palaces, gilded coaches, and operatic paraphernalia were not regarded as very important assets.

After more than ten years' labor, and the display of an energy and perseverance on the part of its chief promoter that formed not the least heroic feature of the undertaking, the new Bosporus between Africa and Asia was ready in 1869 for traffic.[1] The magnanimous Oriental, plundered as he had been on an unprecedented scale, determined to make the event of the opening so resplendent as to prevent the world from soon forgetting it. The inauguration of the great enterprise, in November, was made the occasion of such festivities as rivaled the traditions of Harun-al-Rashid and Akbar. The presence of the Empress of the French, the Emperor of Austria, the Prince and Princess of Wales, and a score of royalties from Continental courts, statesmen, ambassadors, and celebrities beyond count, and representative squadrons from the navy of every important government, rendered

[1] "On March 18, 1869, the water of the Mediterranean was allowed to flow into the nearly dry, salt-incrusted basins of the Bitter Lakes, portions of which lay thirty or forty feet below the level of the sea. The first encounter of the waters of the two seas was by no means of an amicable character; they met boisterously, and then recoiled from the attack; but soon, as if commanded by a *quos ego* of Neptune, they peacefully mingled, and the ocean once more gained possession of the land which it had covered at a very remote period, but only on condition of rendering service to the traffic of the world."—Stephan.

Story of the Suez Canal

the occasion a veritable "triumph" to the great Frenchman. Forty-eight ships conveyed the illustrious guests of the khedive—for Ismail was footing the bill—through the canal; and, as if illustrating the irony of fate and presaging the future, the first vessel that paid dues after the formal opening flew the British flag. The fêtes in Cairo, transforming the capital into fairy-land for a month, at Ismail's bidding, cost that forgiving prince or his government twenty-one million dollars.

There was a movement in France at about the time of De Lesseps's death to have his name formally given to the canal, but the negotiations to that end were never realized. Surprise had before been felt that this had not been done, and but for the lamentable Panama affair, impoverishing thousands of French homes and smirching the reputations of many statesmen, M. de Lesseps would probably have had the satisfaction, while still in the full enjoyment of his faculties, of seeing his name indissolubly linked with his work. It is not strange, however, that while Saïd Pasha gave his name to an important town and harbor,[1] Ismail

---

[1] The Port Saïd entrance of the canal is protected by two massive piers, the eastern running out into the sea toward the north for a mile, and the western running toward the northeast for nearly two miles. Where they start from the land these piers are fourteen hundred and forty yards apart, but their extremities approach within seven hundred and seventy yards of each other. The most serious risk to which the harbor is exposed is that of being choked with Nile mud, deposited on the Pelusiac coast by a current in the Mediterranean constantly flowing from the west. The western pier is intended to ward off these accumulations of sand and mud, and also to shelter the harbor from the northwest winds which prevail during

Present-Day Egypt

Pasha to Ismailia, and Tewfik Pasha to Port Tewfik, nothing in Egypt beyond a public square in Port Saïd bears the name of De Lesseps. The Suez company is erecting a bronze statue at Port Saïd of the author of the canal, modeled by M. Frémiet; but as the appropriation for this was paltry, its importance cannot be deemed commensurate with the achievement it is planned to commemorate. At the opening of the canal everybody expected that some distinction would be conferred on De Lesseps, the general opinion being that he would be created Duc de Suez; and astonishment was felt at his being merely given the grand cordon

two thirds of the year. Both piers were constructed of blocks of artificial stone, manufactured of seven parts of sand from the desert and one part of hydraulic lime imported from France. The concrete was mixed by machinery and poured into large wooden molds, in which it remained for several weeks. The molds were then removed, and the blocks exposed to the air to harden more thoroughly. Each block weighed twenty tons, and thirty of them were manufactured daily. In all twenty-five thousand were required. Above the wooden molds, which covered an extensive piece of ground, was constructed a railway, bearing a steam-crane, which could be moved to any required spot, for the purpose of hoisting the blocks and conveying them to their destination. After having been hoisted by the crane, the blocks were transported to a boat, where they were placed on an inclined plane in twos and threes, and secured by means of wedges. They were then conveyed to the place where they were to be sunk, the wedges were removed, and the huge masses slid down the incline, splitting the wood and emitting sparks of fire on their way, and plunged into the water with a tremendous splash, while the boat staggered from the effects of the shock and was lashed by the waves thus artificially caused. These huge *pierres perdues*, as they were technically called, were thus gradually heaped up until they reached the surface, and the last layers, rising a little above the level of the water, were finally deposited by means of a crane erected on a steamboat.

Story of the Suez Canal

of the Legion of Honor. The omission was never fully explained. Some thought that, as he had no personal fortune, this stood in the way of his receiving a French dukedom: provision for himself and his heirs would have been necessary. Others thought that the success of the canal was too doubtful for a high honor to be based on it. However, in view of the disgrace that De Lesseps fell into over the Panama scheme, it is fortunate for the French nation that the dukedom was never given to him. If it can be said of any man that he lived too long, that surely can be said of Ferdinand de Lesseps.

The canal destroyed Egypt's important railway traffic between Alexandria and Suez, besides bringing to the land that foreign domination foreshadowed by the oracle consulted by the ancient Necho. Of the never-ending throng of humanity that passes through it, few, probably, think of, or know, the pathetic chapters of its history. It has revolutionized shipping methods, driven the stately sailing-ship from the ocean, and some years ago had developed as much traffic as can be expected to come to it under normal conditions.

The canal's value to the commerce of the world is sufficiently proved by the saving of distance effected by it, as compared with the route around the Cape of Good Hope. By the latter the distance between England and Bombay is 10,860 miles, by the canal 4620 miles; from St. Petersburg to Bombay by the Cape is 11,610 miles, by the canal 6770 miles; and from New York to Bombay by

Present-Day Egypt

the Cape route the distance is 11,520 miles, while by the canal it is 7920 miles. How rapidly the traffic attracted by the economy of distance thus effected has developed, is illustrated by the following statement, taken quinquennially from the company's returns:

Year.	Steamers.	Tonnage.	Receipts in Francs.
1871	765	761,467	7,595,385
1876	1,457	2,096,771	27,631,455
1881	2,727	4,136,779	47,193,880
1886	3,100	5,767,655	54,771,075
1891	4,206	8,699,020	83,421,500
1896	3,407	8,594,307	79,652,175

Eight or ten years ago three quarters of the vessels passing the Suez Canal flew the British flag; but in recent years there has been a slight falling off in the number of English ships, the result chiefly of the determined effort Germany is making to secure new markets in the East. But the British flag represents still two thirds of the total traffic. Next to England, Germany is the principal user of the canal; the Dutch flag comes third, while the tricolor of France is fourth in the list. Not for many years, I am sorry to say, have the Stars and Stripes of our country been seen in the canal over a commercial vessel. A couple of warships and two or three yachts usually comprise the annual volume of American representation. This is a sad commentary on the decline of our mercantile fleet, and demonstrates in no equivocal manner how completely our flag has disappeared from the seas. The records of the United States consular agency at Port Saïd disclose the fact that about eighty American-

A SIMPLE FORM OF IRRIGATION.

Story of the Suez Canal

bound cargoes—sugar from Singapore and the Dutch colonies, and tea from China and India—pass the canal each year; but these, in nearly every instance, are borne in British bottoms.

Our military operations in the Philippines gave an impulse to the canal receipts hitherto never enjoyed from this source by the company, and the United States government, in the closing months of 1898 and the first half of 1899, paid more in tolls for warships, transports, and men, going or coming from Manila, than it had hitherto paid the canal in twenty years. It is truly an ill wind that brings nothing to the Suez company. Every year or two its tribute upon commerce is substantially augmented by the presence of armed strife somewhere in Asia or Africa, in which Europe is taking a hand. The years when Italy was hopelessly fighting the Abyssinians were among the most remunerative in the company's history.

The economy in using the canal is in the saving of time only. The present toll is $1.90 on vessel tonnage, and $2 for every passenger, not counting the ship's crew. The toll on tonnage is equivalent to the cost of about three thousand miles of ocean transportation, it is estimated. Since electric lights for night steaming came into use, it requires from seventeen to twenty hours to make the passage of the canal. The cost for a large steamer, like a liner of the P. & O., the Orient or British India companies, or a troop-ship filled with soldiers, is not infrequently ten thousand dollars. I first made the trip from Port Saïd to the Red Sea in the yacht

Present-Day Egypt

Sagamore, under the flag of the New York Yacht Club, and for this comparatively small craft the toll was four hundred dollars.

The Suez company's capital—bonds and shares of every character—is practically one hundred million dollars; and the length of the canal is just under a hundred miles. In average years the gross revenue is about 16 per cent. on the capitalization, and the net earnings about 7.6 per cent. These figures indicate a remarkable prosperity, and explain the popularity in which the securities are held by Frenchmen and other investors. I recall an interesting conversation with a clever American engineer, two or three years ago, who assured me that by employing the hydraulic excavating machinery of the present day he could make a canal from the Mediterranean to Suez, as wide and deep as the existing canal, for twenty million dollars; and he regretted that international agreements and vested rights rendered it impossible to "parallel" the Suez waterway. The machinery with which his name was associated had done wonders in making the Chicago drainage-canal, and his estimate of the cost of dealing with the sands of the Egyptian isthmus seemed reasonable.

It is too early for speculation as to the reversionary value of the Suez Canal. Many persons, knowing how Egypt is mulcted in most matters, claim that it will never be turned over to the Egyptian government, predicting that in time it will be thrown open to the world, and supported by a nominal tax on vessels using it, after the manner

Story of the Suez Canal

in which lighthouses are maintained. Of course this is conjecture, pure and simple. Many things can happen in the space of seventy years, and before 1968 conditions may prevail that no one now foresees. The Suez Canal will doubtless be as useful then as now, but the term "Egyptian government" may have a meaning foreign to that expressed by the words of the concession under which the canal was made. There is little prospect that this most important artery of marine travel will ever bring substantial benefit to the Egyptian people. Yielding an income in these times of sixteen million dollars a year, the Egyptians would be receiving two million four hundred thousand dollars annually from the stipulation of the concession giving them fifteen per cent. of the gross revenue, had not Ismail thrown away their rights in his mad craving for money.

When United States capital and skill join the Atlantic with the Pacific, let the canal be our own, under whatever guaranties of its neutrality in time of war!

CHAPTER VII

ISMAIL PASHA AS KHEDIVE AND EXILE

BUT for two great errors of judgment, Ismail might have ended his days in Cairo, as Egypt's khedive, instead of in Constantinople, an exile. The first and greater of these mistakes was the exaggerated estimate formed of the resources of Egypt. Coming to power at a time when the prices of agricultural produce, and especially of cotton, were unduly inflated by the Civil War in the United States, he sprang to the conclusion that he could indefinitely draw a vast tribute from the Nile land. He claimed proprietorship of twenty per cent. of the cultivable acreage of the country, and what was not his belonged to his subjects. These beings, he argued, were his indisputably, soul, body, and all that belonged to them. By this process of reasoning the doughty pasha felt that "Ismail" and "Egypt" were synonymous words.

His second error was that of exciting the jealousy and ill will of the Sultan, his political master. Had Ismail been properly advised, neither of these mistakes would have been made, and his history would not be so fraught with pathetic contrasts. But half-way measures were unknown to him. His

Ismail as Khedive and Exile

generosities were as magnificent as his vices, and he consulted neither law nor reason in discharging his khedival prerogative, for he was a law unto himself.

When General Sherman informed him that American military men could give Egypt a capable army, he brought thirty or forty of these specialists to the country and paid them lavishly, instead of fifteen or twenty as advised by the great general. When Ismail sent a wedding-gift of a handful of diamonds to General Sherman's daughter, later on, the value of the dazzling jewels was found to be so great that the limited Sherman fortune was menaced by the New York customs collector. Asked to present an obelisk to New York's Central Park, Ismail promptly authorized the removal from Egypt of the monolith of red syenite granite that Julius Cæsar had brought from Heliopolis to adorn the approach to the Cæsarean temple in Alexandria, forgetful of the fact that it was covered with hieroglyphs of the reigns of Thothmes III, Rameses the Great, and Seti II, that it antedated the Christian era fully twelve centuries, and was for other reasons an object of priceless value to students of Egyptology. But there was nothing petty about Ismail, and when he admired a nation as he did the American, he would have given away a pyramid with as little concern as he would a blooded horse from his stable.

Ismail was born in Cairo on the last day of the year 1830, and died on March 2, 1895. His father was the warrior son of Mehemet Ali, Ibrahim

Present-Day Egypt

Pasha, from whom he inherited that reckless courage so discernible in every important action of his life. Caution and prudence were altogether overshadowed by the daredevil quality descending from men knowing only the law of the sword. He came to the viceroyship on January 18, 1863, inheriting from Saïd, his uncle, the *damnosa hereditas* of the Suez Canal. Ismail found himself pledged to the undertaking of his predecessor, and the excuse for the vast debt which accumulated during his reign may partially be found in these obligations.

Prince Ismail was sent to Paris in 1843 to receive a French education, and was authorized to attend the classes at the Polytechnique. He spent every Thursday evening at the Tuileries, and generally dined with the royal family on Sundays. He had been nearly seven years in the French capital when, in 1849, his education was thought to be completed, and he was recalled to Egypt. His sojourn in Paris was coincident with the ferment into which the railway movement, by exciting greed to the utmost, had thrown all France. This was one of the underlying causes of the revolution of 1848, which Ismail witnessed, and the young Egyptian went home with his head filled with ideas derived from Louis Philippe and his courtiers.

Being learned in mathematics and all the sciences that could be acquired in a few years, Ismail thought he was better qualified to reign in Egypt than his uncles, Saïd and Abbas—both younger sons of Mehemet Ali. The youthful Comte de Paris,

OBELISK AT HELIOPOLIS.

Ismail as Khedive and Exile

figuring as prince royal and taking precedence of his uncles, was an object-lesson over which young Ismail pondered, for he was full of the idea of substituting the European order of succession for the Mohammedan. Yet he was not the eldest son of Ibrahim Pasha, for Achmet was the first-born.

Ismail had not been at home long before he conceived a fondness for Nubar, a crafty and accomplished Armenian, who had lived on the viceroyal family from the hour that he was appointed reader to Mehemet Ali. At this time Nubar was director of the railways, and it will ever be suspected that he had much to do with the tragedy that placed Prince Ismail in line to succeed Viceroy Saïd. A special train was ordered to convey the princes and their suites from Cairo to Alexandria, where the viceroy was to give a great garden-party. Strangely enough, Ismail excused himself at the last moment from going, on a plea of sudden illness, the story is told, while, by odd coincidence, Nubar, whose duty it was, as head of the railway administration, to accompany the princely party, pretended, just as the train was about to steam out of the station, a similar indisposition, which forced him to remain in Cairo. The train, in addition to carrying the heir apparent, also conveyed his uncle, Prince Halim. It proceeded safely on its way until reaching Kafr-Zayat, a point about half-way between the two cities, where the road passes over a drawbridge spanning one of the arms of the Nile. As the train bearing its precious freight rushed around the curve leading to the bridge, the engineer saw to his horror that the draw was open, leaving a yawning space over the muddy and eddying waters forty feet below. It was too late to avoid the catastrophe, and the whole train was hurled into the river. Halim Pasha, a splendid swimmer, managed to extricate himself from the wreck and get ashore; but Achmet was drowned in his compartment, thus leaving the succession to the throne of Egypt clear for his younger brother. Nubar found himself disgraced temporarily, and with circumstantial evidence pointing to him as a murderer, he found it prudent, the tale runs, to betake himself to Europe. As soon as Ismail ascended the throne, he summoned Nubar Pasha to his side, and named him prime minister, besides bestowing magnificent presents of land and money upon the friend who, so Cairo gossips say, had served him well.

Another instance of Ismail's disregard even for human life, when seeking to attain an important object, was furnished by the taking off of his quondam favorite known as the "Moufettish." This functionary, holding the purse-strings of Ismail's government, was living in a splendor at times eclipsing that of the khedive himself, and to do this was plundering the people and the official cash-box with a recklessness that promised to hasten the impending national bankruptcy. Whether this man was more the *âme damnée* or the pernicious counselor of his master is a point never fully settled. In all probability he acted in both capacities, for which his duplicity and cunning qualified him. Ismail, having made certain that the Moufettish

Ismail as Khedive and Exile

was robbing him, invited him to Ghizereh Palace to discuss affairs of state. The man went, as he had done scores of times before, but was never seen again. A small government steamer started that night for Upper Egypt, a brief notice was published to the effect that the Moufettish had been sent on an important mission to the southern provinces, and that was all. The opinion was that the minions of the khedive strangled him as soon as he passed the portals of the palace, and that his corpse was carried to the bottom of the Nile so carefully weighted that the evidence of the crime would be concealed for all time. The palaces of the dishonest minister of finance were confiscated, and his harem of four hundred women was broken up, most of the beauties being sent back to Europe. The tale of the Moufettish ceased years ago to interest Cairenes, and is now resurrected only when some one wishes to show the summary method Ismail Pasha chose to employ in dealing with an official who had betrayed his trust, as had Saddik Pasha.

When Ismail came into power, he found his people living in the middle ages of orientalism, but practically free from debt. Every pound of cotton that his country could send to England brought a dollar; and this condition spurred Ismail at once to set to work to develop every resource of the Delta and valley of the Nile,—to bring Egypt abreast of the Western countries that he had visited,—with a lordly disregard of cost. Railroads were built, and bridges and docks constructed; sugar-factories sprang up along the Nile like mushrooms, and be-

Present-Day Egypt

fore cane-cultivation had practically begun; new sections of Cairo were laid out and the land donated to those promising to erect houses; the harbor of Alexandria was deepened and enlarged; elaborate schemes for irrigation were organized; and, in fact, everything appropriate and inappropriate was done to transform Egypt into a part of Europe, as far as enlightenment and prosperity were concerned. Money was borrowed and spent blindly. Much of it stuck to greedy and dishonest hands, and Ismail's reign may be said to have been the golden age for the most clever and unscrupulous adventurers from every part of the world.[1]

At length came the inevitable day of reckoning. Egypt was no longer able to pay the interest on the enormous foreign debt of five hundred million dollars that had been piled up in the space of a few years. When the khedive made known the fact that the interest coupons on the debt could no longer be paid in their entirety, the governments of Germany, England, and France stepped in, on behalf of their subjects who had invested their savings in Egyptian state bonds. They protested that

[1] "Generous and open-handed, Ismail's mania was giving; his great fault, never to think of the liabilities incurred. In accepting the financial aid of the Continent, he did not discern the political consequences, nor the jealous intrigues which were to turn his monetary difficulties into a source of international meddling and encroachment. Blindfolded, he allowed himself to fall into the hands of the money-lenders; from high to low, all Continental usurers threw themselves upon Egypt as an easy prey. So long as he had securities to of the anterooms of his ministers were overcrowded with bankers ious to lend him millions at a percentage prohibited by the penal of their own country. . . . Cringing as long as they could hope

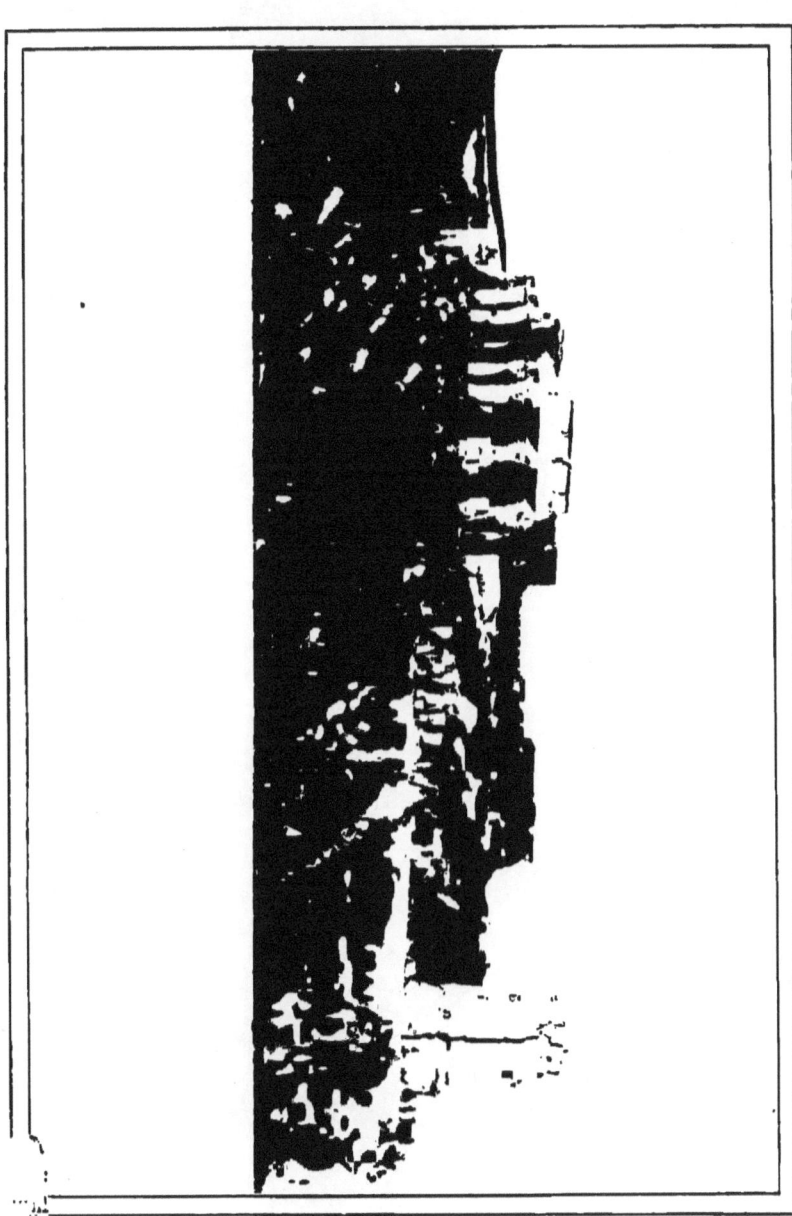

Ismail as Khedive and Exile

Egypt was solvent, whereupon Ismail invited them to appoint a commission to investigate the financial condition of his country. This commission proved his ruin; for, while it acknowledged that the country was unable to pay the rate of interest until then demanded, and reduced it from seven to four per cent., it likewise declared that the economic crisis was due wholly to the extravagance of Ismail.

To prove his good will and patriotism, the khedive surrendered private estates and plantations to the value of twenty-five million dollars; but this was not all that the foreign governments and bondholders demanded. They insisted on further sacrifices, not only of a financial but also of a political character, to which the khedive could not agree; whereupon they invited the aid of the Sultan, who had always resented the spirit of independence displayed by his powerful vassal, and obtained a firman deposing Ismail, and placing on the throne his eldest son, Prince Tewfik. This was in the closing days of June, in 1879; and within a week of his degradation Ismail left Egypt for Naples.

To the last, Ismail seemed unconscious of having

<small>something out of him, they continued to push him to take their gold, and to mortgage Egypt, to pawn his state and his private properties up to their utmost value, renewing greedily his bonds until they found it more advantageous to liquidate his estate. Had his been the case of an ordinary mortal, a court of law would have reduced the outrageous claims to fair and just proportions. But he was a sovereign, and his creditors were the kings of Jews, or rather the Jews of kings, and powerful enough to bring to bear the authority of their respective governments to enforce their claims by every means available."—Baron de Malortie, in "Native Rulers and Foreign Interference."</small>

committed wasteful extravagance, and only a few hours before his final departure from Cairo pleaded guilty to but one piece of lavish expenditure—that of the colossal sum devoted to the Suez Canal fêtes.

Ismail did not leave his country empty-handed. Though he had hoped to remain in power, yet he was prepared for an adverse decision at Constantinople before the receipt of the fateful telegram. He caused portable articles of value in his many palaces—and they were veritable treasure-houses—to be prepared for shipment, and it was estimated that these belongings were worth millions of dollars. The women of the harem were compelled to hand over their jewelry, and thus he obtained a quantity of property easily convertible into cash. Seventy of the harem women were selected to accompany the exile. Those to be left behind did not relish the situation, and they are said to have shown their displeasure by smashing mirrors and articles of a fragile nature, as only a thousand angry women could. Ismail's reign had been an orgy of despotic plunder, so to speak, and when he had no throne to sit upon, or palaces to occupy as master, he appropriated and carried off as much of the khedival property as the time and facilities at his command permitted. A long baggage-train was packed with pictures and cabinets, dinner-services and rare carpets, bronzes and silver candelabra, and plate of solid gold, much of it inlaid with jewels. At Alexandria everything was hurried on board the yacht *Mahroussa*, a steamer as big as an Atlantic liner. Ismail followed in a special train,

Ismail as Khedive and Exile

with two of his sons, a small suite of attendants, and the chosen ladies of the harem. As soon as the passengers were on board, the yacht started for Italy.

At Naples the ex-khedive occupied a royal palace and maintained a pretentious court. He made frequent excursions to Paris, where his fat, dumpy figure and intelligent face, surmounted by an unusually large tarboosh, were familiar to habitués of the boulevards; for Ismail was very fond of sitting for hours at a time at one of the little tables in front of the Café de la Paix, sipping coffee and watching the passing throng. Tortoni's was another of his haunts; and there, too, he would sip his coffee by the hour, musing, perhaps, on the proud empire that had passed away, and which, in its fall, had crushed his friend Napoleon III, driving him likewise to an exile from which he could never return.

The wanderer grew in time to dislike Naples; the neighborhood of Vesuvius affected the nerves of the ladies of his household, and all wanted to go elsewhere. His pleading with the Sultan for permission to visit Constantinople was finally favored, and he was later "induced" to establish himself in a pretty palace on the European side of the Bosporus, where he might the better be watched by the Sultan and, possibly, the British government. As he was a vain man, he suffered greatly from being deposed, and for years was hopeful that he might be permitted to return to the khedivate. But when he realized at Constantinople that he was a

Present-Day Egypt

prisoner in a gilded cage he surrendered himself to the situation and made the best of it.

A few years after his deposition, Ismail presented to the Egyptian government a claim for twenty-five million dollars, alleged to be the value of personal property he had been deprived of by his expulsion from the country, and more than half this amount was secured for him through the efforts of his counsel, Sir William Marriott.

Like most imaginative persons, Ismail possessed a keen sense of humor, which disappointments and troubles did not altogether smother. It is related that when in the midst of the depression following the French emperor's surprising award over the canal matter, a certain European was having an audience with him at Abdin Palace, to discuss something connected with the khedive's financial operations; although the temperature was ideal, with not a breath of wind stirring, Ismail was observed to rise from his divan in the midst of the conference and close a window behind the caller. "Monseigneur, why did you do that?" asked a friend who had witnessed the incident. "Because," answered the khedive, "if that sharper could allege that he had sat in a draft and caught cold in my palace, it would take at least a quarter of a million francs to meet the demand that he would make for satisfaction. I am beginning to understand these European business gentlemen," he added sadly.

In examining the correspondence files in the American diplomatic agency in Cairo, I came upon a record that served as a vivid illustration of

EXTERIOR OF TEMPLE AT DENDERAH.

Ismail as Khedive and Exile

Ismail's love for doing things that would attract notice and make talk. It was a document relating how one of my predecessors, twenty or twenty-five years before, having business at Ras-el-Teen Palace in Alexandria, was invited to defer his return to the capital, and dine that night with the khedive. The American representative stated that he was unprepared, having brought no evening dress. "That will be all right," exclaimed his Highness. "At seven o'clock you will find your clothes at your hotel." A telegram was despatched from the palace to Cairo, and a special messenger, traveling by special train, brought the desired raiment. It cost somebody—probably the Egyptian taxpayer—a considerable sum for running the train a hundred and thirty miles, and was wholly unnecessary, for the resources of Alexandria could have produced a dozen suits of evening garments in no time. But that was Ismail's way of doing things.

In Ismail's character there was little that could be commended, yet one could not wholly withhold admiration for his grandeur of thought and intrepidity of action. He was a ruler of magnificent but inchoate ideas, in which he often got bewildered; and he invariably embarked in enterprises without thinking of the cost. To deal adequately with a character so regal, egotistic, masterful, and subtle, to extenuate nothing, and at the same time set nothing down in malice, is a task not easily performed. He certainly left his impress on history, and had he not lived it is doubtful if Cairo would to-day be half as acceptable to its winter

Present-Day Egypt

sojourners. There might be no opera, no boulevards, no Ghizereh drive, and no real comfort. What he did for the city might be compared to what "Boss" Shepard did for Washington, "Boss" Tweed for New York, and Napoleon III and Haussmann for Paris. In his brief rule of sixteen years Ismail incurred for his people a debt of more than four hundred and fifty million dollars—a greater obligation than any other person that ever lived has succeeded in creating; but to accomplish this he mortgaged the souls of generations of Egyptians yet unborn.

Half the royalties of Europe helped Ismail to spend twenty-one million dollars in celebrating in Cairo the opening of the Suez Canal. The opera of "Aïda" was composed to his order, and produced as an incident to the entertainment of the Empress Eugénie and other guests. When it was discovered that there was no suitable building in the capital for the opera's production, the khedive ordered the present opera-house to be erected. Workmen toiling day and night accomplished this in a few weeks. "Aïda" had a cast composed of the greatest singers of the period, the Egyptian Museum was ransacked for jewels and "properties" to be employed in its production, and so delighted was the Egyptian ruler with the work of the composer that Verdi was handed a purse of thirty thousand dollars after the opera's first presentation. Mariette Bey, the savant in Egyptology, occupied himself with the reconstitution of the era of the Pharaohs, and it is to his skill and learning

Ismail as Khedive and Exile

that opera-goers owe their enjoyment of the marvelous picture of the temple of Ptah in the second act. Perhaps no opera was ever put on the stage in such elaborate fashion or with such scrupulous regard for archæological accuracy. Planned to stand but a few months, the theater has since been the home of opera in Cairo, and Verdi's masterpiece is given therein several times every winter. The composer's original manuscript of "Aïda" is among the treasured archives of the opera-house.

It was Ismail's dream to make an Oriental Paris of Cairo. The French metropolis, he argued, could be reproduced: it was simply a question of finance. A goodly portion of the money borrowed by the khedive was spent at Gizeh, nearly opposite the spot where tradition says Moses was found in the bulrushes. Half a dozen lath-and-plaster structures, with walls painted in a style suggesting solidity, went up there, with accompanying gardens like the Tuileries ranging from the Nile nearly to the Libyan desert. One of Ismail's ruling passions was for building palaces, and another found expression in the way he surrounded himself with everything deemed fitting to the court of a mighty personage—a king among kings.

To this day, hidden away in Cairo cellars, are miles of iron fencing made to his order in Europe, a conspicuous feature of whose ornamentation is the royal cipher "I. R.," surmounted by a monarch's crown. This was to inclose palace domains, and the design had been agreed upon in anticipation of the successful outcome of negotiations pending at

Present-Day Egypt

Constantinople for absolute independence. So certain was Ismail Pasha of positive rulership, perhaps deceived by the wily Nubar, who was concerned in the negotiations, that it is related that a banquet was given to a group of favorite functionaries in celebration of the news that he believed was forthcoming from the Sublime Porte—that the Sultan had at last consented to give him full sovereignty of the Nile country. The dinner was Lucullian in character, each dish a gastronomic triumph, and the program called for a *surpris* at the end of the feast. What it was to be, only the khedive and his chef knew. Clothed in immaculate white satin, the chef, wielding an enormous wooden knife, lifted the crust of a huge pie placed in the middle of the festal board, and out stepped a sprite in pink fleshings, dainty of face and form. With simulated bewilderment, she scanned for a moment the faces of those at table, and, her choice decided upon, she stepped over dishes and decorations to the head of the table, and placed a kingly crown upon the brow of Ismail.

But an edict of another sort issued from Constantinople, and a few weeks after the historical feast Ismail was sent away from Egypt, never again to see his beloved capital. When dying, he pleaded to be taken back to Egypt; but not until he was dead was the consent of the Sultan and the powers granted.

A specially chartered steamship brought the body of Ismail, accompanied by Princes Hussein and Fouad, his sons, from Constantinople to Alexan-

dria. The obsequies in Cairo (March 12, 1895) were marked by all possible pomp and circumstance. Funeral pageants and the stately etiquette of European court mourning are entirely foreign to the spirit of Islam; but the Egyptian capital has long been accustomed to compromises, which are lamented only by the strictest Mohammedans.

At an early hour in the forenoon the funeral procession, which must have numbered ten thousand people, began to muster near the new railway-station, in one of the private rooms of which the coffin had rested through the night, watched over by old retainers of the dead pasha. Egyptian and British troops lined the sides of the streets from the station, past Shepheard's and the opera-house, up the Boulevard Mehemet Ali, to the Rafai mosque under the citadel. Along the whole route, a distance of three miles, the pavement, windows, balconies, and housetops were thronged with spectators, blending the bright colors of the East with the more somber raiment of the West. But, save for a few flags draped with crape, and the shrill lamentations here and there of native women, it was difficult to realize that this chattering, laughing, indifferent crowd was gathered together to witness a pageant of death.

The procession itself, which defiled for almost an hour in one unbroken column, presented the same strange contrasts, the same curious jumble of Eastern and Western life. Its very composition reflected all the anomalies of modern Egypt. Behind detachments of mounted police and Egyptian cavalry came Major-General Sir Herbert Kitchener, the sirdar of the Egyptian army, with his staff—unmistakably English in spite of their Egyptian uniforms. Immediately behind them walked readers of the Koran, reciting the sacred verses in a high nasal chant; deputations from the native guilds and corporations, bearing flags and banners with embroidered religious devices; descendants of the prophet, in green turbans and flowing robes; mollas and ulema, in long caftans; dervishes, in tall felt hats; students from El-Azhar—in fact, the militant and uncompromising Islam in all its old-world picturesqueness. Then, in sharp contrast to the medieval scholasticism of the great Mussulman university, came hundreds of black-coated boys and youths from the modern schools and colleges, with their European teachers. Behind them again, in curious alternation, walked native and European notables: judges from the native and international courts; gold-laced pashas and beys; British officials, in the Stambouline coat, indicating their Egyptian employment; the six European commissioners of the public debt; long-robed clergy of the different denominations, and rabbis of the Jewish community; and red-coated officers of the British army of occupation, led by General Sir Frederick Forestier Walker.

Behind this medley of humanity walked the diplomatic corps, headed by the doyen of the body, Lord Cromer. Save the United States diplomatic agent and his secretary, all were in the spectacular uniforms prescribed by their governments, gold lace,

Ismail as Khedive and Exile

feathers, and orders of chivalry making them doubly conspicuous. It seemed to me that the black civilian garb of a diplomatic official of the great republic harmonized with the ceremonial better than the gorgeous costumes of the representatives of divine-right rulers. Had a United States congressman seen the procession from Shepheard's terrace, I am certain he would have returned to the halls of legislation a lifelong opponent of the movement to dress our foreign representatives in tinseled coats and cocked hats.

Next to the diplomatic and consular body came the khedival ministers, and the English advisers for finance, justice, and the interior; and then came Khedive Abbas, walking with Ghazi Moukhtar Pasha, the Ottoman high commissioner (the hero of Kars), at his side. Following his Highness were fully thirty princes of the khedival family. Behind these mourners and the household of the deceased ex-khedive, a double row of youths sprinkled perfumes and burned incense in front of the coffin. Covered with an embroidered pall, on which were displayed the uniform and decorations of the deceased, the mortal remains of Ismail were borne on the shoulders of twenty troopers from the khedival body-guard, hard pressed by a weird crowd of female mourners, rending the air with their shrieks of woe. Another body of troops, with arms reversed, closed the strange pageant.

The ladies and women attendants of the ex-khedive's harem, to the number of some eight hundred, had expressed their intention of following barefooted the remains of their former lord and master; but orders from Abdin Palace ultimately forbade so public a manifestation of their grief. For fully a week before the funeral there had been a nightly "wake" at Kasr el-Ali Palace by these women.

When abreast of the heroic statue of Ibrahim Pasha, Ismail's father, in the opera square, Khedive Abbas left the cortège, and was taken to Abdin by carriage. The diplomatic body and many of the Europeans left the procession at the same time, while the thousands wended their way slowly to the mosque of Sultan Hassan, where the usual prayers were recited, and then to the mosque of Rafai, opposite. There, beside the tombs of his mother and two of his daughters, Ismail was finally laid to rest in the mausoleum which he had designed for himself, but which will probably never be completed. The foundations of the huge pile are already showing signs of subsidence—a monument perhaps not altogether inappropriate to the man whose life, after a brief period of artificial splendor, ebbed drearily away amid the ruins of his shattered ambitions. Ismail had planned to have the new Rafai mosque eclipse in beauty and vastness the Sultan Hassan mosque, long regarded as the most perfect example of architecture in the Mussulman world; but his financial disaster interrupted the work when only the outer walls and roof had been completed.

CHAPTER VIII

TEWFIK PASHA AND THE ARABI REBELLION

FEW events in modern history are more pathetically dramatic than the substitution of Tewfik for Ismail. The Turkish grand vizir despatched two telegrams to Cairo on June 26, 1879. One was to "Ismail Pasha, ex-Khedive of Egypt"; the other to Mohammed Tewfik, his son. In the former it was stated that his Imperial Majesty the Sultan, as the result of a decision of his council of ministers, had formally decided to request Ismail's retirement from the khedivate, in favor of the next in succession, his Highness Tewfik Pasha, and that the *irade* to this effect had been issued. While Ismail was reading this decree at Abdin Palace, the son was reading the other message at his country-seat a few miles out of Cairo, to the effect that "his Imperial Majesty the Sultan has named you by imperial irade Khedive of Egypt, and the firman will be delivered to you with the customary ceremonial. Convoke the ulema and functionaries, the chief men of the country, and the government employees, and communicate to them the stipulations of the decree relative to your succession, and at once relieve his Highness Ismail

Present-Day Egypt

Pasha from the direction of the affairs of the government."

It was a matter of great importance to be arranged by telegraph, this change of rulership in almost independent Egypt; but thus it was done. The Sultan's aversion to the mysterious electric current is known to exclude the telephone, the electric light, and even the trolley-car from Constantinople; but in matters of state, when urgent, his Majesty is a liberal enough user of telegraph and cable.

In Eastern countries it is a coveted privilege to convey good news to any one. I have the story of the telegrams from a distinguished journalist who was behind the scenes in the abdication affair. He describes, with some license, perhaps, the consternation at Abdin when the message was delivered with the words "ex-khedive" so boldly penned on the envelop that there could be no mistaking the purport of the inclosure. The grand master of ceremonies would as soon have fondled a viper; and one and all of his assistants thought of pressing matters demanding their presence in other parts of the palace. The keeper of the seals said emphatically that the delivering of telegrams was no part of his duty; and the officer of the khedival guard could not be cajoled into doing this errand. Everybody agreed that a message to his Highness at this particular time must be a matter of state, and no one of less rank than a minister could appropriately have anything to do with it.

At this moment bluff old Cherif Pasha, peren-

Tewfik and the Arabi Rebellion

nially minister of this or that, strode into the palace. With some reluctance he consented to take the fateful telegram up-stairs to the khedive. Ismail's face changed a little as he read it. "Send at once for his Highness Tewfik Pasha," was all he said. Then he folded the message and laid it on the table by his side. A moment later he handed the bit of paper to Cherif to read, saying as he did so: "I can't go to the investiture; I do not think that can be expected of me. But I shall be the first to salute the new khedive of Egypt, and wish for him a more successful reign than his father has had." Then, drawing the table nearer, he said to Cherif Pasha: "Now we will have a game of backgammon."

Tewfik's message was hurried full tilt from the telegraph office, the messenger making a record for speed, wondering as he ran if he would be made a pasha or a bey.

True to the habit of punctilious politeness acquired in France, Ismail determined to maintain his savoir-faire in the hour of adversity. He quickly cabled to Constantinople that he submitted to the will of his sovereign Sultan; and, Tewfik Pasha arriving at the palace shortly after, Ismail is said to have greeted him with the words, "I salute my effendina," bowing low to his successor and covering his hands with the kisses of submission.

Tewfik's account of what passed immediately following the greeting in their altered stations is told by Alfred J. Butler, an English tutor in the Tewfik household, in his volume of reminiscences of court life in Egypt. "When I came to the throne," Tewfik is reported to have said, "I received the news without joy. Sympathy with my father's fall, and the great sense of responsibility, left me no room for rejoicing. After my father's courtly salutation, acknowledging me as his effendina, he heaped reproaches upon me and accused me of having at last intrigued successfully. I then produced two letters from one of his former ministers, received when I was acting as regent, in his absence from the country. These offered me the support of the army; and if I consented to the minister's plot, it was proposed to destroy the khedival yacht when it returned to Alexandria, sending Ismail to the bottom of the harbor. My father read these letters, and was much moved. He then kissed me affectionately, saying, 'Forgive me, my son, forgive me!'"

Prince Tewfik was perhaps ten years of age when Ismail became viceroy. He was born in 1852, and his mother was an attendant slave in Ismail's harem. Her princely master acknowledged the child and added its mother to his list of lawful wives, completing the quota of four allowed by his religion. Other sons were born to Ismail shortly after, but no amount of intriguing on the part of their mothers could alter the fact that the child brought into the world by the harem slave was their liege lord's first-born and heir. Ismail from the first could not conceal his dislike of Tewfik; but he disliked even more his uncle, Halim. In applying liberal largess at Stamboul to procure a firman pro-

Mehemet Ali Pasha. Ibrahim Pasha.
Abbas Pasha. Saïd Pasha.
Ismail Pasha. Tewfik Pasha.

PREDECESSORS OF KHEDIVE ABBAS II.

Tewfik and the Arabi Rebellion

viding for the khedival succession from father to eldest son, he believed, doubtless, that he was paying his money for the lesser of two evils; and, besides, fate might remove Prince Tewfik, the intruder, permitting the son of his favorite wife to become heir apparent.

While the other sons were sent to schools and colleges in England and France, Tewfik was kept at home, and little effort was made to give him more than the educational advantages that would fall to the son of any well-to-do Egyptian gentleman. He once ventured abroad, traveling as far as Vienna; but the breaking out of the Franco-German War caused him to return to Cairo, and shortly thereafter he found himself installed at Koubbeh, with a spouse so devoted and good that he was happy to lead the life of a country squire, and leave court intrigue and politics to those caring for them. His princess was the daughter of a man of position, descended from Mehemet Ali, and she possessed a mind and character of an order unusual in the East.

Tewfik never availed himself of the Moslem right to give rivals to the Princess Eminè in the way of other wives. He was an affectionate husband and a model landlord. He took a great interest in the cause of education, and established schools at his own expense, to which not only his own two sons were sent, but the sons of the gentry and officials as well. The educating of children was his greatest hobby.

Ismail had always played as recklessly with the

Present-Day Egypt

tenets of the Koran as with other things, and delighted to jeer at the strictness with which Tewfik discharged his religious duties, telling him he should adopt European modes of thinking and living. "When you come to the throne, pretend to be a good Mussulman, like me; it is good policy, and the people will like you for it," was the father's flippant advice. When Tewfik, on the day he took upon himself the responsibilities of the khedivate, went in state to the mosque and prayed with the faithful, Ismail is reported to have remarked: "You are acting the Moslem very well." The son replied: "Yes, sire; but I am truly sincere."

Tewfik came to the khedivate when it had been shorn of three fourths of its power; and anxious as he was to use his prerogative for the best interests of his people, the new khedive found himself nearly as helpless as Gulliver bound hand, foot, and body by the Lilliputians. The influence forceful enough to remove Ismail had likewise been sufficiently potent to establish the dual control, by which England and France had taken possession of the finances. In no country in the world is everything more vitally dependent on the Finance Office than in Egypt. The ministry of finance is the mainspring of the executive machinery, the fountainhead of everything, without which nothing can be done. The ministry of public works devises schemes of irrigation certain to make the soil profitable to agriculture; but the Finance Office provides the money with which they may be carried into effect. Tewfik might complain, but he could not drive

Tewfik and the Arabi Rebellion

M. de Blignières and Major Baring from the ministry of finance; nor could he procure from these controllers a single piaster for any purpose unless they agreed with him as to the expediency of the appropriation. Foreign intervention had not only removed the cash-box from the custody of the khedive, but commissions of liquidation and restrictive measures had completely changed the character of the khedival office in its transition from father to son.

Hampered thus in the exercise of power, Tewfik made enemies without gaining friends. The ruler who distributes places and pensions has many eulogists. Tewfik Pasha was ready to coöperate in doing away with extravagances and abuses; but the alien controllers—in effect the "receivers" of an establishment from which they wanted to extract every penny possible for their principals, without destroying its future earning power—effected such sweeping economies that thousands of natives went hungry as a consequence of a stoppage of their supplies. A people unfamiliar with diplomatic methods of collecting overdue accounts knew little of the significance of the dual control, and cared less. Believing their khedive governed Egypt, they addressed to him their petitions for relief; but he could give no relief, and discontent followed as a natural consequence. A glimmer of understanding in time coming to the people, the cry, "Down with the foreigners!" rang from the Mediterranean to the Sudan, and was echoed back with the added cry of "Egypt for the Egyptians!"

Present-Day Egypt

Evidences of insubordination in the native army were brought to public notice daily, furnishing a theme of conversation in bazaar and palace. The soldiers had many grievances, the arrears of pay being the most important. Before Ismail had been driven away, the minister of finance had even been mobbed in the street by four hundred desperate officers, demanding the means to supply their families with food. On another occasion an army officer carried a dead child in his arms to the ministry of finance, praying for enough of the money due him to provide decent burial for his little one. When the strain to find funds to pay European bondholders was greatest, the crops failed in Upper Egypt, and there was much suffering among the populace.

Meanwhile the cry, "Egypt for the Egyptians!" was coming to have more than a sentimental meaning. It was maturing into a menace, and one of such force that every intelligent person in Egypt must have recognized its possibilities. I confess that the position of the common people, if truthfully described by impartial witnesses, reflected a cruel disregard of the principles of justice and humanity. I am certain my sympathies would have gone to the poor Egyptians, ground to starvation that distant bondholders might continue to receive an exorbitant and usurious interest.

No universal rule for redressing grievances can be laid down, but there was a right as well as a wrong way of attempting a rational solution of even so complicated a situation as that prevailing

TULIP COLUMNS AT KARNAK.

Tewfik and the Arabi Rebellion

in Egypt in the early eighties. Arabi Pasha was the exponent of the wrong process. The logic of argument, reaching the proper ear, should be more potent in these days than ill-considered revolt. Rebellion is usually destructive in its results, and does not always appeal to the seat of true wisdom.

Ahmed Arabi was constructed on lines too narrow to make it possible for him ever to become a liberator. He lacked every mental attribute requisite to successful leadership, perhaps explained by the fact that he was but a peasant, whose forefathers had never known an hour when they were free from the heel of the oppressor. Arabi talked superficial platitudes that pleased his kind, and their flattery convinced him that he was born for a great part in the world. He had risen from a common soldier to be a colonel, and had a fondness for intrigue. His flowery talk and employment of claptrap dramaticism had lifted him within a year from obscurity to notoriety, and wherever he went he excited the admiration of the common people.

His propaganda of "Egypt for the Egyptians" was hourly exploited. People followed him in the streets singing his praises, and he was undeniably the man of the hour. It is related that, as he once walked along an important thoroughfare, in a manner indicating profound reflection, knowing he was followed by a hundred worshipers, he struck a dramatic attitude, and said, as if speaking to himself, "Here,"—placing his foot over a certain spot,—"buried here is the heaven-sent weapon that will free Egypt from the grasp of the infidels." A dozen eager hands clawed in the earth, and brought to light a Remington rifle, so bright and free from rust as to justify the suspicion that the crafty Arabi had deposited it there but a few hours before.

Tewfik Pasha was a strange combination of courage and weakness. The latter was proved when the spirit of rebellion among his troops first took concrete shape. Arabi had led four thousand soldiers to Abdin Square to demand from the khedive the dismissal of the Riaz ministry, against which great dissatisfaction had been fomented by Arabi and his brother conspirator, Mahmoud Sami. Three sides of the great square in front of Abdin Palace were filled with soldiery and the accompanying rabble, when the khedive, attended by Sir Auckland Colvin, an English official, went forth to meet the insolent Arabi.

The leader rode across the square, sword in hand, to the point where the khedive stood, with his group of palace officials. Arabi was nervous, and the experienced eye could tell at a glance that he could be cowed as easily as a truant schoolboy. " What shall I do ? " Tewfik asked of Colvin. "Tell him to dismount," was the reply. " Iniz il ! " commanded Tewfik. Without a word, and almost with undignified haste, the comic-opera hero was on the ground, but his sword was still drawn. The khedive pointed to it, and Arabi sheathed it promptly. But his hands trembled as he ran the blade into the scabbard, betraying the cowardly heart beating within his jacket.

It was the moment for action. " Demand his

Tewfik and the Arabi Rebellion

sword," whispered Colvin to his Highness. Could Tewfik's lips have uttered these words in a manner carrying authority, the craven would have laid his weapon at the feet of his effendina and kissed the skirt of his garment—and the Arabi rebellion would have been stifled while yet in innocent embryo, and a dark chapter in Egyptian history would have been avoided. But the khedive's tongue was as if paralyzed. A word to the troops, later, would have caused a reaffirmation of their loyalty; and, had their sovereign mounted Arabi's horse and led the regiments through the city, Arabi and the cause he was espousing would have been ridiculed out of existence.

But Arabi saw that he had conquered in this conflict with spineless Tewfik, and from that instant he was master of the situation and the apostle of a movement now grown to national proportions. Arabi had his way, and the khedive dismissed the ministry of Riaz Pasha. Not many months later Arabi was minister of war, and his better-informed ally, Mahmoud Sami, rose to be prime minister.

To Mehemet Ali the incident would have been but a playful moment, and he would have pistoled the leader instantly. Ismail Pasha, even, would have dealt with it no less conclusively, but in a different way. But the father and great-grandfather of Khedive Tewfik were men of impulse and quick action.

After his easy triumph at Abdin, the dreamy Arabi became a bustling bully, full of his own importance, and displaying more than usual ignorance. But to a man the army was with him, and fifty thousand peasant farmers along the Nile were ready to fight under his banner whenever he called for them. Tewfik did many things to placate Arabi, which did much to turn his head. At last the rebel leader forced the khedive to hide himself for safety in one of his palaces near Alexandria, while he became the dictator of the country, basing his authority upon his military prestige. He sent lying proclamations into the interior, and pretended to have divine revelations pointing to a crushing victory over the Christian oppressors of the land. It was his boast that his guns could sink any fleet, whatever its strength; and he assured his followers that a hundred thousand foreign soldiers, if they landed in Alexandria, would be hacked to pieces.

The baselessness of Arabi's opinions was quickly proved, for the forts of Alexandria were able to make only feeble resistance to the modern ordnance of Admiral Seymour's fleet, and were reduced to ruins in short order, with the principal quarter of the city as well. Arabi and his army retreated to the interior in the wildest disorder, and only once made anything like a determined stand against the pursuing British regiments. That was at Tel-el-Kebir, and was of brief duration. The poltroon Arabi a few hours later was glad of the personal safety attending his surrender to the English as a prisoner of war.[1]

[1] "On September 13, 1882, the British army under Sir Garnet Wolseley stormed the earthworks of Tel-el-Kebir, and with one brilliant dash scattered to the winds the forces and the hopes of 'Ahmed

AVENUE OF SPHINXES AND PYLON, KARNAK.

Tewfik and the Arabi Rebellion

But I find myself drifting into a needless description of the rebellion, and the bombardment of the forts of Alexandria on July 11 and 12, 1882, with the wanton massacre of thousands of innocent people by the natives, maddened to frenzy by Arabi and his followers. It is a page of history too well known to be repeated, and has no place in these slight sketches.

Mr. Moberly Bell, a fair-minded English writer on the subject of contemporary Egypt, in recording his opinions of the campaign as he saw it, says this of Arabi: "It may be admitted that the whole country sided with Arabi up to the day of Tel-el-Kebir, but the significance of this fact is apparent when we remember that the whole country was against him the day afterward. Again, the general promise held out to millions of fellaheen that all debts due to Europeans should be canceled would have enabled the devil himself to have made converts. In Egypt, the man who succeeds is always popular; the man who has power leads the nation. Arabi got power, not by his ability, but

Arabi, the Egyptian.' Nine tenths at least of the so-called 'rebel' army were only too delighted at the opportunity of throwing away their arms and their uniforms, of donning once more with all haste their *galabiahs* of blue cotton, and returning to the unconstrained life and patient labor in their beloved fields, which were so much more congenial to them than the duties and the dangers of military service. The next day two squadrons of British cavalry reached Cairo. They had ridden straight across the desert, some forty miles, and both men and horses were nearly dead from fatigue; yet the citadel and city, though occupied by a strong body of Arabi's troops, surrendered without a show of resistance. The 'rebellion' was at an end."—Sir Alfred Milner, in "England in Egypt."

Present-Day Egypt

by the efforts of those supporting him, and by the blunders of his opponents. After Tel-el-Kebir he never uttered one word of regret, never made a single inquiry as to the fate of those poor wretches who were the victims rather of his dunderhead stupidity than of his intentional wickedness."

Many times, before and after the revolt, Tewfik Pasha was deplorably wanting in firmness, and, on the other hand, was more than once as heroic as any man could be when in imminent danger. If compelled to decide quickly, the decision was too often on the side of error; but with time for deliberation, his conclusion was nearly always to do the right thing, unmindful of the peril or the consequences. A man of the greatest genius, however, might have found it difficult to thread his course through such a labyrinth of doubts and misfortunes as that in which the khedive was placed.

If any benefits immediately resulted from England's voluntary aid to Egypt, the breaking of the dual control was the first in importance. French susceptibilities were so irritated by the non-departure of the British troops, sent to the country to restore the authority of the khedive, that the government of France declined to remain a party to the management of Egyptian finances. I do not express an opinion as to the wisdom of this action as a matter of policy, but the withdrawal of France certainly helped the position of the poor Egyptians, for they had then one master less. A single control is preferable to any other form of oligarchy, when the welfare of a suffering people is considered.

Tewfik and the Arabi Rebellion

By the old system, with each side issuing a proclamation almost daily to the other, the patient was in danger of succumbing while the rival physicians were deciding which should take the responsibility of going to his relief.

During the bombardment Tewfik was in his palace three miles out of Alexandria, with his wife. When urged before the shelling of the city to seek shelter on his yacht or on a war-ship, his answer was: "No. I will remain with my people in their hour of danger. I am still their khedive." Within range of shots from the ships in the harbor, and with a bloodthirsty, looting mob near by, Tewfik remained in his Ramleh palace throughout the two days of carnage. Shortly after the crushing of Arabi, cholera broke out in Cairo in its most fatal form. Then this man who had failed to nip a rebellion in the bud by a commanding word to Arabi went deliberately with his khedivah to the capital, against the advice of his suite, and to the dismay of the physicians. He went from hospital to hospital, inspiring courage throughout the stricken city by his example, and helping the bereaved with money from a purse not overflowing.

Called to a heritage of bankruptcy, discontent, and rebellion, Tewfik Pasha was a virtuous and amiable prince, whose failings inspired sympathy. He regretted the ravages of cholera in Cairo and the Delta more than the losing to the Mahdi of millions of miles of valuable territory in the Sudan, chiefly because he had witnessed the horrors of the home calamity, possibly.

Present-Day Egypt

Tewfik preferred the early morning for work, and documents dealing with public affairs were then read and arranged before his secretaries were astir. He always varied his labors with outdoor exercise, and many were the anecdotes related by him of the experiences with soldiers and policemen who did not recognize as the khedive the sleek, rotund little man taking a morning constitutional. He frequently slipped over to the Ghizereh gardens at sunrise to view the horticultural beauties when only the fellah was astir. Returning to the palace from one of these rambles, he was stopped by a good-natured British soldier doing sentry duty at the main entrance, with these words: "Hi, there! Yer can't go in 'ere, yer know."

"But I belong to the palace," said the khedive, enjoying the situation.

"Oh, do yer? Well, what sort of a place 'ave yer got, anyway?" added Tommy Atkins, convinced of his right to have a bit of chaff with any "furriner."

"Very good."

"Ah, fine times, I s'pose; nothin' to do and plenty to eat, from the look o' yer. Would n't mind servin' this chap meself, if 'e 'd find me five bob a day."

A sergeant on his rounds cut short the soldier's lingo, and his Highness went into the palace to his books and papers, enjoying the joke more than the discomfited redcoat did.

When Arabi, Mahmoud Sami, and other ringleaders of the rebellion had been sentenced to death

EGYPTIAN BRIDE GOING IN STATE TO NEW HOME.

Tewfik and the Arabi Rebellion

for treason, Tewfik was the first to speak for a commutation of sentence to life-banishment. Arabi and his surviving fellow-traitors in Ceylon could not have been forgetful of what they owed to the tender heart of the khedive they had conspired to destroy, when they heard that his Highness had died suddenly, while still a comparatively young man, at Helouan, on January 7, 1892.

A brief account of Arabi in his exile may not be out of place in concluding my chapter. It is more than sixteen years since he and the seven other rebels said farewell to their native land, bound for Ceylon, under military escort. Since then Abd-el-Aal Pasha, the most stalwart of them all, and Mahmoud Fehmy, the astute engineer who nearly succeeded in blocking the Suez Canal, have gone over to the great majority. But Arabi himself, as well as Mahmoud Sami, Toulba Osmat, Ali Fehmy, and Yacoub Sami, are still not only in the land of the living, but in very good health and spirits.

There has been a good deal of marrying and giving in marriage since the steamer *Mareotis* took her contingent of prisoners to Colombo. The sons born prior to their fathers' political troubles are, for the most part, serving the present khedive in more or less responsible positions; but many children of both sexes have been born to the pashas since they set foot on British soil, and they consequently are both *de jure* and *de facto* British subjects. For some time there was much grumbling among the exiles, who suffered from the

Present-Day Egypt

marked difference between the dry heat of the Nile valley and the depressing damp heat of Ceylon. They hoped against hope for permission to return to Egypt, and for years Arabi's friends did their utmost to second his efforts to secure a pardon.

From the first the exiles were treated as persons of importance, and they have been the guests of the various governors who have held sway in Ceylon since 1883. Arabi's home has been visited by many thousands of Mohammedans on their road to Mecca, as well as by an immense number of European and American travelers. He is now located in a picturesque bungalow in the ancient capital of the island, Kandy, in the interior, where the temperature is more like that of his native country than that of the coast. Arabi has ceased to find his life in Ceylon either irksome or otherwise unpleasant. His "visiting-book" is in its way a notable curiosity, and he can now talk of the events of 1882 without the smallest bitterness. He has learned to speak English with tolerable fluency and takes a deep interest in the political events of the day. Sometimes his mind wanders back to the much-loved land from which he sprang, and the freedom for which he fought. He is still in the prime of life, for the rebel leader was only just forty when "he surrendered his sword and his honor into the hands of the English" on the morrow of Tel-el-Kebir.

If not such a "dunderhead" in these years as when hatching rebellion in Egypt, Arabi's reflections would be interesting, could we know them. No

Tewfik and the Arabi Rebellion

longer a political issue himself, the administration of Egypt, owing its creation to him, becomes an international issue, as well as an anomaly having no parallel in history. This control of affairs, upheld by four or five thousand British bayonets, on soil not belonging to the British empire, is an institution over which European statesmen have long wrangled. "Advisers" to the khedive, under-secretaries of state, irrigation experts, military and civil servants of high degree and corresponding pay, and small-fry officials by the hundred, owe their employment in the land of the Nile to the muddle-headed Arabi, now dreaming away his days in the hills of Ceylon. The common people of his beloved Egypt, for whom he was so solicitous in 1881 and 1882, are now enjoying a measure of prosperity greater than they had ever known, oddly enough, as a sequence of his efforts to free them from the grasp of the infidel.

Some philosophers, maybe, see in Arabi one who has done his share toward making Britain's foreign policy so successful as to excite the jealousy of half the nations of the Old World. Unlike Clive, Hastings, and Cecil Rhodes, Arabi accomplished what he did for England as the result of bigoted ignorance and blundering, not of clear-sighted intention.

CHAPTER IX

THE PRESENT KHEDIVE AND KHEDIVAL FAMILY

HIS Highness Abbas Hilmi II was born in Cairo on July 14, 1874, and succeeded to the khedivate at the age of eighteen. Estimates of his character are never indefinite, for he is liked or disliked intensely—it depends upon the point of view from which the judgment is formed. The public relying upon English newspapers for knowledge of persons and events has no doubt regarding the intractable nature of the khedive. The human mind in time accepts as facts, concrete and unyielding, what is heard and read for years. The unattractive side of Abbas Pasha from the day he came to the khedivate has frequently been paraded in English prints. Hence the majority of English people do not like him. They believe they know him, but manifestly do not. Yet no people on earth so persistently demand fair play as our British cousins.

The opinion of Abbas held in the British Isles is the outcome of political exigencies. Whenever an Egyptian "incident" calls for official attention in London, Fleet Street is moved to applaud England's foreign policy, and decry the khedive whose rebellious spirit has led him to show by manner or word

The Present Khedival Family

that he would like to guide unaided the government of which he is the titular head. This is an expedient of the moment, defensible, possibly, because patriotic. But when the young Egyptian is forced to repress his desire to rule over his people, subject only to his suzerain, the newspapers forget to neutralize the harsh things said of him in their zeal to promote Britain's foreign interests. It seldom occurs to English journalists that Abbas, too, knows the meaning of the words "fair play."

This young man, the seventh of the Mehemet Ali line to be at the head of the Egyptian people, makes no pretension to unusual wisdom; yet his capabilities are of an order making of him a not unworthy successor to the Pharaohs and Ptolemies, Alexander and Cleopatra. He lacks some of the amiable characteristics of his father, Khedive Tewfik, it is true; but he is incomparably better qualified for successful administrative work. English people approved of Tewfik Pasha, but that khedive never aroused their anger by expressing wishes or opinions. He was pliable as clay in the strong British grasp.

Abbas's faults are neither numerous nor serious. His good qualities exceed in number those possessed by the average prince of his years and experience. The sentiment of patriotism is one that justly claims respect, and that he should desire to be free from foreign tutelage is natural enough. To learn his true character and arrive at a just conclusion of his worth, he must be measured at home, since the opinions spread before readers of English newspapers and books are scarcely ingenuous.

Present-Day Egypt

For four years I endeavored to be a fair-minded student of the character of Abbas Pasha. The letter of credence that I bore from the President of the United States commended me to him as the head of the Egyptian government; and throughout my residence in the Egyptian capital I punctiliously treated him as my instructions demanded. Study my credentials as I would, I could discover no intimation that the khedive was but a nominal executive, and my documents from Washington made no reference to Great Britain as the dominating power in Egypt.

British functionaries of a rank entitling them to come into personal relations with Abbas Pasha form a sincere liking for him. But the petty subordinate, seeing him at a distance, or more likely not at all, is obstinately wedded to the belief that it is his duty as a loyal Briton to utter partizan opinion against the nominal head of the government from which he may be earning his daily bread. Americans, on the other hand, invariably like Khedive Abbas, and as a people they are not incapable of forming sound judgments. They see him with eyes not blurred with political vapors.

Less than eight years ago Prince Abbas was a light-hearted student in Vienna, pursuing a course of study at the famous Theresianum fitting him for the exalted position some day to be his. The Austrian emperor took a kindly interest in the lad being educated to rule the oldest nation in the world, and means were provided for giving him a practical insight into the profession of the soldier,

HIS HIGHNESS ABBAS HILMI PASHA II, KHEDIVE OF EGYPT.

The Present Khedival Family

as well as the calling of the engineer and the skilled artisan. In the midst of these pursuits, at a time when he believed he had many years for study and travel, the news was cabled from Cairo, on January 7, 1892, that Tewfik Pasha had died suddenly, and that Prince Abbas had been proclaimed khedive.

Thus ended abruptly the happy student days, and the prince had to exchange the outspoken language of youth for the carefully considered phrases of the head of a nation to control which several European governments were in jealous rivalry, one of them being represented on Egyptian soil, without any real authority, by an army of five thousand men, and hundreds of officials employed in administrative capacities. It was surely not a promising prospect.

Abbas was taught English as a child, by a governess, and later special tutors were brought from England to perfect his knowledge of the language. An American officer in the Egyptian army was assigned to teach the military rudiments not only to the heir to the khedivate, but to Prince Mehemet Ali, a year younger, as well. At the age of twelve Abbas was sent to the celebrated Haxius school at Geneva to complete the preparatory course fitting him for the Theresianum.

In his student days Abbas visited every capital in Europe, with the exception of Madrid and Lisbon. He went to the North Cape and saw the midnight sun, but, he remarks with a smile, has never made the ascent of the Gizeh Pyramids, which overlook his capital. During his travels he observed closely such institutions as he considered suitable for application to his own country, and the knowledge thus obtained has no doubt contributed in a measure to the progress of present-day Egypt. Plans had been arranged for a protracted visit of the princes to the United States in the year of the Columbian Exposition. The itinerary would have taken them not only to Chicago and Washington, but also to the principal industrial centers. Tewfik Pasha had planned for instructors to accompany the young men, who would have given them an insight into the sources of America's greatness. Abbas Pasha has more than once expressed his keen regret that fate should have deprived him of the advantage of seeing the country with which his grandfather had established valued relations.

Elevation to exalted position has not obliterated the memory of comradeships at Geneva and Vienna; for when the khedive is sufficiently acquainted with his caller to lay aside formalities, and the visitor is American, he will recall many pleasant companionships with American youths, mentioning them by name when speaking of their attractive qualities.

The lingual capacity of the khedive is striking, especially to those who regard a prince's training as purely ornamental. During the course of an "audience-day" it frequently happens that he discusses questions of state with the British and United States diplomatic agents in excellent English, with the representative of France in faultless French,

The Present Khedival Family

and with the German in the choicest language of the Austrian court. Later he conducts affairs with the Sultan's representative in Turkish, and may conclude the day by presiding over a council of his ministry, when all sorts of intricate details of policy are arranged in Arabic, the native tongue of Egypt, and one of the most difficult of languages. The evening may see his Highness at the theater, listening with pleasure and understanding to opera rendered in Italian.

The accomplishment yielding the khedive his greatest pleasure, next to his horsemanship, is his musical proficiency. He is a skilful pianist, and has a correct ear for melody. Included in his entourage are forty or fifty picked musicians, constituting his private band, whose position is anything but a sinecure. At Koubbeh the bandsmen are quartered close to the palace, and an abbreviated rehearsal or a flagrantly false note receives immediate attention from his Highness, it is said.

Abbas Pasha does not claim infallibility, but realizes, like his seniors, that administrative mistakes can be made. He is a very different man from the ordinary type of Oriental sovereign, having no religious bigotry, narrowness of thought, or ignorance of the outside world. A desire to promote the welfare of his people is his controlling thought, and under his guidance their future would be full of encouragement and hope.

The khedive receives a yearly grant from the Egyptian government of five hundred thousand dollars. His private wealth is great, and chiefly invested in productive farms and cotton-plantations in the Nile Delta. His habits tend to thrift, perhaps as the natural result of the downfall of Khedive Ismail, whose extravagance has no parallel in history. In addition to the khedive's grant from the national exchequer, he receives another five hundred thousand dollars for the support of his mother, brother, sisters, and the various relatives of the khedival family, nearly a hundred in number.

He is a strict disciplinarian,—reflecting doubtless his Austrian training,—but is just, considerate, and kind. State and show he dislikes, but insists on receiving the full deference due his rank. In childhood the two brothers, in addressing each other, invariably employed the full title, as Prince Abbas Bey and Prince Mehemet Ali Bey. On one occasion, it is related, however, the latter was inclined to be indolent and shirk his lesson.

"Come, Prince," urged the instructor, "it must be done."

Abbas Bey at once exclaimed: "Prince, indeed! My brother is no prince when idle—he is only a fellah."

One privileged to meet the khedive is led to the audience-chamber through files of saluting guardsmen—in smart blue uniforms if it is winter and at Abdin Palace in Cairo, or in white uniforms if it is summer at Ras-el-Teen in Alexandria. He is greeted at the door in a manner proving the khedive's geniality. After shaking hands the visitor is motioned to a seat on the divan with his High-

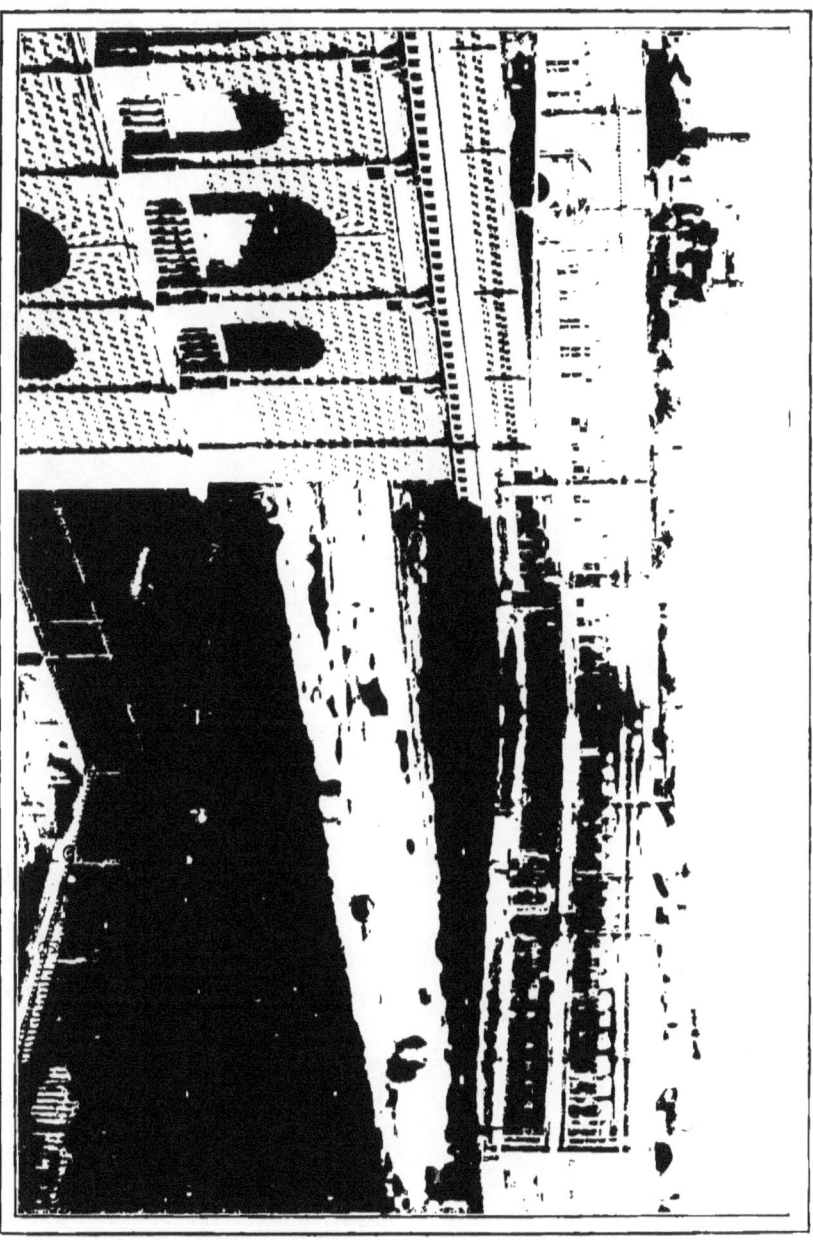

The Present Khedival Family

ness. Khedive Abbas has a pleasing face, full and round, with a fair complexion browned by outdoor exercise. The upper lip is arched and delicately molded; the lower full, but without a touch of grossness. There is a little dark mustache, to which he puts his right hand in moments of animation, twisting its ends.

No portrait gives an idea of the wonder of the face, which comes from eyes of light hazel, and the fair, clear complexion derived from his Turkish ancestors. The eyes mirror every emotion, flashing with the light of laughter, and deepening with the shadow of thought. Photographs of the khedive cannot possibly suggest the charm of face, coming with his mood, and varying therewith. Abbas's figure tends to stoutness, and he is not tall. He is unmistakably magnetic, agreeable, and mentally alert. In his dress there is nothing Oriental, save the red tarboosh, never removed from the head. The clothes might be those of any young American, not particular as to the latest mode, but his coat on ordinary occasions is invariably a frock. Jewelry and glossy boots are never in evidence, except when he wears the uniform of commander-in-chief of the army, with gemmed orders, sword, and accoutrements.

A visitor quickly discovers that he is dealing with no novice of life and affairs, but with one whose responsible position has forced a precocious maturity, for Abbas's manner and words are those of a man of thirty-five. He quickly grasps the point of a question, and a few minutes' conversation shows him to have a good insight into current events.

A remarkable memory enables the khedive to converse effectively on almost any topic. When on military subjects he will speak of the excellent services rendered the Egyptian army by the Americans who placed it on a footing of efficiency in his grandfather's time. It is the firmly set mouth that indicates his determination, inherited from Ismail, and which his own father did not possess. The khedive is by some called stubborn and obstinate; but, like many others, he can be more easily led than driven.

His Highness rises usually at half-past five o'clock, and shortly after is in the saddle for a ride about Koubbeh or Montazah, visiting working parties and stables, and giving orders for the day after the manner of any gentleman farmer superintending his own estates. He breakfasts at eight, after which and up to noon, if it is not an audience-day in town, he is occupied with his secretaries in arranging and considering affairs of state, going thoroughly into details before deciding any matter. After luncheon a secretary replies to letters of a personal character under the khedive's direction, and from three to five his Highness receives diplomatic and other official visitors, and then drives until sunset. It is his custom to appear on the Ghizereh oval, in Cairo, every Friday afternoon in the season. For an Eastern, Abbas Pasha is extraordinarily energetic.

When the Duke of Cambridge was in Cairo, a few

The Present Khedival Family

seasons since, it was arranged that a field-review be given of the Egyptian troops quartered in the capital, in honor of the famous commander-in-chief of Queen Victoria's army. The proposition came from Britishers in the Egyptian service, those who believe that Egypt would go to the eternal bow-wows were it not for the fostering hand of England. His Highness the Khedive was to be present, as nominal commander of the army.

All Cairo was at Abbassieh, on horseback or in carriages, to see the manœuvers. The khedive galloped on to the parade-ground with his aides, and immediately took command of the forces. The spectators were treated to something manifestly not on the bills, for the young Egyptian put the soldiers through their paces in a manner causing consternation to the officials who had intended the khedive to play an ornamental part only in the show.

Infantry and cavalry were hurried here and there, the camel corps was sent across the desert to repel an imaginary foe, and platoons of artillery were ordered into position, and their guns belched forth volley after volley. This mimic warfare, extending over miles of the desert, was kept up for two hours, and waxed so fast and furious that nearly all the spectators had fallen by the wayside, from inability to keep up, long before it was over. His Royal Highness of England had not experienced such a shaking up for years, and when the campaign ended did not hesitate to say that the Egyptian soldiers were a fine lot of men, knowing every detail of a soldier's calling.

Present-Day Egypt

This approving formula had become habitual with him in commending British yeomanry and volunteers, but in this case was uttered with unmistakable sincerity. The old duke had seen more practical soldiering on the plains of Abbassieh than he had anticipated, and from that time he has been an admirer of the young khedive.

Abbas Pasha never disobeys the command of the Koran by tasting wines or spirits, and the example to the youth of his country is carried further, for he is a total abstainer from tobacco, which, in a land where nearly everybody smokes cigarettes from morning until night, means much.

A striking phase of character for one occupying so conspicuous a position before the world is the manner in which the khedive dissociates private life from official station. When his work at Abdin Palace is finished, a cavalry guard escorts him to the palace of Koubbeh, five miles out of Cairo, on the border of the desert. There is little suggesting princely estate about Koubbeh, save the few soldiers of the khedival guard and the musicians and drummer-boys lounging in front of their quarters. The palace looks like the seat of a well-conditioned European family of country tastes. The presence of its master is indicated by the scarlet flag bearing the threefold star and crescent floating over the palace.

The khedive's consort, described by those who know her as an attractive Circassian, and the four little children, are installed at Koubbeh during the winter season. It is likewise the home

THE SULTAN'S HIGH COMMISSIONER IN EGYPT, GHAZI MOUKHTAR PASHA.

The Present Khedival Family

of the khedivah-mère, who, by reason of having been born a princess, takes rank over the khedivah as the first lady of the court. The khedivah-mère is little more than forty years of age, and is said to be charming and accomplished. She was at one time the most beautiful of the princesses of the East. Her lovely, clear complexion, magnificent eyes, with the shape of her face and the carriage of the head, made her a very queen of beauty, it is claimed by ladies having the entrée at the viceroyal court. Living in strict Mohammedan seclusion, and never appearing in public except with veiled faces, the ladies of the khedival family are not subjected to masculine gaze. Their attendance at the opera is concealed from the audience by screened boxes; but flashing jewels and shadowy outlines behind the gossamer curtains tell of their presence.

Up to February 20, 1899, Prince Mehemet Ali was heir to the khedivate; but on that date the consort of Abbas Pasha gave birth to a son at the villa of Montazah, and while the happy event was being celebrated throughout the country, it was formally announced that Prince Mohammed Abdoul-Mounaim, the newborn, was heir apparent to the khedival dignity and estate. This was in accord with the Sultan's firman of June 9, 1873, which provided that the succession to the khedivate of Egypt is exclusively by order of primogeniture in the male line. Should Abbas Pasha die, the firman provides for a regency until the heir attains his legal majority at the age of eighteen years.

Present-Day Egypt

Having no official position in the Egyptian administration, Prince Mehemet Ali passes a good portion of each year in Paris. Every winter sees him in Cairo, where, although a bachelor, he resides in a bijou palace in the European quarter.

The khedive has two sisters. The elder, the Princess Khadija, born in 1880, is married to a Turkish notable, and spends much time at Constantinople; the younger, the Princess Nimet, born in 1882, is wedded to her cousin, Djemil Pasha, an accomplished and wealthy prince, who resides at Mounerah Palace in Cairo.

While a devout believer in the religion of the Koran, the khedive has never taken advantage of its provision that one may have four wives. He is a monogamist, as was his father. The khedive has no harem in the European sense. Each of his palaces, however, has its "harem division," which means simply that portion set apart for the khedivah and khedivah-mère and their enormous entourage. The attendants are young Turkish women, coming chiefly from the provinces of Georgia and Circassia, and are attired in exquisite garb of semi-European character.

Although spoken of in the Orient as "slaves," many of these young women have the simplest duties, and in Europe might almost be regarded as ladies in waiting at court. It was a woman of this class that was taken by the khedive for his wife, and the published accounts of the marriage may have shocked western-world readers, knowing little of actual life in the East. It was in keeping with

The Present Khedival Family

Mohammedan custom, however, and was most popular with the Egyptians.

For the Koubbeh estate the khedive has imported American farm machinery, to illustrate the advantages of tilling with modern appliances. There are extensive stables filled with choice horses from various parts of the world. The position of honor is given to a magnificent Arabian steed with flowing tail, sent to Abbas Pasha by the Sultan. Close by is the English thoroughbred Cedar, presented by the late Colonel North, and in a neighboring stall stands an American trotter, the gift of an admiring Philadelphian.

The dairy, kennels, and poultry-yard at Koubbeh are supplied with selected animals and fowls from every clime, and in them the khedive takes the keenest interest. For the work-people there is a model village, with mosque, school, and meeting-place where discussion is encouraged after the lyceum idea—all supported by the khedive, to demonstrate the benefits of order, cleanliness, and community of interests. The native fire-brigade, with English apparatus, would be creditable anywhere.

So devoted is Egypt's young ruler to horses that from his private purse he maintains a commission to improve horse-breeding. He offers valuable prizes at horse-shows, and himself makes entries for the races during the Cairo season, when it not infrequently happens that his colors are carried to victory by his native jockey. The khedive enjoys driving, and may often be met in the outskirts of

Present-Day Egypt

Cairo or Alexandria, holding the reins over a dashing pair, and accompanied by an aide-de-camp or one of his many relatives.

Before the heat of summer comes, the khedival establishment, with its army of officials and attendants, moves to Alexandria. Six railway-trains are required to transfer the court. The khedive and his ministers and other high officers go in state in an observation saloon-car of American make.

The historic structure, Ras-el-Teen, overlooking Alexandria harbor, is treated by the khedive simply as an official palace, as Abdin is in Cairo. The home-loving instinct has caused the khedive to create a summer retreat at Montazah, snugly nestled on the picturesque Mediterranean coast, a few miles to the east of Alexandria. There the family life, with artistic and musical surroundings, is carried on in charming simplicity. Perplexities arising from conferences at Ras-el-Teen are left in the precincts of the old palace.

A mile to the eastward of Montazah is Abukir Bay, made famous by Nelson's victory over the French fleet little more than a century ago. Although Montazah was reclaimed from the desert only six years since, forests of quick-growing trees have sprung into existence; many varieties of game-birds and animals have been domiciled there, including native antelope and European red deer, for the khedive is an ardent sportsman. In a remote part of the estate is the camp of the khedive's camel-corps, whose Bedouin riders are trained marksmen, and with whom he makes long journeys

BISCHARINS IN UPPER EGYPT.

The Present Khedival Family

in the desert. It is said that his Highness bears any amount of fatigue when on these excursions, and his caravan frequently marches from sunrise to sunset before bivouacking for the night.

Montazah harbor shelters many boats, including a small yacht that conveys its master to Alexandria when he prefers the sea to special train or carriage. Safe anchorage is assured by a breakwater costing two hundred thousand dollars to construct.

The khedival yacht *Mahroussa*, of forty-five hundred tons and four hundred and forty feet long, is the largest in the world, if one excepts the war-ship *Hohenzollern*, on which the German emperor makes summer cruises. For voyaging to Constantinople, cruising in the Grecian Archipelago, or going to Triest or Venice, if the trip may be regarded as "unofficial," the khedive employs a beautiful Scotch-built yacht of seven hundred tons, capable of steaming fourteen knots an hour, and called *Safa-el-Bahr*, the Arabic for "Joy of the Sea."

Khedive Abbas, with his family, spends two or three months each summer in Europe. He is fond of visiting Switzerland incognito for a few weeks' sojourn in a high altitude. His Highness has several times made protracted stays in Constantinople. One of his numerous habitations is a palace on the Bosporus, presented by his august master, the Sultan.

In a nautical talk the khedive told me that he was not the best of sailors, and instanced that sad winter voyage when summoned from Vienna to assume the throne of Egypt. Etiquette demanded

Present-Day Egypt

that the Austrian emperor place a steamer at the youth's disposal, with an escort of dignitaries from the Vienna court. The vessel was old, "perhaps fifty years old, and very small," said the khedive. Violent storms had made the Adriatic and Mediterranean turbulent, and the journey from Triest was disagreeable and trying. High seas retarded progress, and even the ship's officers wished themselves ashore. At Brindisi Prince Abbas begged to have the ship wait for better weather.

"I must not stop, Highness," was the admiral's reply, "for it is the emperor's command to lose no time, and the etiquette must be observed."

When the peaceful harbors of Greece came in sight, the khedive again pleaded for delay. But the punctilious commander insisted that "the etiquette must be observed, for it was his Majesty's order."

This was too much for the poor sufferer, and he remarked to the ceremonious officer: "Etiquette is well enough in its place; but his Majesty Francis Joseph is comfortable in Vienna, and not seasick on this awful ship."

The voyage was successfully completed, nevertheless, and the day after landing on Egyptian soil the illustrious passenger formally took upon himself the rulership of Egypt.

The state ball given each winter at Abdin Palace by his Highness, besides being the most important social occurrence of the year, has a spectacular effect not to be excelled anywhere by any similar function. In its variety and contrasts it eclipses

The Present Khedival Family

the governor-general's at Algiers, so often painted by great artists, and is claimed to be a pageant equal to the viceroyal ball at Calcutta. The khedive's annual ball occurs usually in January or February, and brings together representative types of nearly every race of Europe, Africa, and Asia, with a very liberal sprinkling of Americans.

Conspicuous in the medley of brilliant uniforms are those of diplomatic celebrities and the leaders of the Egyptian army and the army of occupation, glittering with orders. There are present officials of every hue of countenance, including mudirs and omdehs from distant Egyptian provinces, Bedouin sheiks from the Red Sea coast, and perhaps Indian princes breaking their journey to or from England for a few weeks' participation in the gaieties of the khedival city. Abbas Pasha's hostship elicits general admiration. He receives those bidden to the festivity with a graceful cordiality, and makes a point of displaying his gallantry to the ladies of the diplomatic corps, whose pleasant duty it is to stand by his side and receive with him. The dancing begun, he appears to find much satisfaction in watching the moving figures in one of the most beautiful ball-rooms in the world. A box of generous proportions, duly screened, is filled with the ladies of the khedival family, who watch the brilliant scene, unperceived by those participating in it. The supper is a liberal education in gastronomy.

CHAPTER X

GREAT BRITAIN'S POSITION IN EGYPT

THE Egyptian question is perennial, but American readers know only that version of it which British writers prepare, and this, naturally, is apt to reflect their partizan bias. Most published opinion is so treated that the casual reader is led to believe that by some feat of diplomacy, long forgotten by him, the ancient land of the Pharaohs has been segregated from the Ottoman empire and incorporated as an integral part of Queen Victoria's realm. This is in effect what has been done, but accomplished more through the coöperation of circumstances than by any preconceived intention to secure control of the country.

Briefly stated, Great Britain's visible right to wield a dominating influence in Egypt is that she is in "occupation" with an armed force, and this only. In theory, at least, "occupation" means much less than "protectorate," and diplomacy has heretofore regarded it as a word fitting a temporary expedient. But England does not bother about definitions. In point of fact, the Nile country has for seventeen years been more absolutely governed from London than has India, Canada, Aus-

Britain's Position in Egypt

tralia, or any crown colony; yet between England and Egypt there is no tie that is officially recognized by any European power. While Britain is probably permanently established in Egypt, she has yet to legalize her position. Meanwhile, the welfare of the people of Egypt improves each year, England has become indifferent to the expressions of dissatisfaction by her only outspoken critic, France, and the cause of humanity and progress is steadily benefited by the British occupation, anomalous though it be. The Sultan is the only person possessing an absolute right to demand a halt or a declaration of intentions on the part of the British government; and the khedive can make his complaint of abridgment of authority only to his imperial master at Constantinople.

To discuss now the moral right of Great Britain to a foothold in Egypt is as superfluous as for a lawyer to argue in court that the state cannot arrest his client, when he is already a prisoner behind the bars.

Not one Englishman in a thousand has two opinions on the subject of national expansion; if he has views against territorial acquisition, he never parades them in public prints to be read in other countries. This is a basic principle of the Briton's idea of patriotism. Frenchmen twit the British with being afflicted with the square-mile mania, and insist that the excuse for ministering to this is never analyzed so long as an additional foot of soil may be incorporated within that charmed zone of red encircling the earth, on which the sun never sets. On the other hand, Englishmen say with truth that were this instinct non-existent in their race, there would to-day be no British empire, and maintain that the world is enriched through their achievements as empire-builders. It seems to be an impulse difficult of suppression in the Anglo-Saxon, wherever his abode.

Since France withdrew in 1883 from the dual control with England of the finances of the khedival government, Egypt has been in everything but name a dependency of Great Britain, the French in the meantime trying to resume their share in its administration. More than once they have urged the Sultan to interfere and order the English from his domain, and for many years they have doggedly obstructed Britain's conduct of Egyptian affairs, but with little success.

Englishmen deny that there has ever been any serious thought of annexing Egypt; that would be grossly unjust to the Sultan and his vassal, the khedive, they confess, and lead to endless diplomatic controversy. The occupation was entered upon with an unselfish motive, and was dictated by necessity, they say; but temporary expedients have the awkward knack of developing into permanent conditions the world over. The routing of the khalifa and his dervish mob at Omdurman by the Anglo-Egyptian expedition led by Kitchener, the hoisting of the flags of Turkey and Great Britain jointly over Khartum, the entering upon a scheme for constructing Nile reservoirs that cannot be completed for five years at least, and Cecil

LORD KITCHENER, SIRDAR OF THE EGYPTIAN ARMY
AND GOVERNOR-GENERAL OF THE SUDAN.

Britain's Position in Egypt

Rhodes's materializing project for building with British money a Cape-to-Cairo railway, taken together, cannot give the foes of British domination in Egypt much hope for expecting any radical change of program for many years to come. I am told that to this day there is periodical speculation in Spain as to when England may be expected to restore to the Spanish government the rock of Gibraltar. Having this event always in contemplation, the Madrid council has for a century regularly appointed a grandee to the governorship of the rocky promontory that gives Great Britain control of the Mediterranean. The departure of the English from Egypt is as unlikely to happen as their restoration of Gibraltar to the Spaniards.

The statesmen guiding France in 1882 claimed to recognize no necessity for bombarding Alexandria, and when it was decided that England's ships were to fire upon the city, the French admiral was ordered to remove his fleet from the scene of conflict. Frenchmen still insist that the Arabi rebellion could have been successfully dealt with on shore, and that the razing of Alexandria was wanton destruction. When the war-ships of France steamed away from Alexandria they decided the fate of their country as a participator in the affairs of Egypt, and the record of that July day is an eventful page in French history, and marks the beginning of the claim on the part of England to govern single-handed a country forming no part of the British empire.

Present-Day Egypt

It is known that England invited France to share the responsibilities of the bombardment; but it is not known that France was urged to coöperate in the enterprise, or that anything was said on the point of a division of the spoils that would naturally fall to the power or powers undertaking the quelling of the Arabi insurrection. At all events, the French fleet took its leave of the country where French sympathies and influence had prevailed from the going there of Napoleon in 1798. As detailed in another chapter, Britain's fleet remained and reduced the best part of Alexandria to dust, making a prisoner of the rebel leader, and in a brief period stamped out what had been an indifferently planned uprising of that portion of Egypt's population easily swayed to fanaticism.

If Englishmen have any really vital interest in Africa, it is to monopolize the Nile, which means more to their nation than the control of the Niger, the Kongo, and the Zambesi combined; for the Nile is as potential commercially as it is politically, and the country lying at its mouth is the strategical keystone to Britain's Indian and Eastern superstructure. Statesmen and publicists throughout Europe are perpetually discussing what they term the Egyptian question or the Sudan question, and dilating upon the rights of England in Egypt; but these are minor themes and subordinate to the great Nile question.

Great Britain already controls every foot of the Nile valley not in barbaric hands, means to have it all, and has no intention of sharing the river with

Britain's Position in Egypt

any other European power. Khartum now reached, England will stop at nothing to bring the valley intervening between Khartum and the equatorial lakes safely within her dominion. Under no circumstances would Britain share her control of any important part of the Nile with France, and she is ready to resist by force of arms any movement directed at a curtailment of her aspirations. Her attitude at the time of the Fashoda incident proved this, and did much to bring France to an understanding as to the relative spheres of influence of the two governments in Africa.

The southern provinces being now reconquered, and railways from Assuan to Khartum, and from the Red Sea to Khartum, either planned or building, in effect making the Sudan a British colony, England at some time may believe it to her advantage to relax her grip on Egypt and withdraw her troops from Cairo and Alexandria. But diplomatic bickering or pressure will never bring about this result, and no nation is alone sufficiently strong to enter upon actual warfare to oust the British from their position. The strength of the Muscovite may scarcely be expected to be ever directed against England in a contest for Egypt—the stakes would be too small; and Russia, however pronounced her sentimental attachment to France, is not going to embark in war to further the ambitions of her volatile friend. Germany, while perhaps regarding England's methods in Egypt as forming a startling precedent in statecraft, has not sufficient interest to initiate any active campaign in connection therewith. Italy, again, is in spirit England's ally in more than one African enterprise; and Austria, by reason of being the Sultan's nearest neighbor, chooses to keep her hands free from the Egyptian imbroglio from politic motives. Hence it is no longer necessary for Englishmen to pretend that the occupation will end when Egypt "becomes capable of self-government," or when "normal conditions in the country have been restored." Nothing but England's voluntary action can bring about her evacuation of the Lower Nile valley and the Delta.

The Czar aims at becoming the dictator of things Asiatic, possibly omitting India for the present. By brilliant diplomacy Russia acquired nearly all the increment of benefit going to Japan as a result of Japan's victory over China; and her influence in Korea is well-nigh paramount, as it is also in Persia. Russia has various ways of reaching the East independent of the Suez Canal; she employs Persia as a connecting overland link with India, or can even construct a railway from a Syrian port to the head of the Persian Gulf; while England's alternative to the Suez Canal would be the old-time Cape route. But no route can offer a fraction of the advantages, commercial, political, or strategic, of the Suez waterway. That is always going to be the favorite avenue to the East.

Great is the country of the Czar and the marvelous Siberian railway. The country is vast indeed, and is constantly growing—has a chronic taste for expansion, and is yearly exhibiting new evidences

Britain's Position in Egypt

of that phase of its national character. Russia has within a few months, in further development of its expansion proclivities, secured a port on the Persian Gulf,—that is, one that borders on the Indian Ocean,—and, what is vitally important, has come to an agreement with England regarding their respective aspirations in China. The aim of this agreement is to put an end to the battle for concessions, railway and other, which raged acrimoniously for two years. The Russian object is to avoid a conflict which would interfere with the successful exploitation of the transcontinental railway, on which she has spent an enormous sum, and also to get funds from Great Britain when needed for the development of industries at home.

Russia's desire to avoid British opposition may be taken to mean that the Northern Bear will be slow to direct its gaze toward Egypt in a menacing manner. Two centuries ago Russia had but a single sea-outlet, the Gulf of Finland. Later she secured control of the eastern Baltic and obtained a free course to the North Atlantic. Once more she reached out and gained an outlet into the Mediterranean through the Black Sea. Again she reached out for the eastern Asiatic trade and attained that object, and a few months ago she acquired a port on the Indian Ocean and came to an understanding with John Bull respecting Chinese matters; and this can have no other meaning than "hands off" in Egypt.

England has certainly so interwoven the destinies of the country of the Nile with her own that evacuation could be accomplished only with great confusion to a policy under which Egyptian finances have not only been repaired, but placed on a footing of enviable solvency.

The Dongola expedition, a few years since, afforded opportunity for England to show European military critics and strategists the possibilities of her imperial resources in a defensive way, by bringing from India several native regiments which garrisoned Suakim and other Red Sea ports during the months when the entire Egyptian army was concentrated on the Upper Nile. It would not be difficult, at any time, for Great Britain to place a good-sized army of Indians in the Nile valley, independent of her naval position in the Mediterranean, if she dared weaken her strength in India for a time. Rail connection between the Red Sea and the Upper Nile would render this easy.

The reconquest of the Sudan cannot, for a year or two at least, mean that the provinces south of Dongola are open to trade. The whole region about Khartum, and for hundreds of miles up and down the Nile valley, is practically depopulated as a consequence of the years of tyranny and misrule of the khalifa. To bring the natives back to the peaceful pursuits of agriculture and its concomitant interests can be accomplished only gradually by Lord Kitchener and his assistants. Not until this is done, and the Anglo-Egyptian authority organized in all its civil ramifications, can the Sudan be regarded as "open" to the world. It will be a long time, at all events, before the Su-

A NILE FARM.

Britain's Position in Egypt

dan will be able to pay its way; but with good management it should eventually become a contributor to the Cairo exchequer.

It is interesting to observe, by recorded official utterances and the sequence of events, how the retention of Egypt by Great Britain could not have been seriously considered until years after the occupation had been entered upon. Oftentimes it is entertaining to follow the development of an idea, especially one having for its consummation a result or condition the very opposite of the purpose declared at the outset. To begin the evolution of the idea of permanently retaining Egypt, it is instructive to state that the Gladstone government, which sent the troops and ships to Egypt in 1882, asserted that British intervention was made solely in the interests of humanity, and for the purpose of suppressing the Arabi rebellion and restoring the authority of the khedive. These pledges, although addressed to no specific government, were accepted in Europe in good faith.

A few hours before opening the bombardment of Alexandria, the commander of the British fleet said, in a formal communication to Khedive Tewfik: "I deem it opportune to reaffirm to your Highness that the government of Great Britain has no intention to effect the conquest of Egypt, nor to interfere in any way with the liberties or religion of the Egyptians; its sole object is to protect your Highness and the Egyptian people from the rebels."

Admiral Seymour spoke with the authority of his government in this momentous matter, as did

Present-Day Egypt

General Sir Garnet Wolseley, who led the later campaign on shore, when, to hasten the restoration of law and order, after the rebellion had been crushed, he said in a proclamation to the people of Egypt: "The general in command of the British forces wishes to make known that the object of her Majesty's government in sending troops to this country is to reëstablish the authority of the khedive. . . . The general in command will be glad to receive visits from chiefs who are willing to assist in repressing the rebellion against the khedive, the lawful ruler of Egypt appointed by the Sultan."

Even that ablest of diplomatists, Lord Dufferin, then ambassador to the Sultan, formally announced, over his signature, that England, by her interference in Egypt, was "seeking no territorial advantage, nor the acquisition of any exclusive privilege, nor any commercial advantage for her subjects which cannot be obtained equally for the subjects of any other nation."

Arabi was tried in Cairo for treason, defended by English barristers, found guilty, and sentenced to death. His campaign cry of "Egypt for the Egyptians" in a way stamping him as a patriot, and the people enrolled under his banner having some show of reason for their objection to the frequent interference of foreign powers clamoring for money, his sentence was promptly modified to banishment for life.

English influence was responsible for the commutation of the sentence, and Great Britain, which

Britain's Position in Egypt

seemingly takes upon itself the task of policing half the world, sent Arabi and his principal supporters into exile in British territory, for a crime in no sense committed against England. Thus, for usurping the khedival prerogative,—which, plainly stated, can have no other meaning than the right to direct the administration of Egypt,—Arabi was guilty of an offense punishable by death or deportation.

The British government announced, shortly after the crushing of Arabi, that its "army of occupation" would be withdrawn as soon as law and order could be restored, and a date six months thence was actually fixed for the departure of the troops. Her philanthropic task not being completed, in her opinion, at the end of the six months, an extension of time for another six months was made. At all events, the occupation was to last only for the brief period that would be necessary to teach the Egyptians the easy art of self-government. But the soldiers have never left Egypt.

Thus the word "occupation" promises for many years to be applied to a novel operation in territorial expansion, entered upon in the name of humanity; and the right of ruling Egypt, taken from the khedive by Arabi the rebel, and technically wrested from him by Great Britain, will probably never again fully reside in the family of Mehemet Ali. Military occupation indefinitely extended, as illustrated in Egypt, amounts to annexation. The present system is called euphemistically by some a "veiled protectorate."

The mind of the reader is certain to revert to the

utterance of the Congress of the United States, when, in declaring war against Spain to free the people of Cuba, it was stated in language so clear that ambiguity was out of the question: "That the United States hereby disclaims any disposition or intention to exercise sovereignty, jurisdiction, or control over said island, except for the pacification thereof, and asserts its determination when that is accomplished to leave the government and control of the island to its people." The Englishman, alert in seeking instances that tend to justify Britain's position in Egypt, believes and hopes that he is to have a helpful parallel in the outcome of our relations with Cuba.

Englishmen make a point of recalling that the Sultan declined to send Turkish troops to quell the Alexandrian disorders in 1882, and they likewise point to Tunis, when justifying their attitude toward Egypt, and assert that France is doing with that country exactly what the British are doing with Egypt.

There is now and then a spasmodic demand in the British Isles, raised by "Little Englanders," that England's hand be lifted from Egypt, that the Tory policy of grab be reversed. Mr. Gladstone stated on all possible occasions that Britain had no right to remain in Egypt, and politicians of the Dilke, Harcourt, Courtney, Labouchere, and Marriott type frequently raise their voices in condemnation of a continuance of British rule in Egypt. These men talk only when their party in Parliament is in the minority, however; should one of

Britain's Position in Egypt

them find himself a member of the government he would in all probability be as silent on the subject of evacuation as the Sphinx itself.

Does England profit sufficiently from her retention of Egypt to warrant the jealous hatred of France, her nearest neighbor?

Great Britain has well-nigh made an English lake of the Mediterranean; the outlet of this lake, the Suez Canal, is the key to the whole scheme of British rule in India and the East. To control the canal, by force of arms if necessary, is the predominant reason why England remains in Egypt. It serves her purpose perfectly to have five thousand redcoats within a few hours' journey of the great international waterway, and a guardship at each terminus of it. Without the absolute control of this connecting-link between Occident and Orient, thirty-six million people in Great Britain could not expect long to hold in subjection four hundred millions in India, and to govern a quarter of the globe.

Monetary considerations have as much weight with Englishmen as with other people. As perhaps half of Egypt's bonded debt was held in England when the occupation began, the gradual appreciation of the value of Egyptian securities has seemed to Britishers another justification, perhaps of secondary importance, for continuing their sojourn in Egypt. When they went there, it must be admitted, Egyptian credit was as low as it well could be.

In 1882, it is estimated, English people owned

bonds to the face-value of two hundred and seventy-five million dollars, and these could not have been sold then for more than half that sum. "Egyptians" are now quoted at a premium of from three to six per cent., and the difference between the market value in 1882 and the value to-day of England's supposed financial stake in Egypt is the comfortable sum of one hundred and forty million dollars—sufficient to pay for the army of occupation for more than a century! This restoration of Egyptian credit has benefited all bondholders proportionately—French, German, Italian, Austrian, and Russian, as well as English.

An incidental reason why Great Britain retains her hold upon Egypt is that the cotton crop of the Nile valley reduces more and more each year the dependence of British spindles upon the cotton-fields of the United States.

There are also several considerations of minor importance which have influenced the Egyptian policy of England. The reconquest of the Sudan could be prosecuted only from the north, and geographers are agreed that whoever controls equatorial Africa and the sources of the Nile becomes the natural holder of Egypt. Therefore, without Egypt firmly in hand, the ambition of British map-makers for a zone of territory stretching continuously from Cape Town to Cairo, and bringing more than half the African continent under British influence, must of necessity be abandoned.

The statement so often seen in French journals that Egypt possesses a value to England as a dump-

Britain's Position in Egypt

ing-ground for younger sons and a horde of civil and military functionaries, furnishing the minimum of usefulness for the maximum of compensation, is petty, and forms no part of a scheme of such magintude as the practical absorption of Egypt.

The land of the Pyramids has become a short cut to English honors, as the Suez Canal is to the British possessions in the East, and no act of courage, benefit, or policy on the part of a British military or civil official there passes unrecognized by the home government. At least four peerages have fallen to British servants in Egypt since the bombardment of Alexandria, and knighthood and lesser degrees of chivalry have been apportioned to the Briton serving in the Nile land with lavish generosity. In most cases the dignities have been merited, doubtless, under England's system of bestowing rewards. As a recognition for dealing the death-blow to Mahdiism, Kitchener's peerage and the Parliamentary grant of thirty thousand pounds sterling were not excessive.

Are the people of Egypt materially benefited by English rule?

Unquestionably they are. Unpopular as it is with a majority of the people of Egypt, humiliating to the Sultan and the khedive, and at times bitterly criticized in Europe, the occupation has done vast good. No fair-minded investigator can witness the present condition of the Egyptian fellaheen, or peasantry, knowing what it was before the advent of the English, without conceding this. For six or eight years Egypt has fairly teemed with

Present-Day Egypt

prosperity. The story of that country's emergence from practical bankruptcy, with its securities quoted nearly as high as English consols, reads like a romance; and there is no better example of economical progress through administrative reform than is presented by Egypt under British rule.

Security is assured to person and property, slavery has been legally abolished, official corruption is almost a thing of the past, forced labor for public works is no longer permitted, and native courts have now more than a semblance of justice. Hygienic matters have been so carefully looked after that the population has increased from seven to nearly ten millions in a decade or more. Land-taxes have been lowered and equalized and are systematically collected, and scientific irrigation is so generally employed that the cultivable area has been considerably extended. Egypt was probably never so prosperous as at the present time. The debt is being slightly reduced, and will be made less burdensome, as time goes on, by the increased productiveness of the soil. It is indeed a mighty stride from the Egypt of Ismail Pasha to the Egypt of Lord Cromer.

The present external debt of Egypt is approximately five hundred and eight million dollars, and it is a popular error that it has been reduced since the advent of the English. As a fact, it has been increased by forty million dollars. This went to indemnify Alexandrians whose property was destroyed at the time of the rebellion and bombard-

Britain's Position in Egypt

ment, to defray the cost of the military campaign resulting in the loss of the Sudan, for the recent reconquest of the Sudan provinces, and for certain public works deemed imperatively necessary.

By her management of affairs England has, nevertheless, so improved the conditions in Egypt that European bondholders have been satisfied to have the interest on their bonds reduced from seven to three and a half or four per cent.

England possesses a capacity for conducting colonies and rehabilitating run-down countries which amounts almost to genius. Overbearing and arrogant as the British functionary out of England often appears to be, he must be scrupulously honest and generally capable to find a place in the perfectly organized machinery guided from London. Frenchmen say that Egypt's restoration to prosperity could have been better accomplished by them, and some allege that this prosperity is more apparent than real, charging that much is neglected in the desire to make a favorable showing in the yearly balance-sheet. But a frank investigation of what France does with her own dependencies, nearly every one of which is run at a loss, gives support to the belief that Egypt is better off under British guidance than she could be under that of France. No alien power could have done better in Egypt than Great Britain has. But her critics claim to recognize scant justification for Britain's absorption of the country of the khedive merely because of her ability to do good work there, and point to the glaring flaw in her title.

Present-Day Egypt

Has England educated the Egyptians to govern themselves?

Not as yet, certainly.

England's desire to remain in Egypt could not better be served than by making her functionaries appear essential to the well-being of the country; in fact, by making progress dependent upon her administrators, accountants, and irrigation experts. This they have surely done, and the "understudies" of these clever servants, those who could best take their places, are Englishmen, not Egyptians. There are many hundred native subordinates doing the simplest routine work, who perceive the splendid results, but contribute thereto chiefly by their submissiveness. They are not being instructed sufficiently to keep Egypt from retrogressing should they find themselves in charge of affairs.

The khedive is compelled to yield to England in all matters connected with the choice of a ministry, and this necessarily results in a partizan cabinet acceptable to London. On occasions when the khedive has appointed a cabinet officer without first securing the consent of England, he has been promptly called to account, and the menacing display in the streets of his capital of thousands of British guns and bayonets has not abated until the office has been filled by an Egyptian practically named by the British government.

The real business of important executive departments in Cairo is directed by the under-secretaries (assistant ministers), who are English, and their utterances and plans formally receive the sanction

AT THE BASE OF CHEOPS.

Britain's Position in Egypt

of their Egyptian chiefs. The native minister is the visible and signatory power, the creative and actual force being the English assistant. Everything financial is dictated by an "adviser," as is nearly everything judicial, and these functionaries are British. Similarly, the ministry of the interior, presided over by the educated and capable Egyptian premier, is also largely directed by an "adviser."

Lord Cromer is proud of the British assistants who have coöperated with him in the work of rehabilitating Egypt, and especially pleased to inform inquirers that the work has been accomplished by a body of officials not exceeding one hundred in number—a record that we in America, new to colonial administration, will do well to consider. An interesting example of the way in which English officials seek to carry the Egyptians with them is afforded by some recently announced statistics. In the finance ministry, under the strictest British tutelage, 13 English and 513 natives are employed; in the department of the interior, dictated by British rule, 62 English and 784 Egyptians find employment. In the offices under international control the percentage of Britishers is very small. For example, the staff of the mixed courts consists of 242 Europeans (of whom 17 are British) and 101 Egyptians. The Caisse de la Dette employs 50 Europeans (2 being British) and 10 Egyptians, and the quarantine board has 48 European and 19 native employees.

Each year sees a slight augmentation of Englishmen on the Egyptian pay-roll, but always in responsible positions. It is true that one Englishman can perform the work of two native clerks, but he gets usually the pay that would go to three. There are more Frenchmen, Syrians, and Italians employed by the Egyptian government than English, probably. Most foreigners in the Egyptian service are lavishly paid, wholly from the Egyptian exchequer. The salary of an "adviser" is about ten thousand dollars a year, and under-secretaries receive seventy-five hundred dollars.

Seventeen or eighteen years is a considerable lapse of time anywhere; in the East, where people mature at an early age, it represents a generation. Those who were children in the year of the bombardment are now in the prime of their lives, and England has had ample time to fit them for fair administrative work; yet she has done so only in small measure.

Uninfluenced by political motive, the schools of the American Presbyterian Mission have done tenfold more for the cause of education and the spread of the English language in Egypt than has Great Britain. These schools, upward of a hundred in number, are distributed throughout the country, and are yearly elevating thousands of youths to a better condition, teaching them in particular the value of order and system. At Cairo, Alexandria, Mansurah, Luxor, and many other places, these schools for years have done a noble work, and thousands of Egyptians of both sexes owe their well-being to the unselfish devotion of

Britain's Position in Egypt

the men and women teachers of the American Mission. The college of the Mission at Assiut, long presided over by the Rev. Dr. Alexander, is a model institution whose standard of education has few rivals in the Turkish dominions.

Since England has done but little to develop a class that may in time take the positions now filled by her own countrymen, Anglophobe critics point to this as confirmatory evidence of the insincerity of the statement that England ever intends the Egyptians to take the helm of state.

A flagrant error of British administration, until two years ago, was the omission to introduce the English language. Egypt is a polyglot country, and the incorporation of English as an official language might with propriety have followed the introduction of the present system of affairs. French, consequently, remains the only European language known to any extent by the educated natives; and where there is one Egyptian who knows English, forty who read and write French can be found. Only one of the khedive's ministers knows a word of English, yet all six are proficient in French.

The official language of the government has been French for many years. Official publications and correspondence are in French. It is the European language of the railways and postal department. Postage-stamps, railway-tickets, and telegraph forms, actually printed in England, express their values and conditions in French and Arabic. English employees in governmental bureaus write officially to one another in French, frequently to the confusion of the ideas intended to be expressed. An entire department, having charge of museums and the conservation of antiquities, employing thousands of natives, is exclusively French in administration, although supported in great measure by English-speaking visitors. So long as the European language of the Egyptian official remains French, his mode of thought and action will be French also.

In Cairo and Alexandria as many as ten newspapers are printed in the French language, purveying opinion bitterly hostile to the occupation. One of these, published at the capital, printed daily for years in display-type a list of Great Britain's broken pledges in connection with the occupation, quoting from Blue Books and like documents such extracts as appeared to prove its case. Only one English journal is published, and that is forced to print its news and editorials in French as well as English to secure remunerative circulation.

All the journals printed in French are antagonistic to British rule, and being regarded by thousands as oracles, their influence is far-reaching. From their columns European opinion favorable to the anti-English cause is translated into Arabic by native journalists, who read French and know not a word of English, and finds currency in the native papers penetrating every village. Public measures are acrimoniously reviewed and made to appear to the native reader as added evils, and any reform introduced by England can have its merits so distorted as to be always regarded by the common

Britain's Position in Egypt

people as absurd or tyrannical. This is a conspicuous reason why England's work in Egypt has never been popular with the masses.

Two years ago two hundred and fifty-six students from governmental schools presented themselves in Cairo for examination, prior to receiving diplomas. Each had to undergo examination in a European language, chosen with a view to equipping himself for a career of usefulness. Although the British had long dominated their country, and with every indication that they would never retire, only fifty-five of these students had acquired English; all the others, seventy-eight per cent. of the whole, had learned French. Paraded far and wide by French opponents of English influence, the preponderance of students learning French was brought home to those guiding British policy in Egypt, and attention was immediately directed to promoting the study of English in governmental schools. The Egyptian father being not slow to catch an idea that concerns his welfare, the desire to learn English suddenly became almost epidemic with native lads. That they were encouraged in this is proved by the fact that a few months ago the percentage of pupils in governmental schools studying English was sixty-seven, against thirty-three learning French.

From the time of Mehemet Ali the traditions and sympathies of the people of Egypt have been essentially French, and it has long been the policy of the French government to encourage Egyptian youths to enter their educational establishments; the matter of compensation has ever been a nominal consideration.

English has never been made an official language of the international courts of Egypt, yet advocates therein can plead in Italian, French, and Arabic the principles of the Code Napoléon. Steps are now being taken, however, to have English placed on the list of official languages for pleadings, with every prospect of securing the assent of a majority of the governments interested in the courts. The United States will, obviously, assist the movement. A beginning has been made within a few months by the admission of legal documents in English, and by the appointment of several registrars who understand English. Still England cannot hope to rival France in legal matters in Egypt for many years to come, for every young Egyptian aspiring to the profession of law qualifies therefor at the Cairo School of Law, maintained by the French government, and takes his degree in France.

All these conditions, by which France has been hourly in evidence, to the almost total effacement of England, have contributed to the bewilderment of the minds of the natives. British trade follows the British flag, but British opinion never follows the French language, surely.

The administrative blunder of the English in not bringing in their language with the beginning of their intelligent reforms is half responsible for the unpopularity of the occupation, whose benefits would surely be obliterated and forgotten six months after the departure of the last British

GHIZEREH BANK OF THE NILE, CAIRO.

Britain's Position in Egypt

functionary. This is one of the best reasons given by Englishmen why the occupation should not be terminated, and any member of the so-called anti-English party in Egypt, if asked for his opinion, would assert that the omission to introduce the English language into his country was a triumph of statecraft, and not a blunder thereof. "Having no intention of going, the Britishers want an excuse, even a lame one, for remaining; and the influence of the Anglophobe press, which they purposely refrain from counteracting, creates one," this critic would say. Travelers have long known that it was a part of Britain's policy in India to allow native discontent to vent itself through the local press. It relieves the Indian grumbler, and does not hurt the English official.

Is Egypt capable of self-government?

The candor prompting one, after long and disinterested study of Egyptian matters in the country itself, to say that England has performed her self-appointed task better than any other nation could have performed it, likewise compels one to state frankly that Egypt is not capable of complete self-government at the present time, for she has no class of officials trained in the higher ranges of administrative work. No other nation should ever be permitted to supplant England as administrator or "occupier," certainly.

The khedive, in my opinion, is sufficiently earnest and competent to guide an enlightened policy for carrying on the affairs of his country without any European intervention. He would have at his

Present-Day Egypt

command a group of progressive men like Tigrane, Boutros, Mustapha Fehmy, Fakhry, Mazloum, Cherif, and Yakoub Artin, each qualified to render excellent service as an independent minister. As in times prior to the coming of the English, the khedival government could employ expert or technical assistants of any nationality it chose. American military officers, before England's assumption of power, gave Egypt as good an army as it ever had. British and other irrigationists and engineers having services to sell should be as willing to labor for Egypt as a self-governing administration as they are under a régime upheld by British soldiers. In this way perhaps the prerogatives of the khedive might be restored, and the "running shriek of denunciation" of the army of occupation be silenced.

Egypt might, and might not, prosper under these changed conditions. But there is little likelihood of her being permitted to try the experiment, whatever her right, and "Egypt for the Egyptians" must remain, in all probability, a sentimental illusion. The khedive has the undoubted right to govern his country, subject only to his imperial sovereign at Constantinople, at least until it is demonstrated that he is incapable. It is no reckless hazard, however, to predict that a dozen years hence all that portion of the Nile valley from the Mediterranean to Khartum and farther south will be represented in school-books as a pendant from Britain's red girdle of the globe. How it is to be accomplished, legally and morally, is a matter regarding which I can record no conjecture. In time some-

Britain's Position in Egypt

thing may "turn up" helpful to the legal aspect of England's position in Egypt.

To get rid of the present anomalous position, a great many people in the British Isles and elsewhere would be glad if diplomatic fictions could be brushed away, and the whole of the territory tributary to the Nile openly declared to be a portion of Queen Victoria's empire. But at present the British government thinks it wiser to make sure of the substance than to pay attention to shadowy phrases. British withdrawal would be an act of justice to sultan and khedive, but would serve no other legitimate interest. To annex Egypt, as France did Madagascar, would probably stir up animosities resulting in war.

The masterly victory of Turkish troops in the Greek war was a blow to Englishmen and others who believed the disintegration of the Ottoman empire to be near at hand. They had already experienced a set-back when the Armenian disorders failed to shake the Sultan's throne, and the result of the Greco-Turkish war caused a painful awakening as to the true state of the health of the "Sick Man of Europe." A break-up of the Sultan's empire may come in time, and Egypt fall to England, and Syria to France, in the general parceling out of Turkish possessions. But the "Sick Man" keeps such watchful attention on the Bosporus that the scramble for Ottoman territory may be postponed for many a long year.

CHAPTER XI

WINTERING IN EGYPT FOR HEALTH'S SAKE

IN consequence of the warm and chemically pure atmosphere, Cairo and Upper Egypt offer an ideal climate for persons suffering from consumption, anemia, asthma, and rheumatism, as well as for those convalescing from illnesses. The climate is dry and tonic throughout the year, and during the season when travelers are there—from November to the end of March—these characteristics are more observable than in summer. Violent variations of temperature are unknown, and sunshine prevails even to monotony. It may truthfully be said that the Nile valley is as bountiful in rest and recreation to the invalid as in matchless sights to the tourist. That the natural conditions will suit all health-seekers would be a statement too comprehensive for a lay writer to venture. But the ailments that would be benefited by a winter passed rationally on the banks of the Nile greatly outnumber those that would not. The word "miasma" has no place in the vocabulary of Cairo or Upper Egypt.

The annual rainfall in Cairo is scarcely more than an inch and a half. This means, perhaps, but three

In Egypt for Health's Sake

or four rainy days during a winter. At Mena House and Helouan the rainfall is generally less than in the capital, while at Luxor and Assuan a shower is regarded by the natives as a wonder of nature. Alexandria and other places on the Mediterranean do not share the general immunity of the rest of the country from storms. Cairo's mean temperature for November, December, January, and February is about 62° F., as compared with 63° at Orotava, 61° at Madeira, and 49° at Nice and Mentone. Egypt is the winterland par excellence.

On the coldest days in Cairo the thermometer never falls below 34°, and this degree of frigidity occurs only at long intervals. Some Cairenes recall a slight snowfall a half-century ago, and a thin film of ice on pools in the suburbs may be seen several times in the average winter. This is caused by the desert influence on the early morning air, and is of short duration after sunrise. The cool nights of winter give the air much of its stimulating property; and in summer, however hot the days, the nights are nearly always made comfortable by cooling breezes from the desert.

The Egyptian year has but two seasons, summer and winter. The period of warm weather lasts eight or nine months, while winter is confined practically to the months of December, January, and February. It is only in July, August, and September that the heat is intense; the rest of the year is climatically agreeable. When the Nile is high, in the autumn, there is at times sufficient humidity to cause some discomfort, especially when the humidity is combined with a run of abnormally warm weather. The period of comparatively cold weather, six weeks at most, commences early in January. From April until the end of June the increase of heat is gradual, the maximum being reached usually by July 1; but in some years the highest temperature is not recorded until August or September. The so-called khamsin period sets in by the middle of February, with its parching desert winds, freighted with impalpable particles of sand that cannot be excluded by door or window. Wherever air has access, there the khamsin leaves its layer of dust. The word "khamsin" is Arabic for "fifty," and the belief is that this is the number of days prior to the summer solstice when the scorching winds are liable to occur. A khamsin generally lasts two days, but a season seldom sees more than eight or ten days of these sand-storms. It is nothing to be dreaded, beyond making it desirable to remain indoors during its prevalence. Sufferers from certain forms of asthma even profess to enjoy a khamsin day.

It is difficult to believe that the country's increased canalization and the added area of vegetation are contributing to a diminution of the frequency and force of the khamsin, when one realizes the overwhelming expanse of desert in which these winds have uninterrupted play. Like the severity of New England winters, the force of the khamsin in the Nile valley has manifestly been modified in recent years. Those who wrote of Egypt a hundred or even fifty years ago emphasized their

In Egypt for Health's Sake

descriptions of the horrors of this hot wind. If the contemporary development of Egypt is in any way affecting the blowing of the khamsin, as many claim, then the British are responsible for a benefit heretofore overlooked by their championing press. Alexandrian boatmen, a few years ago, in enumerating their reasons for not favoring the English occupation of their country, would claim that fishing had become impossible in certain parts of the harbor. "The fish no longer bite since the British came," they would say. This serious charge, if challenged, would lead to the explanation that the debris gathered after the bombardment of 1882, including hundreds of tons of mortar and plaster, was dumped into the sea at points where navigation would not be impeded, and that the lime drove the fish away, never to return. This is a fact.

If it is believed that Cairo presents too many seductive dissipations for the health-seeker, Mena House, at the foot of the Pyramids, has much to offer to those needing rest with nerve-toning surroundings, and especially those having weak lungs. The neighborhood itself possesses enough to keep the mind profitably employed for weeks; for towering over Mena House are the Pyramids of Gizeh —in fact, the hotel is built with material removed from titanic Cheops, though it is scarcely missed from the king of pyramids. Close by is the Sphinx, as mysterious to the present-day person pursuing a rest-cure as it was to Napoleon on the occasion of his midnight invocation, or to Herodotus, or the

Present-Day Egypt

great Rameses, or Menes himself, nerve-resting in its inscrutability.

The excursion to Sakkarah and Memphis is more easily made from Mena than from Cairo, and the choice of conveyances ranges from camels to broad-wheeled "sand-carts." To the west of Mena is desert, stretching far and wide for thousands of miles, to Tripoli, Algeria, and Morocco, terminating only when the Atlantic Ocean is reached. To the east is the Nile valley, and Cairo ten miles away. Polo and shooting are every-day diversions. More interesting still is the ever-present opportunity to study the human species, from the lordly Bedouin sheik to the highly developed product of latter-day civilization in Europe, who, maybe, has successfully "tooled" a four-in-hand coach all the way from Shepheard's, over a faultless road, to the Mena piazza. Of the two, judged physically, the brown son of the desert is the finer and better-visaged. "Happily possessed of a golfing-ground and a marble swimming-bath, as well as a resident chaplain for the piously inclined, and a 'dark room' for the ubiquitous photographer, what more," asks cynical Marie Corelli in her Egyptian novel "Ziska," quoting from the Mena House advertisement, "can the aspiring soul of the modern tourist desire?"

It surely is a far cry from invalidism to chicken incubators; but persons who have lolled away a winter at Mena can hardly expect to be invalids when February or March comes. By that time daily jaunts have taken the place of physicians' prescriptions. To these I can recommend nothing

In Egypt for Health's Sake

more interesting than a visit to an "incubatory" in any one of the native villages in the neighborhood of the Pyramids. It will be found that the incubatory is constructed of sun-dried bricks, and so arranged internally that the eggs, placed in mud-constructed ovens on trays cushioned with cut straw, are constantly under the attendant's view. No scientific apparatus is employed by this man, not even a thermometer. He knows from experience and his own feeling how much heat is needed, and he systematically turns the eggs several times each day until they are developed into peeping chicks. These hatching establishments exist throughout Middle and Upper Egypt, and in a season bring fully twenty million chickens into the world, that grow up to be scrawny, unattractive fowls. The industry is thousands of years old, and seems conclusively to settle the question of a chicken's maternity by allocating that parentage to the hen laying the egg. The incubator is a foster-mother only, and is responsible for stifling the "setting" instinct with Egyptian hens. The keepers of the incubatories have a system of traffic with peasant farmers by which eggs are purchased outright, or six live chicks given in exchange for a dozen fresh eggs.

Villa life, with quietude and health-giving air, is offered at Matarieh, six or eight miles to the eastward of Cairo. Uninteresting itself, the village is surrounded by points of historical association in sufficient number to keep the attention of sojourners occupied for a few weeks at least. The plain

Present-Day Egypt

of Heliopolis, the Virgin's tree, and the locale of Kléber's victory over the Turkish legion, present possibilities of great scope to the reader of history. The ostrich-farm close by, and the neighboring khedival estate of Koubbeh, are objects of interest, as well. Matarieh has much to commend it to sufferers from incipient consumption and bronchial disorders.

Singly or in combination, the springs and unadulterated air of Helouan are believed by hosts of people to offer a complete cure for rheumatism and neuralgia. To the imagination of some folks, the odor of the place is of a suggestive character, for, set in the middle of the desert, where sulphur-springs abound, the air smells strongly of brimstone whichever way the wind blows. But this effect soon passes off, and to the neuralgic patient in particular, after a little time, the place appears a heaven. Helouan is a gem of a town set in a golden circle of sand, with a grand view of the river, and palm forests bounded by more desert and a number of pyramids in front of you; and behind, the everlasting Mokattam Hills, that run from Cairo hundreds of miles southward, with a branch range extending to the Red Sea. To the left is the desert again, with a view of the pencil-proportioned minarets of the Mehemet Ali mosque in Cairo, fields of intensely verdant green, and beyond, the great silent form of the Cheops pyramid keeping watch over all. At Helouan are comfortable hotels, first-rate bath establishments with capable physicians in attendance, plenty of little white

SCENE IN THE FAYUM

In Egypt for Health's Sake

houses—many of them of bungalow design—in their little gardens, the whole enveloped in the driest, most exhilarating air you can dream of. The Romans, clever fellows as they were, knew the importance of Helouan, and built there grand houses and bathing-places, remains of which the visitor to-day may gaze upon. Did they have neuralgia or rheumatism? Not for long, surely. The hills around Helouan contain many caverns to be explored, many sepulchers to be discovered; there are glorious walks—even the rheumatic can walk here—for those who like exercise, and shady groves of sweet-smelling acacia, verbena, and every flower that grows "in and out of season as the seasons go." For those who prefer rest, a good story-book, or a color-box and sketching-materials, are in order. And all this is little more than a half-hour's journey from the Egyptian metropolis! The medicinal advantages of Helouan, perhaps as potent as those of Aix-les-Bains, are known far afield, in England, France, Germany, and even in Russia.

A district that should be better known to the seeker for health whose invalidism is not too pronounced is the Fayum, accessible from Cairo in two or three hours by slow railway-train. It has more natural beauty than any other place in Egypt, and is not inappropriately called the "rose-garden." If one would combine the pleasure of the artist with the quest of health, and be not too exacting in the matter of hotel comforts, I know of no place so fascinating and fruitful of subjects for

Present-Day Egypt

the sketch-book or camera as El Medineh, the capital town of the Fayum oasis. The journey from Cairo takes the traveler through the heart of the pyramid region, on the west bank of the Nile, affording opportunity for observing at close range nearly every pyramid of renown in the ancient necropolis. I am here tempted to incorporate a gem of a poem by Professor Clinton Scollard, that sings the praises of the Fayum in graceful but unexaggerated language.

THE ROSE OF FAYUM

Could I pluck from the gardens of old
The fairest of flowers to behold,
And fashion a wreath for the shrine
Of the Muses,—the deathless divine,—
A garland I 'd weave from the bloom
Of the redolent rose of Fayum.

Still the hills with their sun-smitten crest
Tower barren and bold to the west,
Still slumbers the Lake of the Horns
'Neath the glory of luminous morns;
Still is attared the glow and the gloom
By the redolent rose of Fayum.

Arsinoë's temples are prone,
And scarce is there stone above stone
Of the palace whose grandeur and girth
Was one of the wonders of earth;
But in triumph o'er time and the tomb
Springs the redolent rose of Fayum.

In Egypt for Health's Sake

>The rose of to-day is a shoot,
>Like the song of a glorious root.
>Side by side, till the ages shall close,
>Go the love of the lute and the rose;
>And my song I enlink with the bloom
>Of the redolent rose of Fayum.

As health-stations, Luxor and Assuan, in Upper Egypt, have every recommendation, and are more and more appreciated each season by rheumatic and consumptive persons, and by healthy people in want of mental rest and physical recreation. To these an entire winter passed in either Luxor or Assuan, or divided between the two places, may lead to the return of mental energy and bodily health and vigor. These up-river places have the purest and driest air to be found in Egypt, being many degrees warmer than Cairo; and fast steamers and all-rail connection with the capital being provided, they have sprung into a popularity not to be wondered at. Their visitors keep better hours, dance less frequently in overcrowded rooms, and take more rational exercise, than do fashionable sojourners in Cairo. And besides, the daily ride on donkey-back, necessary in making excursions to view objects of interest, has a more beneficial effect upon inactive livers than any amount of driving in a Cairo victoria.

Rain is rare in Upper Egypt, and the oldest inhabitant has no recollection of frost. There are no newspapers to disturb one's equanimity, no quotations of the stock exchange; yet the telegraph brings Luxor and Assuan into intimate touch with the world. Luxor has good hotels, a small hospital, and competent medical men. The Luxor Hotel is good enough to satisfy any reasonable person; its gardens include hundreds of varieties of tropical plants and trees. If time presses, the journey to Cairo, four hundred and fifty miles, may be made by train in a day, but not with the comfort to be found on the steamers. In archæological attractions Luxor is without a peer. Karnak is admittedly unapproachable in grandeur and antiquarian interest, and the plain of Thebes rich with storied ruins. An excursion to the Tombs of the Kings, where the royal mummies rested for thousands of years previous to their transfer to Dêr el-Bahari, repays one for taxing strength and energy. From the moment of mounting your donkey on the Nile strand to the final dismount on the return, diminutive Egyptians, not overclad, keep pace with the animal throughout the day, demanding bakshish with smiling faces at every step—and it is a long and tortuous journey to the Tombs of the Kings. However resolute one may be not to give, and although your command to "*imshi!*" has been sternly repeated a thousand times, you generally relent at the last moment, as the youngsters know you will, and shower your millièmes and half-piasters among the descendants of Mizraim. There is something consoling and stimulating to robust sightseer as well as to semi-invalid in this exercise of benevolence.

From Luxor to Assuan is a short one hundred

In Egypt for Health's Sake

and thirty-five miles, yet the journey seemingly takes one into the heart of Africa. Assuan is the frontier of Egypt proper, the first cataract of the Nile being nature's indicated boundary, south of which is the limitless domain of Nubia and the Sudan—Egypt's territorial extension, so to speak. Assuan has many of the characteristics of frontier towns in other countries. One sees there the military side of the governmental administration, and discovers that martial rather than civil law is in force. The temperature is a few degrees higher than at Luxor, abbreviating the season of sojourn by a week or two, many travelers there meeting the tropical sun and moving northward with it. The roomy Assuan Hotel has culinary possibilities and material comforts in sufficient number to make one forget that its location almost borders on the tropic of Cancer. Lacking the unique antiquarian value of Luxor, perhaps, Assuan in these days provides many compensating attractions. It is a center where strange-looking desert people congregate, whose dress and customs admit of no suspicion of being assumed for spectacular effect. Among members of the tribe of Bischarins may be seen boys and girls who would make the sculptor long to reproduce their classical features and graceful poses. If the trip to the island of Elephantine be disappointing, the excursion to Philæ is wholly satisfying, for there exists nothing more beautiful in the domain of ancient art. But the army of dam-builders, engaged in a work meaning much for the country's progress, is destined so to alter nature at the cataract that Philæ's charm must necessarily be impaired. The bazaar in Assuan is essentially African in character, and a mine of entertainment.

If not an out-and-out invalid, one is certain to go several times to Philæ. I should urge the visitor to make at least one trip by donkey-back. In this way one can take in the quarries from which the ancient kings drew the colossal obelisks and stones for their stupendous structures. Great humps of rich red granite crop up through the tawny sand, and here and there are plain traces of the methods employed by these marvelous builders in working and moving their blocks of material. A huge, nearly completed obelisk, as large as the one in New York or that in London, lies *in situ* as it was hewn from the solid rock, from which it has never been quite separated; it still bears the incisions for fastening the ropes and pulleys by which it would have been dragged to the river, half a mile away. Its contour is perfectly outlined by rows of oblong holes for the insertion of blocks of soft wood, which would have been expanded by the application of water, breaking the monolith from the ledge with as much certainty as it could be accomplished to-day by explosives. The ancient stone-workers understood the simple secrets of natural forces, certainly. On the way back from Philæ, if coming by boat, a dozen other places may be seen where vast pieces of granite have been broken out of ledge or boulder by the primitive trick of wetting confined blocks of porous wood. It is good for the moderate invalid to study the curious

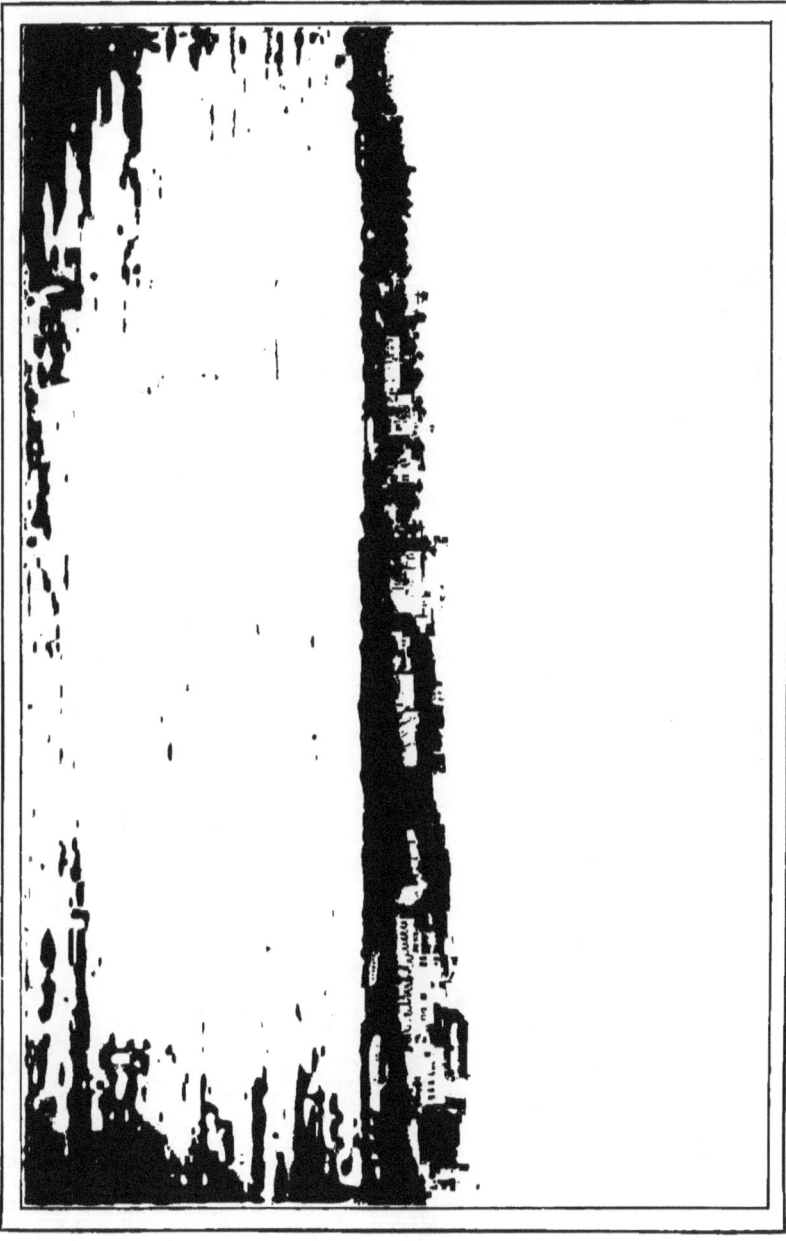

LUXOR.

In Egypt for Health's Sake

things about Assuan, and in the matter of the half-finished obelisk one will speculate why the work was stopped, whether there was a change in the dynasty, or if an appropriation gave out; and it will do no harm, when studying the cartouches chiseled on the boulders along the river-bank, for the mind to endeavor to determine whether they are autographs or were cut by command of kings desirous of leaving an indelible impress of their reigns.

Loiterers about Assuan must not be disappointed when told that the crocodile is no longer to be found within the tourist limits of the Nile. It will be but another illusion shattered, like the popular belief that the tailless Manx cats may be seen in the Isle of Man, or gray Maltese cats in Malta. Outside of a few princely gardens at Cairo not a stalk of the papyrus plant can be found nearer Egypt in these days than at Syracuse in Sicily; and more and better examples of the Egyptian lotus may be seen in August in the public fountain of Union Square in New York than a winter's search in Egypt will reveal.

The evening songs of the Assuan boatmen are soothing to jaded nerves, and the invalid who cannot find peace and benefit at this delightful up-river station can hardly expect to regain health in Egypt.

The health-seeker who desires to linger beyond the usual time for quitting Egypt in the spring or early summer may find comfort and stimulating sea-breezes at Ramleh, the Mediterranean suburb of Alexandria; but dry air must not, of course, be looked for there. It is, nevertheless, a deservedly popular resort, with superb sea-bathing, and a temperature ten or fifteen degrees cooler than Cairo.

I must caution my readers that my enthusiastic statements on the subject of the climatic charms of Egypt must not be accepted to mean that its marvelous air and peaceful environment combine to offer a panacea for all ailments, or that Egypt is a country in which reasonable precautions against colds, chills, and other illnesses are not necessary. There are forms of illness and debility that cannot be benefited by a Nile sojourn, I am assured by medical men long experienced in Egypt. They are few, it is true, but included in the list are advanced heart-disease; advanced organic disease of any organ, excepting cases of chronic and extensive lung-consolidation, tubercular or otherwise, which are often relieved; locomotor ataxia, the lightning pains of which seem to be increased by the electrical conditions incident to the atmosphere of the desert; many forms of skin-disease; insomnia, except when arising from worry or excessive brain-work; forms of neurosis, liable to be irritated by the brilliant sunshine; hypochondria with melancholy tendency; convalescence from acute diseases, where vigorous exercise is essential for recuperation. For these a colder climate is better.

An eminent authority, Dr. Hermann Weber, has prepared the following list of cases that should be cured or relieved by a winter visit to Egypt: "All

In Egypt for Health's Sake

forms of chest-disease where *rest* is desirable—for such cases the climate acts as a charm; all forms of incipient phthisis, where the constitutional disorder preceding the disease is marked, and especially where the patients have still plenty of energy left, and are fond of riding in moderation, and of a quiet life; chronic bronchitis, where the expectoration is more or less abundant, and persons with a gouty tendency; asthma, especially those cases complicated with bronchitis; gout; heart-disease, if uncomplicated with dropsy; all forms of anemia and chlorosis; renal diseases and sufferers from gravel; convalescents from acute diseases, such as influenza, pleurisy, etc., and in the quiescent forms of chronic affection of the lungs, trachea, or bronchi, especially old-standing pneumonic conditions following influenza; atonic forms of dyspepsia; chronic rheumatism and the milder cases of rheumatoid arthritis; chorea, deteriorated health, and general break-up of the system, following overwork, especially in men between fifty and sixty years of age, with gouty tendencies associated with arterial degeneration."

"To persons who are either healthy or merely in want of mental rest and recreation or of healthful occupation—for instance, persons who are socially or mentally overworked, or who have sustained shocks or disappointments, or who have been exposed to one of the thousand forms of more or less prolonged worry, or who are without profession and occupation, and lack either the power or the inclination to procure a healthy substitute for them

—in such persons a winter spent in Egypt may lead to the return of mental energy and bodily health and vigor," remarks the same authority.

It is the duty of any writer on the subject of Egypt as a resort for health-seekers to caution those reading from an interested standpoint, that one may contract a cold there perhaps as easily as elsewhere. The winds of the Nile valley, the marked difference between sun and shade temperature, and the excessive chill coming with sunset, are certain to seize the unwary person feeling that his presence in North Africa gives exemption from such mishaps. A Nile cold has potentialities of seriousness, and cannot be annulled by power of will. On the contrary, an Egyptian cold is stubbornly difficult to be got rid of.

No climate is without its disadvantages as well as advantages, and it is important that a seeker for mental rest and physical benefit should be as cognizant of the former as of the latter. Change of climate, intelligently planned, frequently helps an ailment when other forms of treatment have failed; and in cases where it may have caused amelioration merely, it may by repeated trials eventually effect a lasting cure. Immediate recovery is no more certain to be effected by a change of air and scene than by other remedial agents. Maladies of a constitutional character, such as Egypt is believed to cure, may not even be relieved in a single season, while a second visit may eradicate them for all time. Expert medical opinion is worth securing before setting out for the Nile country, and should be fre-

In Egypt for Health's Sake

quently sought while in that heaven-favored land. A well-known British physician, Dr. James Clarke, writing on the subject of climates in their health-giving aspect, wisely says: "The air, or climate, is often regarded by patients as possessing some specific quality by virtue of which it directly cures the disease. This erroneous view of the matter not unfrequently proves the bane of the invalid, by leading him, in the fullness of his confidence in climate, to neglect other circumstances, an attention to which may be more essential to his recovery than that in which all his hopes are centered." And again: "If a patient would reap the full measure of good which his new position places within his reach, he must trust more to his own conduct than to the simple influence of any climate, however genial; he must avail himself of all the advantages which the climate possesses, and eschew those disadvantages from which no climate or situation is exempt; moreover, he must exercise both resolution and patience in prosecuting all this to a successful issue."

As a rule, robust as well as delicate visitors leave Egypt too early in the spring, thereby undoing in many instances the benefits of their sojourn by encountering the cold weather of Europe. The 1st of March sees a stampede to get away, and every steamer goes crowded to its limit; the up-Nile contingent is seized with a common impulse to get to Rome or Venice or Paris for Easter Sunday, and rushes pell-mell through Cairo to Alexandria or the canal to take ship for the Continent, perhaps

Present-Day Egypt

to find gales and cold storms that effectually undo the physical improvement resulting from the season passed in Egypt. Instead of hurrying away as the first khamsin blows, it is better to remain in Cairo or Alexandria until the end of April. These cities are replete with out-of-season comfort, and no danger lurks in the honest warm weather. March is delightful, and if the midday sun of April is avoided, there is no discomfort worthy of consideration. Strangely enough, the ever-present mosquito is less annoying in spring and early summer than in winter.

As temperaments vary, so differ the ways of seeing the Nile, even of reaching Luxor and Assuan. The trip is in no case inexpensive, unless made by rail; and in a country possessing so many unrivaled interests, no one wishes to travel by railway except in case of necessity. Up to comparatively recent years the voyager to Upper Egypt made the journey only at great expense of time and money. It meant months on a dahabiyeh, generally chartered for an entire season. Nothing more agreeable can ever be devised; but there are stages and conditions of invalidism where it is undesirable to take the risk of being several days between towns, unless the invalid be accompanied by a physician. Steam, under these circumstances, with its definite schedule, is safer. The large tourist-steamers carry medical officers, experienced and efficient, and combine every convenience and comfort of a floating home. Stopping at fewer places, and having no program of excursions to points of interest far re-

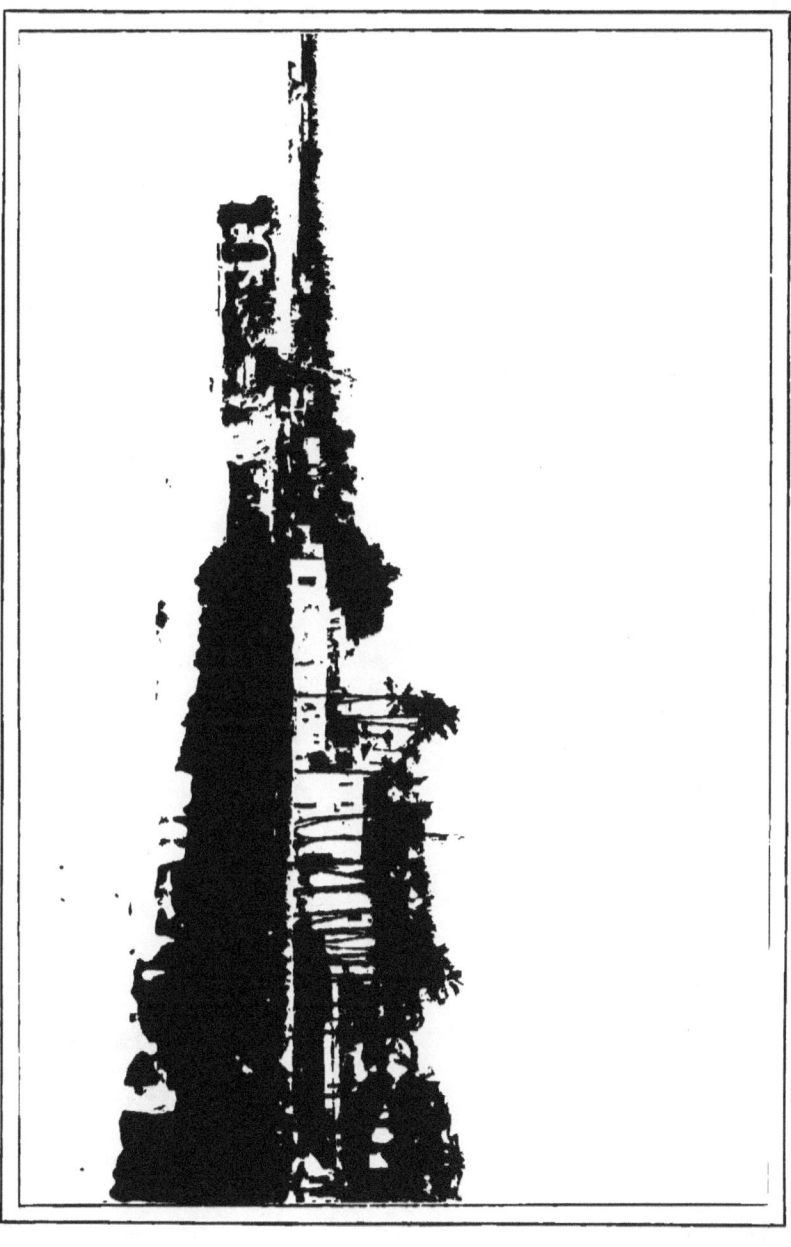

ASSUAN.

In Egypt for Health's Sake

moved from the river-banks, as offered by the tourist-boats, the post-steamers are quicker and much less expensive. In either case, the traveler is seldom out of telegraphic touch with the world for more than a few hours at a time.

Sanitary skill has liberated Egypt from the list of eastern countries where epidemics may rage uncontrolled, and there is no more important item of benefit through British intervention than the introduction of measures which quickly suppress or limit outbreaks of cholera and fevers. A visitation of cholera a generation ago ran riot for many months and decimated the population of Egyptian cities and towns. Dreadful as it must ever be, cholera nowadays is so promptly and intelligently dealt with that well-conditioned people run little risk of contracting the malady. The last serious appearance of this disease in 1896, although requiring months to exterminate, was so skilfully handled that the mortality was kept at an unheard-of low figure; and had it not been for the sensational chroniclings of the press of Europe but few persons dwelling in the European quarters of Cairo and Alexandria would have suffered anxiety. Travelers on the Nile were no more in danger than if making a tour of the fiords of Norway. The international quarantine board in Egypt keeps a vigilant watch of Asiatic epidemics, and apprehends the spread of a virulent disease usually long before it has reached Suez in its western progress. Were it not for the timely work of the international board, whose labors were augmented by those of

Present-Day Egypt

the Egyptian sanitary service—a thoroughly organized department of the national administration—the Nile country would probably not have escaped the recent scourge of bubonic plague originating in Bombay. The presence of a few isolated cases in Alexandria, disquieting as the despatches were, in no way imperiled the country. The time has passed when an ordinary outbreak of cholera or plague can menace winter visitors to Egypt—though the proprietors of Continental winter-resorts are never angry when Continental newspapers announce the appearance of an infectious disease in Egypt.

A good dragoman contributes much to one's comfort and enjoyment. Persons spending the season in or near Cairo, or making the usual tour of the Nile, have no need of a special dragoman. Nearly every steamer provides well-informed guides. For sight-seeing in towns, or brief excursions, one may be taken for the day—and hotels swarm with them. A good dragoman is a blessing undisguised; but one in whom you lack confidence is an unmitigated misfortune. Interpreter-guides proffer their services at steamship landing, railway-station, and even in the street. Most of them are plausible and insinuating, but a display of firmness will protect the visitor from imposition. They are cunning students of human nature, but easily kept in place. It is wise to engage a dragoman recommended by an acquaintance who has tested him, or one guaranteed by a reputable agency. Most of the professional guides are capable, painstaking,

In Egypt for Health's Sake

and honest; but a well-defined written contract aids greatly in keeping them exact in disbursements and duties, and the average man of this calling greatly values money given him as "bakshish." For a dahabiyeh voyage a dragoman-contractor is almost indispensable. With the wane of the Egyptian season, dragomans endeavor to secure parties going to Palestine or Mount Sinai, and have this object in mind while serving winter patrons.

It has become almost a truism that "T. Cook & Son own the Nile." They were the pioneers of systematic navigation on the great river, and for twenty years have conducted their affairs in such a businesslike manner that competition, if existing at all, has been weak and ineffective. Practically every steamer and modern dahabiyeh on the Nile is owned by the firm of Cook, which has a seemingly perennial contract with the government for carrying the mails. This chapter would be incomplete, in dealing with the vitally important subject of the Nile as a resort for health-seekers, if mention of the facilities offered by the fleet of Cook steamers and dahabiyehs were omitted. In Egypt, Cook is unique.

Continuing in the desire to make this chapter valuable to the inquirer for information, I must explain how easily the voyage from New York to Egypt may in these times be made. The route best suited to those willing to sacrifice a few days' time for the sake of comfort in traveling is by the direct service of North German Lloyd steamers to

Present-Day Egypt

Naples or Genoa, changing at one of these ports to a steamer of the same line, that will land passengers at Port Saïd or Ismailia, whichever canal station offers a favorable train to Cairo. If there be no German Lloyd boat sailing from Genoa or Naples at a convenient time, there are several other first-class lines starting from or touching at these ports, and one should find an available steamer without much trouble or delay. In this way the voyage from New York to Egypt is made with the maximum of comfort in from sixteen to twenty days. Every winter offers occasional excursions by the North German Lloyd, Hamburg-American, and French lines from New York to Alexandria direct; and as travel to Egypt grows, which it does by leaps and bounds, the facilities for getting there are sure to increase. A regular direct service between New York and Alexandria, during the winter months at least, is almost certain to be soon established.

The robust traveler bound for the land of the Pyramids can disembark from his Atlantic liner in England or France, as the case may be, catch a quick train to Marseilles, Brindisi, Genoa, Naples, Venice, or Triest, and be in Alexandria or Port Saïd in a few days' less time than if he went by the all-sea route. If he is willing to travel post-haste, he may be in Cairo in fourteen days after leaving New York, or possibly in thirteen.

"He who has once tasted the water of the Nile," says an Arab proverb, "longs for it inexpressibly forevermore."

INDEX

Abbas Hilmi, khedive, 1, 272; criticism of, in England, 273; student days, 274, 277; lingual capacity, 278; civil list, 279; description of, 283; habits, 284; heir of, 289.
Abbas I, viceroy, 220.
Abukir Bay, 92, 95, 292.
Agriculture, value of cotton crop, 133; cane-culture developed by Assuan reservoir, 147; fertilized by deposit of soil from Abyssinia, 164; facility of, in Delta, 170; primitive cultivation, 170; division of crops, 183.
"Aïda," original production of, 22, 236.
Alexander, forethought of, in founding Alexandria, 60.
Alexandria, antiquity of, 78; custom-house, 79, 102; medley of population, 79; ancient Pharos, 80; as seat of learning and great library, 83; Mehemet Ali's interest in, 85; city and harbor of present day, 86, 87; shipments of cotton from, 90; massacre of Christians, 90; railway to Ramleh, 95; Greeks at, 96; port receipts, 133; bombardment of, 260, 263.
American judges in international courts, 116.
American Presbyterian Mission, educational work of, 326.
Anglo-Egyptian expedition, 53, 300.
Anniversaries, 14.
Arabi Pasha, rebellion, 186; lacking in attributes of leadership, 257; demand for dismissal of Riaz ministry, 258; as minister of war, 259; crushing of rebellion, 260, 263, 264; in exile, 269; trial, sentence, and banishment, 312.
Area of practical Egypt, 119.
Assiut, construction of barrage at, 146; cane-culture near, 183.

Assuan, great dam at, 145; reservoir greatly to increase country's producing capacity, 148; dam to be completed in 1903, 151; laying foundation-stone of dam by Duke of Connaught, 151; cost of dam, 153; as health-station, 349–352.

Baksbish, 41, 350, 365.
Barrage, near Cairo, 146; designed by French, made practicable by British, 172.
Bazaars, of Cairo, 41–43; of Assuan, 352.
Bedouins, 5, 292, 342.
Bible, scenes thereof, 6.
British army of occupation, cost of, 55, 186.

Cairo, founding of, 1; quaint life, 2; letter-writers, 7; street scenes, 8, 12, 21; polyglot, 13; confusing calendars, 14; sacred carpet ceremonial, 16; funerals, 20; adornment with statues, 34; tram-cars, 36; bazaars, 41, 42; Mouski, 45; mosques, 47; El-Azhar University, 59; Suez Canal fêtes in, 209; climate and rainfall, 338.
Canals, Mahmudiyeh, 165; early projects for canal from Nile to Suez, 187; prediction of trouble therefrom, 187.
Capitulations, 105; origin of, 106–110.
Census, difficulty of taking, 116; of 1897, 123.
Ceremonials, sacred carpet, 16; cutting of Khalig, 69.
Cigarettes, their manufacture, 75.
Cleopatra, 96; pure Greek, 97, 98; variety of portraits, 98; death by asp-bite improbable, 101.
Climate, 336, 356, 358, 359.
Consular courts, 106.

Index

Cromer, Viscount, able administrator, 140; *de facto* ruler, 143, 320, 325.

Dancing-girls, 30.
Debt, national bonded, 125; per capita, 178.
De Lesseps, Ferdinand, 184; concession for Suez Canal, 192; movement to give name to canal, 209; monument to, 210.
Divorce, simplicity of, 27.
Dongola and Berber, to become important producers of breadstuffs, 182.
Dongola expedition, 308.
Dragomans, 364, 365.

Egypt, involved administration, 104; limited area, 119; origin of name, 120; from insolvency to prosperity, 120; population, 120, 123, 124; improvement of financial position, 125; debt, 125, 320; debt compared with other countries, 126; imports and exports, and Alexandria port receipts, 133; budget and tribute to Sultan, 133; sources of revenue, 134; land-tax, 134, 137; value of land, 139; producing capacity increased by Assuan dam, 148; no benefit from Suez Canal, 184; cost of canal to, 207; reversion of canal to, 216; governed from London, 298; short cut to English honors, 319; present prosperity, 319, 320; self-government, 333, 334.
Egyptian cotton, origin, 89; prolificness, 138; Delta a great cotton-field, 181; advantages of fellah cultivator, 181; necessity in United States and Europe, 182; predicted increase of, 182; importance to Great Britain, 316.
Egyptian question, 298.
Egyptian Museum, 5, 66, 236; new, 69.
"Evil eye," superstitious fear of, 33.

Fayum, 347; Rose of (poem), 348.
France, in Suez Canal affair, 201; emperor arbitrates, 201-204; withdrawal from dual financial control, 300; non-participation in bombardment of Alexandria, 303; invited to share responsibility of same, 304; in Tunis, 314; French as official language, 327; journals in French language, 328.

Great Britain, saving Egypt from bankruptcy, 127; work of regenerating Egypt, 127; territorial expansion, 147; treatment of Khedive Abbas, 272, 273; right to be in Egypt, 298; retention of Egypt not at first intended, 311; official utterances regarding intervention in Egypt, 311, 312; advantage of control in Egypt, 315, 316; not prepared Egyptians for self-government, 322; subjects in administrative offices, 325, 326; introducing English language, 328, 329; anomalous position in Egypt, 335.

Harem, ceasing to exist, 28; description of, 28.
Hashish, 101; how smuggled, 102, 103.
Health, 336, 341, 344; cases not benefited by sojourn in Egypt, 356; cases benefited, 357; Nile colds, 358.
Heliopolis, 48, 344.
Helouan, 344; baths of, 347.
Howling dervishes, 28.

Ibrahim Pasha, viceroy, 219.
Incubatories, chicken, 343.
International courts, 105; originated by Nubar Pasha, 111; procedure and jurisdiction, 112; location, 115; languages of, 330.
International Debt Commission, 105; cost of and limitation of powers, 132.
International quarantine board, 363.
Irrigation, reservoir near Assuan, 145; triumph of science, 147; harnessing Nile to increase country's production twenty-five per cent., 148; contrasting methods of, 165, 166; importance of present, 177.
Ismail Pasha, khedive, beautifying Cairo, 35; entailed rulership, 117; no rule for collecting taxes, 134, 184; interest in Suez Canal project, 185; sale of canal shares to British government, 186; firman from Sublime Porte ordering succession by primogeniture, 199, 200; errors of, 218; education in France, 220; disappearance of the "Moufettish," 224; generosity, 226; surrender of estates, 229; leaves Egypt, 230; at Naples, 231; at Constantinople, 231; character, 235; debts incurred, 236; death, 238; funeral, 241-243.

Index

Karnak, 350.
Khamsin, 338, 341.
Khedivah, 286.
Khedivah-mère, 289.
Kitchener, General Lord, sirdar, 53, 54, 55, 319.
Koran, 24; as text-book, 63; forbidding liquors and wines, 103.

Lake Mareotis, sea admitted to, 91.
Lake Menzaleh, 193.
Luxor, 349, 350.

Marriage, description of, 15; growth of monogamy, 24.
Matarieh, 343.
Mecca, pilgrimage to, 19.
Mehemet Ali, prince, brother of Khedive Abbas, 277, 280, 289.
Mehemet Ali Pasha, founder of dynasty, 1; revels at Shubra Palace 75; interest in Alexandria, 85; connected Alexandria with Nile, 85; revolutionized irrigation, 170; interest in isthmian canalization, 191.
Mena House, 39, 337, 342.
Mohammed Abdoul-Mounaim, prince, heir to khedivate, 289.
Mortality, diminution of death-rate, 124.
Mosques, 47.
Mouski, 45, 46.

Napoleon I, suggested barrage for irrigating Delta, 171; considered canalization between Mediterranean and Suez, 188.
Napoleon III, amazing award of, in Suez Canal dispute, 203.
Nile, travel to, 128; sugar-cane of, 147; alluvial valley of, 148; length, breadth, and fall of, 165; sustained by rainfall of equatorial region, 166; unchangeable features of, 169; waste of water and deposit, 171; monopolization by Great Britain, 304; high, 337; how to see, 360; Arab proverb of, 366.
Nubar Pasha, originator of international courts, 111; difficulty with French newspaper, 118, 223, 224.

Obelisks, none in Cairo or Alexandria, 48, 91; *in situ* at Assuan, 352.
Office-holding, 131.
Ophthalmia, 33.

Palaces, Gizeh, 69; Shubra, 71, 72; Moutazah, 95, 292; Ras-el-Teen, 95, 292; Ghizereh, 225; Abdin, 246; state ball at Abdin, 296; Koubbeh, 251, 268.
Philæ, site of Nile dam, 154; protests against desecration of, 157; date of temples, 160.
Pilgrimage to Mecca, 19.
Polygamy, 24.
Population, 120, 123; density of, 124.
Port Saïd, entrance to canal (note), 209; statue to De Lesseps, 210.
Professional letter-writers, 7.
Professional mourners, 20.

Railways, electric, in Cairo, 36; to Pyramids, 36; from Alexandria to Ramleh, 95; receipts and operating expenses of state, 128; in the Sudan, 128; international aspect of, 132; from Cairo to Suez, 191; from Luxor and Assuan to Cairo, 349.
Rainfall, 336, 337.
Ramadan, 14.
Rameses the Great, 5, 69.
Ramleh, 92, 355.
Religion, devotion to, 23; sects of Mohammedan, 61; classification of, 124.
Rosetta Stone, 66.
Russia, interest in Egypt, 305; Asiatic aspirations, 306; ways of reaching East, 306; desire to avoid British opposition, 307.

Sacred carpet, 16.
Saïd Pasha, viceroy, giving of Suez Canal concession, 185, 192; subscription to canal's capital, 185, 196.
Sakkarah, 342.
Seasons, 337, 338.
Slavery, not obligatory, 28; "slave" palace attendants, 290.
Soldiers, 52; efficiency of, 54; British army of occupation, 55; at Khalig ceremonial, 70; cost of army, 134.
Sphinx, 341.
Sudan, reconquest of, 305, 308, 316; income from, 308.
Suez Canal, 103, 184; concession for, 192, 193; cost to Egypt, 207; value to commerce, 211; nationality of ships using, 212; economy of, 215; capital and profit, 216; reversion to Egypt, 216; advantages of, 306.
Sultan, Egyptian tribute to, 104; deposes Ismail, 243; makes Tewfik khedive, 245; annexation of Egypt

Index

unjust to, 300; declined to send troops to Alexandria, 314; disintegration of empire of, 335.

Taxation, 134; land-tax, 137.
Temperature, 337.
Tewfik Pasha, khedive, favored single marriage, 24; improved method of collecting land-taxes, 134, 229; named khedive by Sultan, 245; birth, 248; difficulties in rule of, 253; wanting in firmness, 264; in cholera-infested Cairo, 265; pleaded for commutation of Arabi's sentence, 269; Admiral Seymour's communication to, 311.
Thebes, plain of, 350.

Tobacco, cultivation forbidden, 75.
Tombs of Kings, 350.

United States, use of Egyptian cotton in, 182; use of Suez Canal by ships of, 212, 215, 217; utterance of Congress regarding intervention in Cuba, 314; Egypt, how reached from, 366.
University of El-Azhar, oldest in world, 59; description of, 60–65.

Whitehouse, Cope, project for storage reservoir near the Fayum, 177.
Women, aversion to European customs, 23; improving condition, 27; graceful water-carriers, 56, 251; attendants in khedive's household, 290.

www.ingramcontent.com/pod-product-compliance
Lightning Source LLC
Chambersburg PA
CBHW030402230426
43664CB00007BB/704